THE VISUAL DIALOGUE

THE VISUAL DIALOGUE

An Introduction
to the Appreciation of Art

NATHAN KNOBLER

University of Connecticut

HOLT, RINEHART AND WINSTON, INC.

New York   Chicago   San Francisco   Toronto   London

Library of Congress Catalogue Card Number: 67–10265
All rights reserved. No part of the contents of this book may
be reproduced without the written permission of the publishers,
Holt, Rinehart and Winston, Inc., New York.
A Helvetica Press production: Printed in
black-and-white gravure by the Presses Centrales Lausanne, Switzerland;
color offset by the Imprimeries Réunies, Lausanne;
bound by Mayer et Soutter, Renens, Switzerland.

90123   75   98765

SBN: 03-059515-0

PREFACE

I N OUR TIME the arts, and particularly the visual arts produced by the contemporary artist, seem isolated from a large portion of society. Yet museum attendance is booming, the sale of paintings has reached impressive figures, and the space devoted to the arts in magazines indicates that editors are aware of unprecedented reader interest in artists and their work. Meanwhile, ironically, many artists find few among the lay public who seem to understand the concepts basic to the arts, few who can recognize the historical ties between present-day art and the arts of the past. To the practicing artist, there appears to be a widespread visual illiteracy, a public generally incapable of "reading" the current visual languages of painting and sculpture and often extremely limited in its ability to "read" the visual languages of the past. This book is the attempt of an artist and teacher to provide the information, the ideas, and the arguments—as well as a beginning vocabulary and syntax —through which there might occur a meaningful, constructive discourse between the work of art and those eager to find significance and satisfaction in it.

The growth of the number of courses in art appreciation and the many texts written on the subject suggest a real desire on the part of the educated public to come to grips with the challenge of the arts. But this desire is frequently thwarted by a kind of cultural barrier which isolates the observer from a response to the art object. It is a barrier constructed in three parts. Part one is formed by the assumption made by many that they can differentiate between a work of art and an object which does not fit this category. They establish a limited conceptualization of the nature and the form of the legitimate painting, piece of sculpture, and well-designed building, and they tend to reject as illegitimate those products of artists which do not conform to the acceptable pattern.

Another section of the wall exists because of the extremely limited contact between most people and actual examples of painting, sculpture, or buildings that would fit the description of architectural works of art. Although it is true that the museums are crowded, the amount of exposure to the visual arts does not compare with the exposure to music or literature. Many reproductions of paintings and sculpture are to be found in books and magazines, but the availability of these references is a mixed blessing, for it gives the illusion of contact with the arts when, in fact, even the most carefully printed publications are unsatisfactory substitutes for painting, and are of course misleading in the representation of the three-dimensional art forms. Some might argue that reproduction of music by tape and phonograph is comparable to the color reproduction of works in the visual arts. But the reproduction of sound is much closer to the original source than is the reproduction of the texture, the scale, and the precise color of painting or the material and the actual three-dimensionality of a statue.

Related to the two parts of the barrier already mentioned is a third element, which is perhaps the most crucial component in the whole matrix. It is the feeling of confusion, the sense of inadequacy, and frequently the feeling of frustration and antagonism toward objects identified as works of art which cannot be confined within the limits of the conceptulization acceptable to the observer.

In my view an introduction to the appreciation of art must begin by attempting to eliminate the barrier of misunderstanding and prejudice found in the untrained viewer. He must find the continuity between the arts of the past and those of the present day. He must be offered a sound, logical exposition of the nature of the visual arts that will help to remove the doubts he may feel about the work of the contemporary painter, sculptor, and architect. Finally, the interested layman must be given a sense of his ability to deal with works of art without the necessity of a third party who will tell him what to look at, why he should look at it, and what it should mean.

The concern I feel for the need to establish a basis for the understanding and the acceptance of the visual arts requires that the first chapters of this book deal with somewhat abstract problems at a length which is unusual in texts concerned with the appreciation of art. My experience in teaching this material has convinced me that it is an illusion to believe it possible to involve students in individual works of art before a preliminary, thorough resolution of their doubts about the nature and validity of the arts in general. This introduction prepares the way for further study by presenting arguments which suggest that there is meaning to be found in forms of art which are at present beyond the understanding of the interested individual.

The book continues with a second section devoted to the exposition of the language of the visual arts. Here I have tried to introduce the reader to the diversity which exists both in the content and the form of the visual arts throughout their history. This section has been written on the assumption that the observer must recognize the interdependence between means and ends in painting, sculpture, and architecture. If he is to understand what a painting means, a viewer must also understand how that meaning is communicated.

In general, it is the thesis of this book that art appreciation is a visual dialogue between each observer and the work of art he confronts—a dialogue which requires an informed, perceptive, and responsive participant on one side and the work of art on the other. A third party, the critic, or the teacher may function to introduce the participant to the work, to prepare him for the appreciation of it, but he can do no more, for art appreciation cannot be taught. It grows within the observer when he is prepared for it, and it has an opportunity to develop only when there is a continuing contact between the perceiver and works of art. It is my hope that this book will help with that preparation and accelerate it, but the responsibility for initiating the dialogue and maintaining it is shared by the artist and each person who stands before his work.

The development of the book's content and organization, and the selection of its examples and illustrations, evolved during the dozen years that I have taught "art appreciation" to undergraduates at the University of Connecticut. The text is illustrated by 244 black-and-white photographs, reproduced in gravure, of objects in painting, sculpture, architecture, and the applied arts, 79 diagrams, and 65 color plates.

N.K.

Mansfield Center, Connecticut
June, 1966

CONTENTS

THE VISUAL DIALOGUE

ART APPRECIATION AND
THE ESTHETIC EXPERIENCE

CHAPTER I

M AN IS an image maker. From the paintings on the cave walls of paleolithic man a record of the visual arts has continued to our own time, and though the motivation for these images appears to change from era to era, there is ample evidence to affirm the need of men to transform their experiences into visual symbols (Figs. 1, 2).

In this span of time buildings and monuments have risen, some to fall quickly, others to remain as evidence of the need of men to protect themselves and to glorify their heroes, their societies, and their gods.

The combination of visual symbols and architectural structures produced by man provides a record that illuminates the past, and many of these artifacts continue to provide the present-day observer with insights and pleasures, rewarding in their own right without reference to their historical implications. The meaning of art does not lie exclusively in its function as a mirror of life; for some it serves primarily as a source of sensuous and intellectual satisfaction that needs no external referent. In the form of a Greek kylix (Fig. 3), the color of a Matisse interior (Pl. 1), or the structure of a great bridge (Fig. 4) there is a potential for awe and delight unrelated to practical value or cultural and historical background.

For those who produce the paintings, sculpture, and architecture of their time, the arts may have a variety of meanings. A work of art may be an exercise in skill and manual dexterity. Perhaps it is a comment on society and morality, wrenched out of the personal involvement of the artist. Perhaps it tells a simple story. Perhaps it satisfies the need to create a mystical token or icon. Whatever the reason for creating it, for many artists the work of art has served its purpose when it is completed. Other rewards may come when the work has found a responsive audience, but the response of the public is so unpredictable that its acceptance can provide only a secondary level of satisfaction for the artist.

For the observers, the consumers of the arts, the meaning of art begins with the work itself. The observer begins where the artist has stopped. The meaning that the layman finds in the art object is dependent upon the work of art, but it is also dependent upon the viewer's own intellectual and emotional condition, as well as his ability to perceive the work before him.

The artist produces a visual statement which in turn becomes the subject matter for a response or reaction from the observer. In this sense the visual arts may be considered a language. As in other languages, there is a source for the

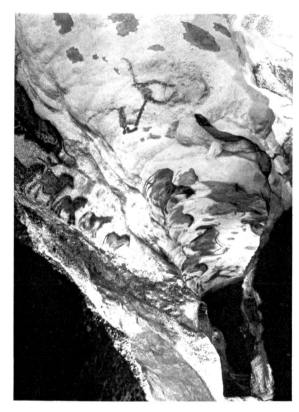

FIG. 1. *Lascaux Cave, left gallery
of chamber A. Rock painting.
15,000–10,000 B.C.
Montignac, Dordogne, France.*

FIG. 2. *Rock painting, detail.
15,000–10,000 B.C.
Lascaux Cave, Dordogne, France.*

FIG. 3. *Athenian black-figured kylix,*
"Little Master" type,
from Monteleone, Italy, showing sphinx
with dead man. 550–540 B.C.
Painted pottery, height 7⁷/₈".
The Metropolitan Museum of Art,
New York (Rogers Fund, 1903).

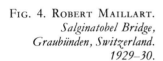

FIG. 4. ROBERT MAILLART.
Salginatobel Bridge,
Graubünden, Switzerland.
1929–30.

communication, the artist; there is a medium that carries the information originating at the source, the work of art; and finally there is a receiver, the observer. Like the reader of a written text, the observer must recognize and decipher the symbols and the pattern of symbols before understanding can occur. Of course, reading and enjoyment are not synonymous. Just as no one reader will find pleasure in each book on a library shelf, so no beholder should expect to find pleasure in every art object or to understand each work of art he sees. Library shelves are filled with volumes beyond the comprehension even of highly educated individuals, and the walls of museums are hung with some paintings which have a similarly limited audience.

It is possible for a layman to have an immediate esthetic response to some works of art, but it is probable that many of the paintings, the pieces of sculpture, and the buildings he confronts will offer him little pleasure. In fact, there may be works of art which disturb and even anger or repel him. Esthetic satisfaction is the result of a complex combination of subjective attitudes and perceptual abilities. No one can state with certainty why certain objects will elicit positive responses while others do not, but if the observer wishes to increase the number of art objects to which he can respond with satisfaction, it will be necessary for him to alter the conditions that affect his response.

The philosopher Albert R. Chandler, in his book *Beauty and Human Nature,* discusses the satisfaction to be found in the arts. He calls this satisfaction "the esthetic experience."

> The esthetic experience may be defined as satisfaction in contemplation, or as a satisfying intuition. When I enjoy a beautiful sunset I am satisfied to contemplate it. My intellectual curiosity is put to sleep—I do not care just then about the physical causes of clouds and light. My practical interests are suspended—I do not care just then whether such a sky foretells dry weather, though my garden may need rain. I am satisfied to contemplate the sunset.
>
> . . . .
>
> The word *satisfaction* may be defined indirectly as the state of mind which is indicated by the willingness to prolong or repeat the experience in question.... The term satisfaction is better than *pleasure,* because *satisfaction* is the broader term. The harrowing excitement aroused by a melodrama is scarcely a pleasure, but it is undoubtedly a satisfaction, since people seek to prolong or repeat it. The same might be said of pathos in music and poetry. It may reduce us to tears, but our experience is nevertheless a satisfying one.[1]

It takes very little special training to react to the colors of a sunset or the forms of clouds or mountains, yet many people find it difficult to have a pleasurable experience from some works of art. Why ? An examination of the factors which can lead to an esthetic experience may develop an understanding of this problem and provide a guide for the discovery of satisfaction in art objects that offered little to the observer before.

Initially, the esthetic experience is the result of an interaction between an art object and an observer. This interaction cannot take place unless the conditions for its occurrence are present. These conditions are *the ability of the observer to perceive and comprehend those aspects of the object or experience which contribute to esthetic satisfaction* and *a receptive attitude on the part of the observer.*

Before going on, let us limit the definition of the esthetic object. It has been suggested that the esthetic experience may be initiated by a response to both natural and man-made stimuli. The study of the esthetic response in all its forms is a formidable task and not the purpose of this text ; we are dealing here with the response to a work of art, and we shall restrict our definition of the esthetic stimulus so that it becomes synonymous with works of the visual arts. Though this restriction eliminates many possible areas of discussion, it still leaves a large body of work for examination. Traditionally the visual arts have been divided into the fine arts and the practical, or applied, arts, the major branches of the fine arts being generally catagorized as painting, sculpture, and architecture. It is possible to argue that there is a potential for esthetic satisfaction in every man-made object, from a can opener to a skyscraper, from a postage stamp to the ceiling mural of a great church, but an attempt to cover the entire range of the visual arts would not permit us to focus on the essential problem that concerns us—the achievement of an esthetic response, an *appreciation* of art.

---

[1] Albert R. Chandler, *Beauty and Human Nature,* (copyright, 1934, D. Appleton-Century Co., Inc.), Appleton-Century-Crofts, Inc., New York, pp. 9, 10.

PL. 1. HENRI MATISSE. *Goldfish and Sculpture*. 1911. Canvas, 46 x 39⅝". The Museum of Modern Art, New York (Gift of Mr. and Mrs. John Hay Whitney).

PL. 2. MASACCIO. *The Virgin and Child Enthroned*. 1426. Panel,
53¼ x 28¾". National Gallery, London.

PL. 3. RAPHAEL. *Madonna del Granduca* (so-called). c. 1504–05. Panel,
33 x 21½″. Pitti Palace, Florence.

PL. 4. JOHN SINGLETON COPLEY. *Portrait of Mrs. Thomas Boylston.* 1766. Canvas, 49 x 38″.
Fogg Art Museum, Harvard University, Cambridge, Mass.
(Bequest of Ward N. Brown, 1828).

The basic problems which arise in the appreciation of sculpture, painting, and architecture have their counterparts in all the visual arts, and the exposition of these problems will apply to other areas of the visual arts which may become the concern of the reader.

THE RECEPTIVE ATTITUDE

What is the attitude essential for an esthetic experience? First, it is necessary that *the observer's attention be directed toward the object before him.* The person looking at a work of art must give it his full and undivided attention.

Some degree of interaction with a work of art is possible without the complete attention of the observer. Many people who live in rooms hung with paintings may rarely stop to contemplate them. Others listen to music while performing their household chores, combining concert-going with cooking and dusting. Both instances are examples of contact with a work of art without a direct, "face-to-face" relationship. Other examples are less obvious but produce similar results: the casual stroll through a museum or gallery without taking time for a reflective pause; the interference of noise and crowds, which hampers concentration; bad lighting; conflicting backgrounds—all these may create a partial barrier between the work of art and the viewer.

The photograph (Fig. 5) of a nineteenth-century interior gives a sense of the chaos that can result from the haphazard display of bric-a-brac, paintings, sculpture, furniture, and fabrics. Hidden within the confusion of this conglomeration are

Fig. 5. *Drawing room. 1889. Museum of the City of New York (The Byron Collection).*

FIG. 6. *Newsstand.*

individual items which may have a high degree of artistic merit, but it is nearly impossible to isolate them from their surroundings. In total, a group of objects may create an atmosphere, set a mood, but as the group becomes more complex, the individual parts of that group lose their separate identities. Much the same condition exists in the photograph of a newspaper-and-magazine stand (Fig. 6). Desiring to display all his wares, the newsdealer has succeeded in hiding them, for they have become a part of an allover pattern in which the individual item is lost in the confusion of the whole display.

The marginal contact produced by limited interaction between art object and viewer may give a certain amount of satisfaction which can be called a form of esthetic experience. However, it is often an esthetic experience without a direction. The experience is diffused and becomes a part of the general activity that is taking place.

The sense of well-being and the pleasant atmosphere that are often the result of "background" music or "background" interior decoration can be valuable. An environment which satisfies the practical and sensuous needs of those who operate within it is important in daily living, but when the identity of a specific work of art is lost in the total effect of a room or gallery, an observer cannot be said to have a response to that particular object. Only an intimate, concentrated contact between observer and object can produce the full potential of esthetic experience from their interaction.

Lack of attention may interfere with the interaction between object and observer that must precede the esthetic experience, but of equal importance to the achievement of esthetic satisfaction is the observer's willingness to take the work of art at its face value; that is, to accept it as a serious, rational effort of a serious, rational person. At one time this requirement would have seemed an unnecessary, and perhaps even bizarre, suggestion, because the public concept of the nature of serious art closely paralleled the appearance of the paintings and sculpture produced by artists. In the last century this condition has changed. The consistency between public expectation and artistic production no longer exists. We need only compare a group of paintings spanning the period from the fifteenth century to the beginning of the nineteenth with a group dating from the end of the nineteenth century to the present to see the evidence of the remarkable expansion of artists' concept of the nature of a painting.

The Virgin and Child Enthroned by Masaccio, dated 1426 (Pl. 2); Raphael's *Madonna del Granduca*, about 1505 (Pl. 3); John Singleton Copley's *Mrs. Thomas Boylston*, painted in 1766 (Pl. 4); and Edgar Degas's *Nieces of the Artist*, about 1865 (Pl. 5) share a common mode for the representation of form, space, and texture as found in nature. The methods of painting differ stylistically, but in each instance it seems that the artist wants the viewer to be concerned with the representational image and not with the means employed to produce that image. Paint has been applied to a surface to produce each of these paintings, but the painting method is relatively unimportant.

Edouard Manet's *Bar at the Folies-Bergères*, which dates from 1881-82 (Pl. 6); Paul Gauguin's *L'Appel*, painted in 1902 (Pl. 7); *Girl Before a Mirror* by Pablo Picasso, dated 1932 (Pl. 8); and Willem de Kooning's *Woman I*, completed in 1952 (Pl. 9) are examples of paintings produced within a span of less than seventy years. Methods of representation and the application of paint differ markedly in these four works. It is possible to discuss stylistic differences in the works of Masaccio, Raphael, Copley, and Degas, but those differences seem slight when compared to the dramatic contrasts between one and another of the later works.

The reasons for the changes in the visual arts will be discussed elsewhere, but the fact does remain that works of art now being offered to the public, by serious artists, often leave the uninitiated confused and sometimes antagonistic. A contemporary observer, confronted with the profusion of approaches used by present-day artists, may question the values and the intentions that allow the wide range of styles and techniques. Questions such as, "Which approach is to be used as a standard for judgment?," "Which technique demonstrates a skillful use of materials?," perhaps even "Am I being hoaxed?" are typical of those which express the present division between the community of producing artists and potential consumers. A bridge over this chasm can be built, but it must be preceded by an attitude on the part of the observer which will allow the introduction of esthetic forms foreign to him. When faced with objects which at first glance may seem meaningless, the observer who seeks to understand contemporary art must give the artist the benefit of the doubt. The observer must grant the possibility that his inability to comprehend the works in question is due to an inadequacy in himself and not in them. He must assume, at least temporarily, a certain humility, a willingness to reserve judgment until he can be quite sure that his attitude is based upon a clear understanding of what he sees. What has he to lose? Whatever his possible loss, it should be measured against the enrichment that can occur when the chasm is breached and the observer finds in a work of art a meaning that once eluded him.

THE PERCEPTION OF THE OBSERVER

The deaf cannot react to the sounds of a Brahms symphony. The blind cannot know the sensation of a bright-red area juxtaposed to a green one of equal brilliance. Between the observer and the object are the limitations imposed by the ability to perceive.

Except for the blind, perception of the visual arts would seem to pose no difficult problems, but few persons of normal vision realize how limited their perception really is.

Perception, our awareness of the world around us, based on the information that comes through the senses, is too often considered a natural, matter-of-fact attribute of the human being. The assumption is made that everyone sees the same things, that the world, as we know it through our sight, hearing, touch, and ability to smell, is the same for all. This is not so.

For some time psychologists and physiologists have known that there is a considerable difference between the raw information given to the brain by the senses (sensations) and our awareness of the world based on this information (perceptions). Professor J. Z. Young, an English physiologist, describes a number of experiments performed with individuals born blind who, in their later years, were enabled to see. Under these conditions the scientist has an opportunity to study the phases of visual training normally passed through by children, because the adult, unlike the child, can describe with accuracy what is happening to him.

The once-blind person, now physiologically normal, does not "see" the world immediately.

> The patient on opening his eyes for the first time gets little or no enjoyment; indeed, he finds the experience painful. He reports only a spinning mass of lights and colours. He proves to be quite unable to pick out objects by sight, to recognize what they are, or to name them. He has no conception of a space with objetcs in it, although he knows all about objects and their names by touch. "Of course," you will say, "he must take a little time to learn to recognize them by sight." Not a *little* time, but a very, very long time, in fact, years. His brain has not been trained in the rules of seeing. We are not conscious that there are any such rules; we think that we see, as we say, "naturally." But we have in fact learned a whole set or rules during childhood.[2]

Young goes on to say that the once-blind man can learn to "see" only by training his brain. By expending a considerable amount of effort, he can gradually understand the visual experiences of color, form, space, and textures.

These experiments suggest that the sensations we receive have no meaning for us until we know how to order them into a coherent perception. Sensation is only one part of perception. Also included in the construction of a percept is the past experience of the observer and his ability to combine sensations into a meaningful form. To perceive something requires that the observer make a selection of the numerous sensations transmitted to him at any one time. He must select those sensations which are significant for the construction of a particular experience and disregard those which are irrelevant. As Young points out, this requires training. The untrained observer cannot make sense out of what he sees before him.

---

[2] J. Z. Young, *Doubt and Certainty in Science,* Oxford University Press, London, 1951, p. 62.

The Visual Dialogue

FIG. 7. JUAN GRIS. The Man in the Café. *1912.*
Canvas, 50¹/₂ × 34⁵/₈". Philadelphia Museum of Art
(The Louise and Walter Arensberg Collection).

FIG. 8. GEORGES BRAQUE. Man with a Guitar. *1911.*
Canvas, 45³/₄ × 31⁷/₈". The Museum of Modern Art, New York
(Acquired through the Lillie P. Bliss Bequest).

Many kinds of visual training take place in the normal process of growing up in a world already organized into a particular physical and cultural structure. The child learns to see objects that obstruct his movements. He learns, after falling numerous times, to step over his toys. He learns to recognize his parents and to interpret other visual experiences which are a part of living in his world. As he matures, the number of these experiences grows very large, and their recognition will appear to be automatic, but in every case they are learned, because they are important to him in his need to get along in his world. In a similar way the observer of the visual arts develops a perception of this area of his experience through a variety of learning methods.

The perception of pictorial images which are a part of everyday activity, photographs and drawings of ordinary objects and their function in everyday life, develops in the first years of childhood. But when the person trained to perceive the ordinary visual symbols is confronted by the paintings of the cubists (Figs. 7, 8), the rules that apply to the perception of a photograph do not work to give meaning to the picture. Juan Gris and Georges Braque use different structural patterns from those which would appear in a photographic representation; their patterns cannot be understood if the observer's visual training has been limited to that required for the perception of photographs. The chaos that may appear to exist in the cubist painting can be seen as a coherent image by the viewer who has been taught to "read" cubist paintings. Repeated exposure to this kind of painting may result in a form of understanding even without the benefit of formal training.

Cultural differences can train different people to perceive differently, so that identical sensory stimuli will produce different perceptions in a person born and brought up in the city and one who has lived on a farm all his life. The meaning produced for each person will depend on what he requires and expects from the world around him.

This process of perception can be diagramed in the following way (Diag. 1): O represents an object or experience existing in the world outside the observer. It may be a single work of art or a complex pattern of interrelated events. Information about this object is gathered by the sense organs S. In the case of the visual arts the organ would most often be the eyes of the observer, but it could also be the finger tips, which might move across the surface of a piece of sculpture. In the design of certain buildings the sounds of water or the rustle of the wind through the branches of trees have been considered important elements of the plan, requiring the use of the ears as information receivers.

The sensory input S is sent to the brain, where it is interpreted. The interpretation is affected by the past experience of the observer, which may be labeled E. This experience would include the accumulation of daily interactions with the environment in which the observer has lived, his geographical location, his economic and political background, his religious involvement, his friends. Included also would be the formal training given to him in schools. It is important to note that past experience is not a static quantity or quality. It changes with time as the observer lives, reads, observes, and is taught. E is different for every person, for though there may be great similarities between the past experience of individuals within a common cultural environment, no two persons can ever have identical past experiences.

Interpretation of the sensory input is affected also by factors other than past experience. Intelligence is at work here, as are the emotional attitude of the moment and the intensity of concentration. Even the observer's physical state may cause the input to be colored in one way or another. Thus a combination of sensory input, past experience, intelligence, and attitude operate to produce the perception P that was initially stimulated by the object O.

The value of this brief analysis is to be found in the steps indicated between the originating object and the final perception. Too often the assumption is made that object and perception are one, that individuals will perceive a single object or a single experience (which may be considered an object in our diagram) identically. Of course, this is just not so, and, in fact, it is possible that any one person may have different perceptions of the same object at different times. A change in experience or a more sympathetic attitude may change a perception so that a new vision or insight occurs. Like the subjects in the experiments described by Young, the observer, once "blind," may be given sight.

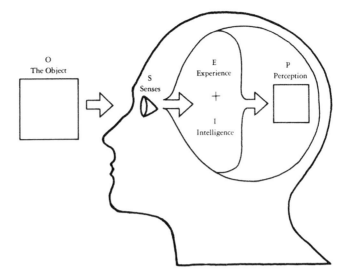

Diag. 1

The perception of meaning in a work of art is not automatic, even though it appears to be so for some works. The training and effort required of the artist for the production of his work often requires a parallel preparation in the public which expects to respond to it. The creative artist begins the chain that leads to esthetic experience, but his responsibility ends in the studio. At this point the responsibility shifts, and it is the observer who bears the burden. If he is satisfied that his perceptual training is equal to the demands made by the artist, then he can question the content and the values implicit in the objects before him. If not, the serious observer can react only to what he finds meaningful; many paintings and pieces of sculpture will remain enigmatic to him until that time when he is prepared to respond to them.

APPRECIATION AND VALUES

We are continually making judgments—deciding which action is right, which article of clothing suits the demands of a social situation, whose opinion is valid. This concern for values finds its expression in the public response to the visual arts as it does in other areas of activity. The questions most frequently heard are: "How do you know it's good?" and "Who decides what is good or bad?" In a society which places a premium on making the *proper* choices there is a natural desire to establish a basis for choice in the area of the arts. Should art appreciation have as its goal the development of the ability to make esthetic judgments, to tell a bad painting from a good one, to recognize a poor building, a mediocre piece of sculpture? What do words which connote value, "great," "good," "bad," "poor," "mediocre," mean when applied to the visual arts?

If it is assumed that there are universal, precise criteria which may be applied to the visual arts, then the application of value terms such as "good" and "bad" suggests that the critic who makes the evaluation is familiar with the terms, is capable of analyzing the work in question, and can apply the terms with objectivity. The question of absolute values in the area of esthetics has concerned philosophers for centuries. Many estheticians have attempted to construct value systems for the arts. None of them has proved adequate. Inevitably the judges are confronted with the application of the rules they have constructed, and it is at this point that major problems arise, for it is impossible to eliminate the personal responses of the viewer from his function as a judge.

Also difficult is the application of rules that were adequate in the past to new works of art, which appear to deny, or even to defy, tradition. The classic example of the confusion which can occur when traditional values are applied to new art forms is to be found in the general critical response given the works of the impressionist painters in the latter half of the nineteenth century. The paintings of these artists were rejected by the large mass of the public, the critics, and museums because they introduced methods of paint application and color usage which were not consistent with previous practice. Paintings by Monet, Pissarro, and others, which now seem unquestionably fine works of art, were reviled and damned as the products of charlatans or madmen (Pls. 10, 11).

There are estheticians who deny the importance of external criteria. They insist on personal, subjective responses as the basis for judgment in the arts. Their judgment becomes a form of communion between the work and the observer. If the observer is moved—if he feels an emotional, an esthetic, or a moral response to a painting, a building, or a statue—it becomes good. Works which do not fulfill this expectation fail and are therefore placed in the lower levels of esthetic achievement. Here again the assignment of values to art objects has obvious difficulties. The very personal responses in one critic carry with them no assurance of similar reactions in others. Even if it is assumed that all those who examine the body of work to be found in the visual arts have a similar educational and social background, there must be differences of intellect, personality, and physical make-up which will affect attitudes and judgments.

Obviously the assignment of values in art is a complex and often confusing business. Yet critics do operate in the visual arts, and though an examination of their writings reveals many areas of conflict, areas of agreement do exist. Certain works of art can be valued more highly than others as esthetic objects. The recognition given to them is achieved because they have been considered by those with extensive experience in the field, over an extended period of time, the best examples of work in their area. This judgment is not the expressed opinion of the general public but the evaluation of specialists, individuals who have made the study of art their life's work. Whatever criteria have been employed by these judges, they have arrived at areas of agreement. They do say, as a body, "This work is good," and their opinions joined in a composite judgment constitute a significant comment upon the arts.

We must recognize, however, that these are opinions and no more than that. They represent individual personal attitudes, whether taken singly or as a part of the judgment of history. These experts bring to their judgments a vast accumulation of experience. They have seen many works of art and can make comparisons between a specific work and thousands of other paintings and pieces of sculpture. When they say that a work of art is good or great, they are, in effect, saying that, compared to the many similar works they have seen before, this particular example communicates its message in a manner equal to or better than the others. Nevertheless, one must always remember that not even experienced critics can make absolute judgments, though their opinions may sometimes carry great weight. Their statements are subject to review, as are the opinions of all of us. The critical limitations of those who condemned the impressionists are to be found exemplified in many other instances. Tastes and values can change. All esthetic judgments may eventually be re-examined and re-evaluated in terms of new cultural relationships. Yet the attitudes of the trained critics are valuable. The critics' contact with art is many times greater than that of the average museum visitor. They have studied the art of the past and are aware of the current work in their fields. Because of their preparation and experience, they can guide the untrained observer to an understanding of art of the past and the present by enlightened comment and a cultivated choice of exhibition material. They can say to the novice, "Here are the works of art which have given me an esthetic experience. In my considered opinion they are the best of their kind. Perhaps you, too, may find in them the satisfaction they gave me."

The answer to the question, "Should art appreciation have as its goal the development of the ability to make esthetic judgments?" must be in the negative. The confusion and uncertainty that surround the problem of values in the arts when specialists deal with it would be compounded when left to the nonspecialist. Of course, no one is barred from the game of awarding critical accolades to the particular works of art which strike their fancy, but the significance of the award is doubtful.

One should not confuse art appreciation with art evaluation. The goal of art appreciation should be the achievement of an esthetic experience. An individual may be guided toward this experience by the knowledge and sensitivity of others; he may help himself by learning the language of art; but in order to achieve this experience he should look at art to react to it, rather than to judge it. If he responds to works of art which are considered mediocre, or even bad, by the experts, the works may still have value for him. Given the opportunity to see a large number of paintings and pieces of sculpture, and given the training to perceive the significant relationships within them, the observer may eventually find that the objects once important to him no longer satisfy his esthetic needs. The forms, colors, and images that prompted his initial reactions may in time lose their impact. To find other, still effective esthetic stimuli he will have to extend his search to areas once meaningless. At this point the example of the trained observers can prove valuable, for if their esthetic needs have been satisfied by certain art objects, it is possible that, in time, the less experienced observer will find satisfaction there too.

The importance of an evaluation depends on the experience and the ability of the judge. Intelligent evaluation may be a guide to appreciation, but it should not be considered the ultimate goal of the person who seeks meaning in the arts.

THE ART OBJECT

CHAPTER II

Wʜᴀᴛ ɪѕ a work of art? In general usage the term "work of art" may include the products of a wide area of human activity, from the use of the spoken and written word to the use of the body in movement. It includes objects of minute size and delicate craftsmanship and constructions of huge proportions.

The objects in Figures 9 and 10 are both examples of the art of the ancient Greeks. One is a bronze figurine from the sixth century ʙ.ᴄ., the other, a great temple of the goddess Athena, the Parthenon, built in the fifth century ʙ.ᴄ. Both are considered works of art, and yet they have obvious differences in size, material, and function. Compare these two examples with a painting by Pablo Picasso (Fig. 11) and a piece of sculpture by Peter Agostini (Fig. 12), both produced in the twentieth century, and the dissimilarity between works of art can be seen even more strikingly.

Fɪɢ. 9. Draped Warrior. *Greek. 6th cent.* ʙ.ᴄ. *Bronze, height 7¹/₂". The Wadsworth Atheneum, Hartford.*

FIG. 10. ICTINUS.
*The Parthenon, on the
height of the Acropolis,
Athens. 447–438* B.C.

A definition of "art object" requires a definition of "art." Many definitions of the word "art" in current use may be found in British and American dictionaries and encyclopedias. In addition there are a large number of personal definitions and theories presented by individual writers and philosophers. Dictionary and encyclopedia definitions tend to be neutral in their point of view, with little or no area for argument. On the other hand, estheticians tend to define their own personal concepts of art and its functions, often stressing some particular facet of the definition which seems important to them in the context of their own philosophical preference. The great variety of meanings attributed to the word "art" emphasizes the desire of men to explain what appears to be a universal human activity. Social groups throughout time, in every part of the earth, have channeled some of their energies into the production of esthetically satisfying objects. Why do they do this,

FIG. 11. PABLO PICASSO. The Painter. *1934.*
Canvas, 39¹/₄ × 32".
The Wadsworth Atheneum, Hartford.

FIG. 12. PETER AGOSTINI. Saracen II 1215 A.D. *1960.*
Bronze, height 29³/₄".
Collection Joseph H. Hirshhorn, New York.

and what qualities inherent in the objects produced separate them from purely utilitarian products ? These questions and others intended to define the nature of the esthetic object and our response to it have produced no absolute conclusions, but certain concepts do recur in most definitions, so that it may be possible to develop a single definition broad enough to include most of the individual concepts.

Differences in the definition of art are concentrated in two major areas : there are those who see the work of art primarily as a means of expressing and communicating ideas and emotions and those who look at the work of art as an object to be perceived as a thing in itself, with little or no reference to other areas of experience. The first group of writers consider the storytelling or imitative aspects of art to be its essential characteristic. What is the artist saying ; what sort of picture of the world does he present ? These are questions the writers ask. Often the estheticians in this group expect the message communicated by the artist to have special qualities : "moral" or "real." They expect to find a meaning in art with a reference to the life and experience of those exposed to the art object. Lev Tolstoi, a nineteenth-century Russian author, reflected this point of view in his book *What Is Art ?*, 1896, when he made the following statement : "To evoke in oneself a feeling one has experienced, and having evoked it in oneself, then by means of movements, lines, colors, sounds, or forms expressed in words, so to transmit that feeling that others may experience the same feeling that is the activity of art."

In direct contrast to the position taken by Tolstoi and those who agree with him is that of Clive Bell, an English esthetician. Bell is known for his defense of the work of the young European artists of the early twentieth century who rejected the traditional, academic storytelling art that was then held in high regard. These artists de-emphasized the importance of representational subject matter and placed a stress upon formal design. In effect these artists were more concerned with the appearance of the object they were making than they were with what it represented. In stating the position of the esthetic he championed, Bell wrote :

> What quality is shared by all objects that provoke our esthetic emotions ?... Only one answer seems possible—significant form. In each [object], line and colors combined in a particular way, certain forms and relations of forms, stir our esthetic emotions. These relations and combinations of lines and colors, these esthetically moving forms, I call "Significant Form" ; and "Significant Form" is the one quality common to all works of visual art.
>
> . . . .
>
> Let no one imagine that representation is bad in itself ; a realistic form may be as significant, in its place as part of a design, as an abstract. But if a representative form has value, it is as form, not as representation. The representative element in a work of art may or may not be harmful ; always it is irrelevant.[1]

In the painting *The Starry Night* by Van Gogh (Pl. 12) Tolstoi might have emphasized the expression of emotion, which seems to have filled Van Gogh prior to or during the painting of this picture ; the swirling movements of the sky, which seems to pulse with all the excitement of the imagination of a mystic who searches the heavens, aware of the invisible forces in the vastness of the universe ; the sense

---

[1] Clive Bell, *Art,* 1913, in *A Modern Book of Esthetics,* ed. Melvin M. Rader, Holt, Rinehart and Winston, Inc., New York, 1935, pp. 247, 252.

of the contrast between this drama in the heavens and the peaceful unawareness of the sleeping village on earth. For Clive Bell the facts of the sky, the moon, the cypress tree, and the village would have been unimportant in comparison with his own excitement as he reacted to the spiral forms, the repeated curved movements, and the contrast of the rich blues and the yellows juxtaposed in agitated brush strokes.

Tolstoi's approach emphasizes the expressive or communicative side of art; Clive Bell's attitude emphasizes the formal side of art. Estheticians agree that these two points of view are not mutually incompatible.

It is possible, perhaps even necessary, to have both the formal and the expressive, or communicative, elements in a single work of art. There is growing evidence that the insistence on formal and expressive elements in art is based upon something more substantial than the personal intuition of philosophers. Psychological studies in recent years have given new insights into the human esthetic impulses, relating them to the human need to communicate and to structure experience. The growing catalogue of psychological studies of the creative expression of the human being suggests that all men have within them the potential seed of this formal communication which we have labeled "art." The difference between the artist and any other human being with this dormant potential is to be found in the facility of the artist to bring forth what the others are incapable of producing. The artist, for one reason or another, develops the manual facility and the intellectual and emotional capacity to produce that which in its essence is a part of all human beings. Henry Schaefer-Simmern, in *The Unfolding of Artistic Activity*, says:

> All normal children display this inner drive for pictorial creation. Drawings on walls, doors, pavements, are visible proofs of the child's inborn creativeness. But because, in the general education, attention is still mainly directed toward acquisition of conceptual knowledge, the child's spontaneous drive for genuine visual cognition is neglected. As he grows older, the creative urge diminishes. It is therefore understandable that in most persons visual conception and its pictorial realization are not developed beyond the stages of childhood. But the ability itself has not vanished. It is always latent and can be awakened.[2]

Schaefer-Simmern's comment on the child's need for pictorial expression is illustrated by the examples of children's spontaneous drawings found in the streets throughout the world (Figs. 13–16).

The visual arts may be considered as communication, as formal organization, or as a combination of both, but it is also possible to examine the products of the artist as the results of a skilled manipulation of materials. Artists find pleasure in the act of applying paint or cutting into the resistant surface of a granite block, and the viewer can also respond to or empathize with the manner in which materials have been manipulated and combined in the process of forming the art object.

No art object can exist unless someone has formed it. The wood or stone which eventually becomes the statue, the paint and canvas which fuse to form the painting, and certainly the many materials which are combined to construct even the simplest building must be worked, manipulated, and controlled to produce the forms that constitute the work of art. As a manipulator of materials, the artist becomes the craftsman. He must know his materials and how to work them. The artisan or

---

[2] Henry Schaefer-Simmern, *The Unfolding of Artistic Activity*, University of California Press, Berkeley, Calif., 1948, p. 29.

Figs. 13–16. *Children's street drawings. Chalk.*
(13) Exterior doorway, Cornelia St., New York. November, 1956.
(14) La Sposa (The Bride). *Pavement in Anguillara, Lazio, Italy. 1959.*
(15) Barred and shuttered window, Ronda, Andalusia, Spain. January, 1958.
(16) Sidewalk, Cornelia St., New York. April, 1955.

The Visual Dialogue

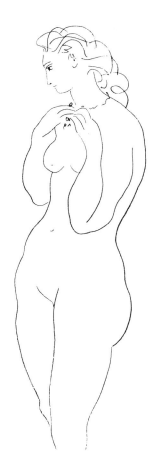

Fig. 17. Pablo Picasso.
Girl with Necklace. *1944. Pen drawing.*
Private collection.

craftsman differs from the artist in that the craftsman's concern is almost exclusively the manipulation of the materials. He learns to control his materials and to exploit their surfaces, structures, and forms. The artist requires these skills too, but they are only a part of his art. They must remain the means by which he achieves the end of his work, which is communication and/or esthetic organization.

How much skill is required? Obviously, enough to do the job. The measure of the skilled use of materials in a work of art is directly related to the intention of the work. When a limited skill in drawing, painting, or carving causes an artist to produce work that is obscure in its intent, when a limited understanding of the structural and visual qualities of his building materials limits the resolution of the architect's design, then the artist is not the craftsman he should be.

On the other hand, a viewer must recognize that the fulfillment of the artist's intention may require a use of materials that departs from tradition. The application of minute areas of paint to a smooth surface with almost invisible brush strokes may indicate a consummate craftsmanship on the part of the painter, but it does not set an absolute standard for the measurement of skill in painting. In another time, for another purpose, the skilled artist may require an application of paint in large, obvious splashes, or perhaps he will need the surfaces and textures of paint dripped or sprayed. The choice of the technical means to produce his work is the artist's.

The two drawings by Picasso illustrated here are examples of the extremes to which the manipulation of material can be carried. In the drawing *Girl with Necklace* (Fig. 17) the flowing, graceful line is carefully and accurately inscribed. The sensuous, curved forms are traced without a single misstep. No superfluous mark

FIG. 18. PABLO PICASSO.
Head *(study for* Guernica*). May 24, 1937.*
Pencil and gouache on white paper,
11'/₂ × 9'/₄".
The Museum of Modern Art, New York
(on extended loan from the artist).

detracts from the continuity of the edge. In total, the quality of the line adds to the image of serenity and grace. The artist's skill is obvious in the control of the line and in the accuracy of its placement in the space of the paper.

Contrast this figure drawing with the study *Head* (Fig. 18). The scrawled, crude areas are shocking in their apparently careless forms. Gone is the controlled, studied grace, and in its stead is an example of what appears to be a drawing produced in an uncontrolled emotional frenzy. We know that Picasso has the skill to draw with grace and accuracy. Can both drawings be the result of a skillful use of the materials? The answer is to be sought in the intent of the artist. What is Picasso attempting to do in the second drawing? Could he have produced the anguish he wished to communicate by drawing his forms with a graceful, flowing line? The drawn line has the potential of being used in many ways. The choice Picasso made in each of the two drawings was based upon his awareness of the material he was using. The use of that material in one drawing is no more skillful than its use in the other. It is the intention that controls the technique, and it is difficult to separate intention from technique in the appreciation of any work of art.

Summarizing then, we may say that a work of art can be described as *a product of man which has a defined form or order and communicates human experience.* To this may be added that it is *affected by the skilled control of the materials used in its construction to project the formal and communicative concepts that the artist wishes to present.*

PL. 5. EDGAR DEGAS. *Double Portrait: The Nieces of the Artist.* c. 1865. Canvas, 23⅝ x 28¾".
The Wadsworth Atheneum, Hartford.

PL. 6. EDOUARD MANET. *A Bar at the Folies-Bergères.* 1881–82. Canvas, 37½ x 51″. The Courtauld Collection, Home House, London.

Such a definition is broad enough to include, within its limits, a great many man-made objects and creative activities. Commercial advertising design, interior decoration, industrial design of commercial and personal objects, sewing, pottery making and other crafts—even the writing of a letter—can fall within the definition suggested.

The inclusiveness of this definition recognizes the potential for esthetic experience in many products of human activity, but no attempt is made in the definition to provide a guide for the establishment of value in the visual arts. It does not separate great art from the mediocre. Each of the art forms within the definition has the potential for a superior esthetic achievement. Some forms may seem more limited in possibilities for full exploitation of one or more of the facets of the definition. Sewing and weaving for instance, would seem to have greater limitations in communication than does painting (Figs. 19, 20); pottery, too, would

FIG. 19. *Friendship quilt, from Baltimore. 1844. Chintz appliqué on muslin, 74¹/₂ × 74¹/₄".*
City Art Museum of St. Louis (Gift of Mrs. Eugenie Papin Thomas).

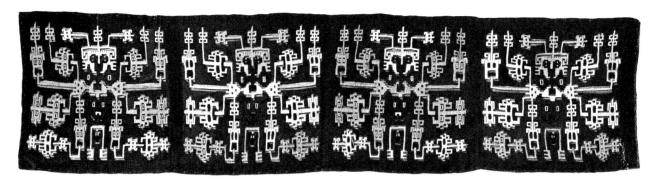

FIG. 20. *Nazca fabric in tapestry weave, from Peru, detail. Pre-Columbian,* A.D. *400–1000. The University Museum, University of Pennsylvania, Philadelphia.*

seem to be less effective than sculpture as a means of expressing ideas and emotions; and yet in the hands of a sensitive artist these art forms do affect a viewer, and certain examples rise above the level of craft objects to become works of art (Fig. 21).

The definition of a work of art suggested here will be that understood through‑ out this book. Though it will be applied only to the arts of painting, sculpture, and architecture, the reader should remember that the statements made in reference to these particular art forms will have application to all the visual arts.

BEAUTY

Nowhere in this definition is the idea of beauty included. This may seem a strange oversight, for the word "beauty" is almost always found in conjunction with art in casual discussions of the subject. The concept of beauty is one of those silent attendants to be expected beside the person who looks at a work of art.

For many people a work of art must be beautiful, but, faced with some con‑ temporary paintings, buildings, or sculpture characterized as works of art, these people feel confused and disturbed, for what they see before them they consider not beautiful, but ugly. Since it is ugliness they recognize, how can they reconcile this disturbing conflict between art and the absence of beauty?

The questions that must be asked are: "What is meant by the words 'ugly' and 'beautiful'?" and "Do these qualities belong in a definition of a work of art?"

There are two basic concepts of the meaning of beauty. In one point of view beauty lies in the subjective response of a person upon contact with an external stimulus: the sense of the beautiful lies within us. Something outside ourselves can make us feel this sense of beauty, but the feeling is not a part of the object that triggered this response; it is solely and completely within the onlooker. In the second point of view beauty is an inherent characteristic of an object or an experi‑ ence. It is the relationship of the individual parts in their combination that is recognized as beauty by a viewer.

These two definitions appear to approach beauty from two opposite poles. Those who think of beauty as existing solely within the responses of the individual are examining the experience from an observer's point of view. Those who think of beauty as inherent in an object or experience are seeing it from the point of view of the creator, the person who must decide how to make his work beautiful.

The Visual Dialogue

The first attitude was expressed by Edgar Carritt, about 1914: "We cannot reflectively think of beauty as an intrinsic quality in physical objects or even in human actions or dispositions, but only as a relation of them to the sensibilities of this or that person." Following in the tradition of Immanuel Kant and George Santayana, Carritt considers beauty a response to a visual, aural, or tactile sensation that gives pleasure.

What of the person who is trying to produce a beautiful object, sound, or movement? For him it is not enough to know that beauty is a subjective reaction within the observer. Such a definition leaves him helpless when he wishes to create something beautiful. The choreographer who must plan a ballet finds it necessary to decide how to group his dancers so that the ensemble will arouse a feeling of delight in the members of the audience. The composer must select, from the resources of orchestral sound, those particular sounds and rhythms which can give the listener the satisfaction of an esthetic experience. The painter, within limits of the edges of his canvas, must place color and textures so that the viewer will feel within himself a surge of delight, which in turn will cause him to exclaim, "Beautiful!" To recognize beauty is one thing, but to produce it is another.

"I shall define Beauty to be a harmony of all the parts, in whatsoever subject it appears, fitted together with such proportion and connection, that nothing could be added, diminished or altered, but for the worse."[3] Leon Battista Alberti, an Italian architect, wrote this definition of beauty in the fifteenth century. Today the same attitude prevails within a large group of the working artists and many of the foremost writers on art. They believe that beauty is the result of a controlled relationship among the separate parts of a work. This definition does not tell the artist how to create beauty, but it does direct his energies toward that goal. It can also direct the observer to the essential elements in a work of art, which in turn may give him that experience of beauty which is called the "esthetic experience."

Both points of view noted above seem valid. It is difficult to refute the argument that beauty, for the observer, is a personal, subjective response, but it can be maintained, on the other hand, that the response requires an initial stimulus with the potential to trigger the esthetic experience.

In the past the esthetic experience was almost always equated with a reaction to beauty. In discussing the sources of esthetic feeling, writers were interested in

[3] Elizabeth G. Holt, *A Documentary History of Art,* Doubleday and Company, Inc., Garden City, N.Y., 1957, Vol. I, p. 230.

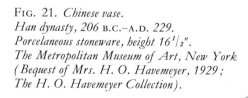

FIG. 21. *Chinese vase.*
Han dynasty, 206 B.C.–A.D. *229.*
Porcelaneous stoneware, height 16¹/₂".
The Metropolitan Museum of Art, New York
(Bequest of Mrs. H. O. Havemeyer, 1929;
The H. O. Havemeyer Collection).

the aspects of beauty and in what produced it. Since the turn of the century, under the influence of psychology, the term "esthetic experience" has more often been interpreted to mean something more than a response to the beautiful.

As noted in Chapter I, Chandler and others feel that an esthetic experience can be, at the same time, unpleasant and disagreeable—that it can include the ugly, the repulsive, and the painful. In effect, many contemporary estheticians and psychologists say that our reaction, pleasant or unpleasant, to art, a reaction we may wish to repeat over and over again because it gives us emotional satisfaction, need not be limited to a recognition of beauty in the work; it may also include areas of human response which are almost opposite to what is generally thought of as beautiful.

With reference to the two questions, "What is meant by the words 'ugly' and beautiful'?" and "Do these qualities belong in a definition of a work of art?" it can be stated that the identification of the ugly and the beautiful is recognized as a personal, subjective response to outside stimuli. Therefore, the recognition of the beautiful by different persons may be motivated by different experiences. Experience, effective at one particular time as an esthetic stimulus for a particular person, may, in time, lose its efficacy for him, to be supplanted by other esthetic stimuli. This evolution affects both the observer and the creating artist who attempts to produce something beautiful by controlling the relationships among the parts of his work in progress. However, the creation of beauty in the usual sense is not the sole consideration of the artist. He may sometimes relate the parts of his work to produce something that is not beautiful. It may be an image more expressive than those created before; it may be a combination of forms or colors in an unexpected and startling composition. The word "beautiful" is tied to the past. It harks back to the established and accepted images and esthetic orders. The new, the startling, the disturbing is rarely seen as beautiful. When the observer approaches a work of art with the attitude that beauty and art are one, he may be imposing upon that work a restrictive demand, forged by tradition, which cannot be fulfilled. In consequence he may be cutting himself off from an esthetic experience which could offer rich rewards.

The conclusion of philosophers that the identification of beauty varies from person to person has been reinforced by psychological studies showing that the esthetic reaction is similar to other emotional reactions and that the individual reactions differ considerably. From infancy on, each person receives innumerable sensations which form within him a potential response to certain stimuli. Some of these responses will be identified as a perception of beauty. Because these emotional reactions are so varied, because there are so many unknown quantities in the creation of the sense of beauty within all people, it is impossible to establish absolute criteria for the identification of the beautiful. The questions always arise: "Beautiful to whom?" "Beautiful when?" To demand that art be beautiful is to reduce the definition of the word to such a personal level as to render it meaningless.

We return then to our original definition: *Art is a product of man in which materials are skillfully ordered to communicate a human experience.* Within these limitations it is possible for some observers to find beauty, for others to find intellectual and emotional satisfaction, and for still others to find a disturbing enigma.

ART AS COMMUNICATION

CHAPTER III

COMMUNICATION BETWEEN PERSONS of wholly dissimilar backgrounds can occur only on an elementary level; separated by the barriers of language and by the absence of common customs and attitudes, the participants in the dialogue may find that their only basis for communication exists in their common experience of the immediate physical world.

Even between individuals who share a common heritage the exchange of ideas, information, and feelings is often difficult. How many arguments are the result of a confused transfer of information? Who has not felt the frustration of trying to express the taste of food, the scent of a garden, or the love of a child? Often the inadequacy of communication is the result of a limited ability to use the available language, but it is also possible that the language itself is incapable of transmitting the information desired.

Nevertheless, communication does take place. The complex process of living in social groups requires a continuing interaction among the members of a group. We seem always to be telling someone something or listening to someone. To keep a society functioning, its members must exchange a great deal of practical information, but it is just as important for each member of the group to be able to express those intimate, personal reactions to life which give him a sense of his own humanity. Wilbur Urban expressed the same idea as follows:

> Life as it is merely lived is senseless. It is perhaps conceivable that we may have a direct apprehension or intuition of life, but the meaning of life can neither be apprehended nor expressed except in language of some kind. Such expression or communication is part of the life process itself.[1]

To point or to scream is to communicate, but the need for more complex communication requires a process or method which is itself more complex.

Communication is a transfer of information or ideas from a source to a receiver. Some vehicle or medium is required for this exchange. We usually refer to this vehicle as a "language." Two persons, looking at the same object, share the consciousness of it. By a series of manual signals they may refer to that object and

---

[1] Wilbur Marshal Urban, *Language and Reality*, The Macmillan Company, New York, 1939, p. 21.

exchange a limited amount of information about it. Once these individuals are separated, or the object of their reference is removed, some systematic combination of sounds or marks must be used to span the distance between them. This more complicated "language" requires the development of equivalents which stand for the object, or the information about it, so that the message may be carried from the speaker to the listener. In communication these equivalents are called "symbols." All those persons who wish to take part in the process of communication, to speak together or read the same paper, must have a knowledge of the language and the symbols that are a part of it. As the communication becomes more complex, as the descriptions become more precise, the language must be developed to represent the specific information and express it. This process requires a language of many individual symbols and a systematic means for combining them into significant and understandable relationships.

To understand a system of language it is necessary to know the specific sounds that have been assigned a definite meaning in it. When it becomes necessary to communicate these sounds beyond the limits of hearing, written symbols, a combination of lines or marks, must be used; and these, too, require a common understanding on the part of the communicators. Thus the sound represented by the word CAT refers to a species of four-legged animal with pointed ears and a tail. The sound itself is not an attempt to imitate the noise made by the animal. The word that identifies this particular animal in the English language differs from the one used in Swedish or Hindustani. It acquires its significance only because we, who speak English, agree to its meaning.

DIAG. 2   DIAG. 3

Similarly, when we wish to express the sound that stands for this four-legged creature, we combine the lines shown in Diagram 2 to produce the symbol shown in Diagram 3. Note that, just as the sound does not imitate the cry of the animal, the lines do not portray it visually. Their meaning exists because it has been arbitrarily assigned and we have been taught to use it.

When a child learns to read, he goes through this process of combining separate elements into a single meaningful unit. At first the separate parts of a letter must be consciously combined to form its shape: a "T" is laboriously constructed with a horizontal mark placed rather precariously over a vertical mark. Then the separate letters are combined to form a word which carries another kind of meaning. In time, the elements that form the letters "C-A-T" and then the word "CAT" lose their separate identities and are seen as a pattern which is readily identified and associated with the animate object in the experience of the child. A good reader will rarely have to consider the separate letters that he combines to form words. Most often he will react to the pattern of the letters and recognize the entire word as a single unit. It is not unusual for rapid readers to identify whole groups of words as a unit, because of the pattern they create. Whether the size of the pattern is large or small, it is his ability to recognize it which allows the reader to understand the meaning of that particular combination of elements.

The sentence, **"THE CAT IS ON THE FENCE,"** is a grouping of separate elements which the reader has learned to combine in a particular way. If the accustomed pattern is broken, even though the individual elements are unchanged, confusion can result:

THEC ATIS ONTH EF ENCE.
CAT FENCE ON IS THE.

Both of the above letter groupings are confusing, for they do not fall into a pattern which has a familiar appearance. To understand the meaning carried by these elements, a reader must stop the normal flow of his reading and attempt to puzzle out the proper relationships for the separate parts. He must, in effect, place them in a new order which makes sense to him. Similarly, in the arts, the person confronted by a new experience must place it in an orderly context with the experiences he has had in the past. He looks for some form of meaning, and always he seeks it in those terms already familiar to him. In painting and sculpture the terms are frequently those of the representation of the physical world, the shape and color of a tree or the size and proportion of a house in its surrounding landscape. The question is often asked by untrained observers of a painting or sculpture, "What is it supposed to be?" These two art forms traditionally have been concerned with the physical appearance of things, and a viewer quite understandably may try to fit the several parts of a painting or piece of sculpture into a pattern based upon the appearance of objects he has seen. He has been trained to do this from childhood, just as he has been trained to read.

As in the case of reading a written language, an untrained observer is usually quite unaware of the separate elements which have been combined to form the symbol of the object he recognizes, nor is he aware of the way in which they have been combined. Like the reader who has progressed from the tedious conscious process of combining letters into words and words into sentences, the untrained person before a work of art often assumes that "reading" a work of art should be a natural, automatic ability, a function of all who can see.

In actuality the artist uses separate elements to construct pictorial symbols in much the same way as a writer combines parts of the written language to produce his method of communication. The following diagrams will demonstrate the similarity between these two processes.

The ten linear elements in Diagram 4 are similar to those used to construct the word "CAT." When they are combined as in Diagram 5, their identities as separate parts give way to a group identity as a pictorial symbol, a house. As in the

Diag. 4   Diag. 5

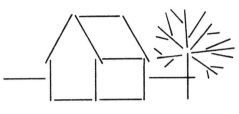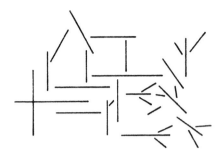

DIAG. 6   DIAG. 7

case of the word formed by separate elements, the new pattern takes on a meaning of its own, which does not normally require the viewer to go through the relatively laborious process of conscious organization.

Again, as in the case of the word symbols, this pictorial symbol may be combined with others to form a larger unit, and this unit, too, has a meaning, because the viewer is able to sense a pattern, a set of relationships, which mean something to him (Diag. 6).

As in the case of the jumbled sentence, this pattern, once broken, may result in confusion (Diag. 7). Because the parts are not arranged in a pattern which has a meaning for the viewer, communication is interrupted; and, as in the word puzzle, no communication can occur again until these elements find their place in a new pattern.

The example of the pictorial symbol used above is a simple demonstration of the organization of one of the artist's plastic elements, *line*. Every work of art, no matter how complex, which uses line as its sole or primary element derives its meaning from the way the lines have been combined. At times the patterns of lines are so complex that the viewer may not consider them as separate and distinct parts. The etching by Rembrandt (Fig. 22) is a picture of Dr. Faustus. Within a darkened room the aging man turns from his desk to see a glowing inscription. He is dressed in heavy robes, his face modeled by the light of the apparition. Form, light, the textures of cloth are all the result of the artist's use of the etching needle. In an enlarged detail of the etching (Fig. 23) the folds of cloth lose their identity and are seen as what they are in actuality—groups of lines. Each of these lines was placed in its particular position by the artist so that it joined with others to create the desired effect. Just as the ten lines of the demonstration drawing were combined to form a house, the lines of the etching are organized to produce their more complex meaning.

What holds true for line is equally true for the other plastic elements, *color, form,* and *texture*. Once again the example of a work by Rembrandt can be used to demonstrate the creation of a symbol used to express the appearance of objects. The *Portrait of a Young Man* (Pl. 13) is an oil painting. When seen from a short distance, the chain that circles the shoulders of the figure appears to be constructed of separate metal segments, glistening in the light. A detail of the painting (Pl. 14) shows a portion of the chain as it has been formed by the artist, actually a number of rather broad strokes of a brush loaded with pigment, which combine to mean "metal chain." Both examples emphasize a basic fact of representation in the visual arts: *the representation of an object is not the object*. The artist did not glue a chain on the canvas when he wished one there. Like the writer, who uses words which are symbols for the things he wishes to communicate, the artist uses the elements of painting and sculpture for communication. The combination of these elements produces equivalents for the subject matter, but the equivalents are always just that—combinations of elements joined to produce an order which must be recognized by an observer before their significance is comprehended.

Consideration of the problems of equivalency will quickly make the following facts apparent. First, *there may be a number of equivalents for the same object in nature.* Line may be used to produce an equivalent, or color, or form. A change in the medium employed by the artist will inevitably change the appearance of the equivalent; that is, oil paint will produce forms, colors, and textures which differ considerably from those produced with water color or mosaic tile. Second, *the appearance of an equivalent may be affected by factors which have nothing to do with the subject matter represented.* Just as there are many different languages in use throughout the world at the present time, each utilizing equivalent combinations of written symbols to represent the objects and experiences of the communicators, there are different visual equivalents in use for communication in art.

Differences of time and tradition may affect both the written and the plastic languages. Even in the expression of persons who share the same language, the same traditions, and the same time in history there is a possibility that, wishing to say the same thing, they will say it in different ways. Finally, it can be said that *each object of experience in nature may be understood or seen in a number of ways* and that *it is impossible for an artist to express simultaneously all the possible meanings potentially in his subject matter.*

FIG. 22. REMBRANDT. Dr. Faustus. *c. 1652.*
Etching, 8 ³/₁₆ × 6 ⁹/₃₂". The Metropolitan
Museum of Art, New York (The Sylmaris
Collection; Gift of George Coe Graves, 1920).

FIG. 23. *Drapery detail of Fig. 22.*

FIG. 24. PIET MONDRIAN.
Tree II. *1912. Black crayon
on paper, 22¹/₄×9⁵/₈".
Haags Gemeentemuseum,
The Hague.*

FIG. 25. PIET MONDRIAN.
Horizontal Tree. *1911.
Canvas, 29⁵/₈×43⁷/₈".
Munson-Williams-Proctor Institute,
Utica, N.Y.*

FIG. 26. PIET MONDRIAN.
Flowering Apple Tree. *1912.
Canvas, 27¹/₂×41³/₄".
Haags Gemeentemuseum,
The Hague.*

Three studies by the Dutch artist Piet Mondrian (Figs. 24–26) are examples of the response of this artist to a tree. What is the tree to Mondrian? Is it a complex arabesque of silhouetted branches, stirring with the forces of life within it; or is it a logical series of rhythms, movement against countermovement, an organic structure? Each painting isolates a portion of the many possibilities that the tree presents to a viewer. By selecting and emphasizing certain parts of the object before him, by reducing the importance of other parts, eliminating details that tend to obscure the statement he wished to make, Mondrian was able to produce three different equivalents for the same object.

It is impossible to say that one of the renderings of the tree is more accurate than the other. Is the plan of a house more accurate than a photograph of its exterior? Does the painting of an animal by an aborigine of Australia (Fig. 27) tell more or less of the truth about that animal than could be shown by a detailed scientific drawing? The detailed drawing might delineate an exterior view of the animal, but the native has tried to combine what he sees of the outside with what he has seen within the animal.

FIG. 27. *Kangaroo-like animals, tribal painting from Arnhemland, Northern Territory, Australia. 19th cent. (?) Painted bark, height 40³/₁". The Museum of Primitive Art, New York.*

Fig. 28. Neb-Amun's Gratitude for His Wealth. *Egyptian wall painting, from the tomb of Neb-Amun, Thebes. 18th dynasty, 16th–14th cent.* B.C. *Painted copy, tempera. The Metropolitan Museum of Art, New York,* Egyptian Wall Paintings, *1930, n. 84.*

Anyone wishing to produce a visual symbol for an experience must be selective. From his consciousness of color, light, form, texture, movement, and even those nonvisual experiences of sound, touch, and smell, he must choose those few characteristic qualities which suggest the essentials of the reality apparent to him at the time he begins to work. This choice may be complicated even further if the artist decides that his subjective responses to the world about him are important factors in the "real" world and that they, too, should be a major constituent of his work.

Selection of the pertinent aspects of reality is not always a matter of free choice. Enmeshed in his own time, the artist perceives and reacts in a manner controlled in part by the traditions and patterns of his cultural environment. The artist who painted the Egyptian wall painting (Fig. 28) was a part of a tradition which existed before he began his life and continued, essentially unchanged, for hundreds of years after his death. The medium he used, the symbols he employed to represent human forms, even the subject matter itself, all were given to him as a part of a tradition. His counterpart in seventeenth-century Holland, the painter Vermeer van Delft, worked within another tradition, one which is closer to present-day

The Visual Dialogue

photographic forms of representation (Pl. 15), but he, too, was faced with technical and symbolic precedents and passed them on with little alteration to those who followed him. If the work of Vermeer is compared with paintings by his contemporaries and with Western artists who came later, it is possible to identify similarities in the representation of form and space which tie these artists into a long and continuing tradition. This tradition has much in common with the kind of visual equivalents produced by a camera.

In Europe, for four hundred years prior to the nineteenth century, the methods for representing form and space in the visual arts had remained essentially unchanged. Though there were stylistic differences between artists and between national or cultural groups, the similarities between the methods of representation outweighed the differences. Linear perspective, aerial perspective, and shading were the prime methods for indicating natural space and form. (See Chapter VI for description of these terms.) These methods had been used so long and so widely that they took on the value of absolutes. That is, they were assumed to be the standard by which all methods of representation were to be measured. Late in the eighteenth century photography was invented, and it was subsequently developed in the nineteenth century into a practical and relatively simple method of creating a visual equivalent for the "real" world. The introduction of the photograph gave additional importance to perspective as the standard method for producing visual equivalents of the artist's perception of form and space in the physical world. The fact that the camera produced an image in linear perspective by an optical-chemical process seemed to be a scientific confirmation of the validity of the perspective system of representing space.

During this same period of time a minority of artists began to experiment with new methods of representation. Stimulated by scientific and technological developments, which were progressing at a startling pace, and influenced by examples of art from the East, from Africa, and from the Americas, these painters and sculptors sought to extend the traditional equivalent forms beyond their representational and expressive limits. These artists had a perception of color, light, and movement which differed from that of their predecessors, and new visual forms were required to communicate this new world. Of course, they did not actually see the world differently from the artists of the preceding generations; the optical-neurological process of sight remained the same: reflected light from the forms before them was focused on the retina of the eye, and the information was transmitted to the brain. But that portion of the information which was given special importance was different from the portions which would have been important to the earlier artists.

If we imagine a scene, a boy flying a kite, what will the visual sense information tell us about what there is before us? The wind is blowing; the sight of leaves trembling and being blown about indicates the presence of the wind. The boy runs across the field, the string of the kite clutched in his hand. The line leads up into a blue-violet sky to a glistening spot. The sun fills the sky with a luminous glow. It casts strong shadows on the boy and turns the green of the field into a series of shifting planes—blue-green, yellow-green. The high grass moves with the wind, and its movement causes changes in the color of the field. There is a sense of connection between the figure in the field and the kite struggling to break the cord which ties it to the boy and to the earth, and yet both of them together, in and above the field, seem isolated from all the rest of the world.

Fig. 29. *Impressionist painting.*
Claude Monet. Rouen Cathedral,
Cour d'Albane, Early Morning. *1894.*
Canvas, 41³/₄ × 29″. Museum of Fine Arts,
Boston (Tompkins Collection).

Fig. 30. *Pointillist painting.* Georges Seurat. Entrance to the Harbor, Port-en-Bessin.
1888. Canvas, 21⁵/₈ × 25⁵/₈″. The Museum of Modern Art, New York (Lillie P. Bliss Collection).

FIG. 31. *Fauve painting.* ANDRÉ DERAIN. London Bridge. *1906. Canvas, 26 × 39".*
The Museum of Modern Art, New York (Gift of Mr. and Mrs. Charles Zadok).

In this imagined scene we are aware of color, light, movement, form, texture. We are aware of our own response to the scene and of the response of the boy. What portion of this reaction is to be selected as the essential portion—the luminosity of the sunlight; the movement of the wind, the boy, and the kite; the specific information about the boy, such as the color of his hair, his age, his weight, the nature of his clothing; perhaps the triangular shape made by the land, the boy, and the kite as they are seen against the horizon? Perhaps the most important part of the whole experience is our own response.

In the relatively short period from the middle of the nineteenth century to the first two decades of the twentieth there arose in succession the impressionists, the pointillists, the Fauves, the cubists, the futurists, and others—groups of artists all attempting to find an adequate equivalent for the communication of the world they perceived about them (Figs. 29–33). Each group found it necessary to construct a visual vocabulary and grammar which differed from those available to them. In their own time the equivalents produced by these painters and sculptors were, quite naturally, compared to the traditional standard, the perspective image, and found wanting. The differences in application of paint, in the use of color, in the representation of form and space were frequently attributed by the critics to inadequate ability or arbitrary idiosyncracies, sometimes even to madness.

FIG. 32. *Cubist painting.* JEAN METZINGER. Tea Time. *1911. Panel, 29³/₄×27³/₈″.*
Philadelphia Museum of Art (The Louise and Walter Arensberg Collection).

PL. 7. PAUL GAUGUIN. *L'Appel.* 1902. Canvas, 51¼ x 35½".
The Cleveland Museum of Art (Gift of the Hanna Fund).

PL. 8. PABLO PICASSO. *Girl before a Mirror*. March, 1932. Canvas, 63¾ x 51¼".
The Museum of Modern Art, New York (Gift of Mrs. Simon Guggenheim).

PL. 9. WILLEM DE KOONING. *Woman I*. 1950–52. Canvas, 75⅞ x 58″.
The Museum of Modern Art, New York.

PL. 10. CLAUDE MONET. *Old St. Lazare Station, Paris.* 1877. Canvas, 31½ x 23½". The Art Institute of Chicago.

Now, however, it is possible to see all these approaches, including that of the traditionalists, as legitimate attempts to reduce the experience of the three-dimensional world of actual experience to the symbolic expression of paint, clay, and stone. The present-day viewer of art can no longer assume that the photographic image is a standard by which other images are to be judged, a language acting as the measure of other communication systems, for he finds himself in a multilingual visual world, a world in which all languages have a value measured by their ability to communicate a significant image of some portion of human experience. Both the the artist and the viewing public are faced today with problems of communication which rarely affected their counterparts in the past. Because they are aware of so much of the world, because they can perceive it historically, scientifically, psychologically, and because the personal perception has been given a value which it did not have in the past, the representation of that perception and the comprehension of what has been represented becomes a complex process. The artist who initiates the communication must use a system that is adequate to say what he has a need to say about experience, and if he cannot find an existing method of visual communication adequate for the job, he must devise one. The viewer comes to the work of art with the knowledge that there are many ways of looking at the world and many ways of communicating what has been experienced. If the artist has used one of the

FIG. 33. *Futurist painting.* GIACOMO BALLA. Dog on Leash. *1912. Canvas, 25 × 42¹/₂″. George F. Goodyear and the Buffalo Fine Arts Academy.*

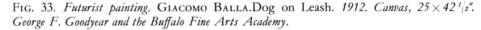

systems of visual communication with which the viewer is familiar, there is a probability that there will be an exchange of information, but if the artist has used a method of expression foreign to the viewer, confusion can and often does occur.

THE SUBJECT MATTER

What can the artist communicate ? This question is related to another : what does the artist wish to communicate ? To judge by the evidence of the work of artists throughout history, the subject matter of the arts may be broken down into three categories : *the world of perceptual reality, the personal response to experience,* and, finally, *the communication of order.* These three areas are not mutually exclusive. Many works of art combine all of them, but there are art forms which appear to emphasize one to the exclusion of the others, and it is important for the spectator to attempt to identify this initial intention of the artist when confronted by a painting, a piece of sculpture, or even a building.

THE WORLD OF PERCEPTUAL REALITY.   Human beings living on the earth in the present have certain basic similarities : the shape and function of their bodies, their primary human drives, and, within the limits of their geographical locations, those aspects of nature which have significance in their lives.

The seas, the land, the skies, and the creatures living in them are a large part of the common inheritance ; they are physical aspects of the world around us. They can be seen, touched, heard, and smelled. Man has added to the physical world structures demonstrating his ingenuity and industry—buildings, bridges, roads, and machines—which seem to increase in numbers by the hour, until in some places they fill the land to exclusion of grass and trees.

This physical world is known to each human being through his senses. The retina of the eye reacts to light energy reflected from objects. Vibrations of air on the drums of the ears are received as sound. The skin reacts to changes of temperature and to contacts with other surfaces. Odors are registered and responses are made to them. In total, this stimulation of the sensory organs provides the raw material that is synthesized within the mind into a personal perception of the external world. J. Z. Young explains the process :

> The essence of the whole process is learning to conform to the conventions of the group in which the individual lives. When we ask a child to name something, we are teaching him to make a response that ensures communication. We are also passing on to him our own ways of observing. We have various means of rewarding him when he is right, punishing him when he is wrong. We can do it by feeding or beating him, but the first can only be infrequent and the second tends to cut off all connexion with him. We do it much more subtly by establishing a special behaviour sequence, that of communication. The child's most important lesson is that the fitting of stimuli into a communicable form produces "satisfactory" results. It is difficult to appreciate how deeply this first way of responding controls all the others, which are later learned through it. Once this is established it is not necessary to set up an elaborate apparatus of rewards and punishments to teach each new association. By giving the signs of approval or disapproval we can show the child instantly whether he has produced the right reactions or not. His whole brain system is trained so that it seeks to organize all the sensory input into

some communicable output—to put it into words. From his earliest days cutting off means hunger and cold, whereas communication means satisfaction. The smile becomes the symbol of completion and satisfaction and the cry that of disorder and pain. By association with these signs that communication has or has not been achieved, the names that are "right" are built into the brain system; the child learns to select and observe "correctly." [2]

Coming into a new world, the child does not experience ordered sensations. He slowly learns to see as his forebears saw, so that he can get along in their world. For this he is in their debt. At the same time, by teaching him to see their world, they have restricted his vision. He is denied the freedom of ordering his own sensations (if this were possible) and seeing the world in his own way. His reactions to the colors and sounds are limited, and, since the pattern of sensation to perception is set in a specific mold, it is difficult to change.

A thousand or even five hundred years ago, men were more isolated from each other than they are today. Separated by the miles and days of difficult transportation, they lived their lives insulated from others who were unlike themselves. The world about them was a small place, and all those who were a part of it were much like themselves. When someone from "another world" did enter their own, he was recognized as different, but the differences did not suggest other worlds, with other ways of living and other ways of seeing; they were seen essentially as eccentricities, in contrast with the "normal" way of saying or doing things. Even the differences that had existed in the past history of the group were not generally understood. Books were available to only a few, and those which were in circulation could not accurately describe the world and manners of former times.

Today there are few places on this earth which are hidden. Through the media of mass communication—television, the movie camera, radio, newspapers, and books—all so readily available, the world has become smaller and smaller. Anthropologists, archeologists, and explorers have roamed the earth to examine man and his environment. The past as well as the present has been opened to investigation. Man has been revealed as a creature of many faces, with many ways of seeing the world. Concepts of morality, of social and economic organization, and of the relationship of the human being to his habitat have been shown to differ widely. Art and the expression of beauty have been found to take many forms. Even the casual reader cannot fail to recognize the vast differences which can separate one cultural group from another.

However, an awareness of the differing cultural forms of human life is not the only way in which the view of the world has been broadened. Developments in the sciences have extended the limits of the senses to a tremendous degree. The eye, aided by the microscope, can see into a world of complex and amazing forms (Fig. 34). The telescope can reach into the heavens to examine the vast spaces among the stars and the patterns of the nebulae (Fig. 35). The x-ray tube permits exploration of the intricate inner forms of familiar objects and creatures (Fig. 36). The oscilloscope reveals patterns of sound and other invisible energies (Fig. 37). The motion-picture camera makes possible the capture of even the swiftest of movements for study at leisure.

---

[2] J. Z. Young, *Doubt and Certainty in Science*, Oxford University Press, London, 1951, p. 92.

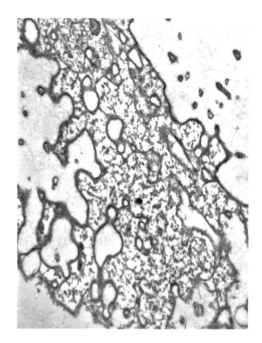

FIG. 34. *Electromicrograph, section of the nerve ending on an electric cell of a Narcine (torpedo fish). Magnification, 19,000 diams.*

FIG. 35. *Great Nebula in Orion (Messier 42). Photograph, 100″. Mount Wilson and Palomar Observatories.*

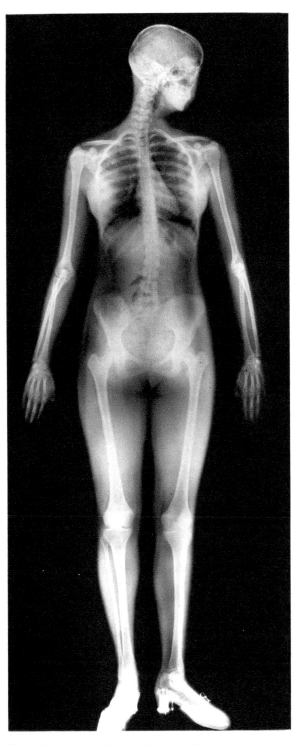

FIG. 36. *Radiograph of the human body.*

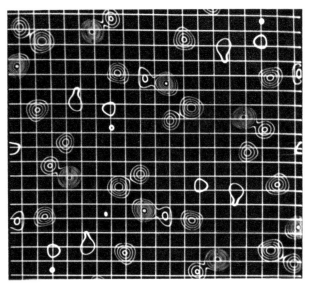

FIG. 37. *Photograph of an oscilloscope screen,*
showing an electron-density contour map of the primary unit
of a crystal of tris *(thiourea) copper (I) chloride,*
constructed with X-ray diffraction data
and the analogue computer X-RAC. Department of Physics,
The Pennsylvania State University, University Park, Pa.

FIG. 38. *Contour farming, Nottingham, Pa., aerial view.*

The landscape of today is not restricted to a view from a hilltop; it can be seen from a plane far above the earth (Fig. 38) or from a bathyscaph a mile beneath the surface of the sea. The dimensions of the perceptual world have been increased many times over in the last few years, and they now continue their expansion into outer space. Each day brings with it a new world to see.

For Renaissance man the forms of the outer world were restricted to what he could see with his unaided eye. When the painter of the fifteenth century conceived of a landscape, he saw it in terms of trees growing over him and mountains rising up over the fields in distant blues and violets. Today the world is a different place for the artist. His vision is no longer confined to the limits of the earth. He may paint what he sees, but now what he sees has been extended to the microcosm and macrocosm that science has revealed to him.

A part of the traditional function of art has been the representation of perceptual reality, and it is important to note that our awareness of the nature of our physical environment is constantly changing. We must recognize also that the conception of this real world may differ with individuals and groups.

There are many approaches to the representation of what we perceive. We all have conceptions of things. These conceptions may vary from time to time, but at any given time we can visualize images of a great many objects. Some of these

The Visual Dialogue

images may be the result of careful study; some may be the result of a careless, passing observation. Some conceptual images have been acquired without direct observations, by contact with images already conceived and produced by others. Photographs, paintings, sculpture, motion pictures, and other image-making media can create ready-made conceptions of objects and experiences for those who cannot create their own.

The world can be thought of as a series of limited conceptual realities, objects which exist only in certain defined and static shapes and positions. A person who conceives of the world in this way sees it in terms of stereotyped concepts. It is often quite difficult for him to recognize representations of physical reality unless they closely approximate his conceptual images. A tree is always *the* tree, a bird is *the* bird, grass is always green, and the sky is always blue.

Children conceive of the world in this way, and their art is an excellent example of *conceptual representation* (Figs. 39–42). As they grow and become aware of themselves and their social groups, their art changes to include the new concepts they develop.

Fig. 39

Figs. 39–42.
*Changing conceptions of the
human being in a child's drawings.
(39) Age 3. (40) Age 3¹/₂.
(41, 42) Age 5¹/₂.
Courtesy Lisa Terenzio.*

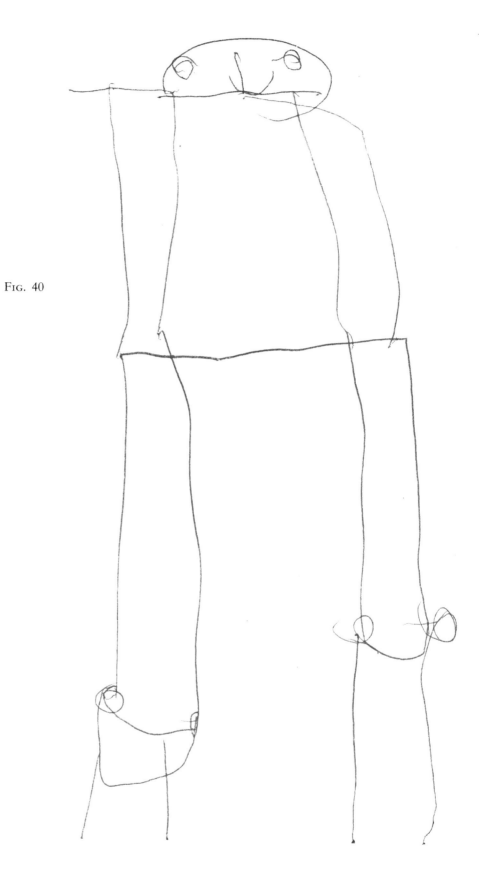

FIG. 40

FIG. 41

FIG. 42

Much visual art falls into this category—the art of conceptual representation. The artist represents what he *knows* about reality, rather than what he *sees*. Like the child, he records those aspects and segments of his world which are meaningful to him, putting together separate conceptual elements to form the entire representation of an experience. Early Egyptian art is conceptual. To depict a man the Egyptian artist selected the most representative concepts of the separate parts of the body and then combined them to form the complete figure. He chose a profile view of a head and placed within it a front view of an eye. He usually indicated the shoulders in a frontal position and the hips and legs from the side view. The resulting image, as exemplified in Figure 43, may not satisfy the demands of other cultures for the representation of a human figure, but its conventions were accepted by the artists and their patrons in Egypt, so that variations from it became the exception rather than the rule.

FIG. 43. Offering Bearers. *Egyptian wall painting, from the tomb of Sebekhotpe, Thebes. 18th dynasty, 16th–14th cent. B.C. Tempera on mud plaster, width c. 30". The Metropolitan Museum of Art, New York (Rogers Fund, 1930).*

FIG. 44. DOROTHY DOUGHTY.
Male Redstart. *1935.*
English Royal Worcester figure.
Bone china, max. height 8$^{15}/_{16}$".
The Metropolitan Museum of Art, New York
(Gift of Mr. and Mrs. Thomas F. Staley, 1950).

Contrasting with the conceptual representation of physical reality is a system intended to reproduce the perceptual experience derived from careful observation of the physical world. In this approach a bird is not always *the* bird. It may be a dot, or a flash of light, or perhaps even the path of a spiraling glide as seen in the sky. Physical experience is communicated in *perceptual representation* as a visual image which, under certain conditions, may be interpreted as a bird, or a man, or an ocean. The senses give the viewer the raw material of his concept. He sees the world in flux, and nothing in it appears twice in exactly the same way. The variables of distance, time, light, movement, and background affect the appearance of all

objects so that they may be represented differently at different times. Even the attitude of the observer at the time of the observation can make a difference in the image created. The resultant representation of this perception may be a three-dimensional replica of the subject or it may be as simplified as a single flashing piece of metal, in which the artist attempts to express the movement, the grace, and the speed of a bird in flight (Figs. 44, 45).

Neither conceptual nor perceptual representation of the physical world is in itself superior to the other; both exist and are to be found in the art of the past and the present.

THE PERSONAL RESPONSE TO EXPERIENCE.   The physical environment comprising the world of actual experience is considered to be the *real* world. In this context the word "real" is used to differentiate that part of experience which seems to occur outside ourselves from that which is confined to our inner person. But the separation of reality from what is unreal is often an artificial division, for there are many subjective attitudes, responses, and images which carry as great a sense of reality as that part of life which is confined to external experience.

The world of subjective reality has been a major influence on much of the visual arts. Constructed of the thoughts and feelings of men, it is shaped by their social values, their emotions, their ideas on life, and their own existence. As William James puts it : "Every exciting thought in the natural man carries credence with it. To conceive with passion is *eo ipso* to affirm."   For many persons their subjective consciousness is more vital, more meaningful, than their contact with the perceptual environment about them, but the communication of this consciousness, this inner reality, often creates problems which are not associated with the communication of experience grounded in the physical world. When a person wishes to say something about a tree, or a cloud, or perhaps even personal relationships, he knows that he is dealing with material common to the conscious experience of many within his society. When he wishes to communicate his own inner experiences, he can never be sure that the images he produces to represent his subjective reality will have meaning for others. In the attempt to express what is real but unseen, the lack of universal symbols creates problems of ambiguity and confusion of meaning and limits comprehension and acceptance.

Museums abound with examples of paintings and sculpture which communicate the forms and experiences of the physical world. The arts that the public generally associates with the communication of abstract realities are music, poetry, and some forms of prose ; in these art forms it expects to find expression of intimate areas of human experience. That the visual arts have also been used for this purpose is not always recognized. For centuries painters and sculptors have tried to express their personal reactions to their subject matter ; and in recent times the communication of the artist's subjective world has become more and more prevalent. There are constant efforts to find a means of communicating these unseen realities in visual terms. The two drawings by Picasso discussed in Chapter II (Figs. 17, 18) may be used again to exemplify the differences between art which has a representational emphasis and art which emphasizes the expressive, subjective response of the artist. The differences between these two drawings are dramatically obvious. The *Head* for *Guernica* does more than describe ; it involves the viewer in the passion that the artist must have felt at the moment he produced the drawing. One cannot imagine Picasso as an uninvolved observer when he began this study. It is much easier to assume a certain detachment on his part when he executed the nude study. Yet an argument could be made that here, too, the artist was emotionally involved and that the drawing is expressive of a quite different concern. Often it is difficult to isolate the representation of perceptual reality from the subjective response of the person who records his perception. Complete objectivity is an impossible goal, and even in the painting of such an artist as Bronzino (Pl. 16) one can find a sense of the involvement of the artist.

Compare the Bronzino painting with Ingres's portrait *Louis Bertin* (Fig. 46), another painting that appears to be an attempt at objective representation. Though

FIG. 46. JEAN AUGUSTE DOMINIQUE INGRES. Louis Bertin. *1832. Canvas, 46×35¹/₂″. The Louvre, Paris.*

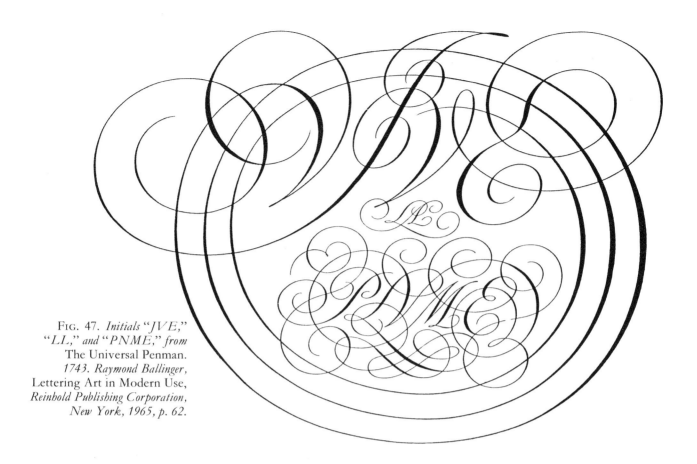

Fig. 47. *Initials "JVE," "LL," and "PNME," from* The Universal Penman. *1743. Raymond Ballinger, Lettering Art in Modern Use, Reinhold Publishing Corporation, New York, 1965, p. 62.*

quite similar in style, there are stylistic differences between them which indicate that the two works are the products of different hands.

THE COMMUNICATION OF ORDER.   Many works of art present no parallels with the experience of an observer because they were produced in a period, geographical location, or culture remote from his own. What can they mean to the contemporary person who does not share the background of the artist who produced the works? A study of history may supply some of the meaning. The similarity of emotions which men have shared throughout time may reveal other meanings. The ability to recognize the representations of physical reality may seem to give another kind of understanding.

An examination of Plate 17 can give a revealing insight into this problem. This work is from the Herat school of painting in Persia during the sixteenth century. What does it really mean to a contemporary Western museum visitor? Certainly it is possible to recognize the representation of figures, a paved court, and what appears to be a building with two figures dining within it, even though the form of representation does not conform to the style commonly seen in Western painting. Once this level of understanding is achieved, what other meaning is to be found in this work? The painting is titled *Bahram Gur in the Turquoise Palace on Wednesday.* Who is Bahram Gur? Who are the others in the courtyard? Is this a simple private meal between two friends, two lovers, two philosophers? The sixteenth-century Persian miniaturist wanted to convey some meaning to his coeval audience. Can the meaning derived by a contemporary viewer who passes the work in a gallery make this painting a significant work of art in the last half of the twentieth century? It may be suggested that much of the narrative meaning and the historical setting of this work can be gathered by research in libraries. Books can surely be found to explain the storytelling element, and this kind of information will offer the viewer some satisfaction of a literary order. Yet even without such background knowledge the painting can give a high degree of esthetic satisfaction to persons of the present day. The differences of time, place, and culture have not markedly affected the human response to color, form, and texture, which constitute the primary reality of the work. The contemporary viewer can find pleasure and meaning in these elements and in the recognition of the way they have been organized.

It is just this sense of order to which Alberti referred in the definition of beauty quoted in Chapter II, and it can be, for the observer, a kind of special communication which can bridge the gaps of time and geography and give him a sense of satisfaction and pleasure.

Rarely do we find a system of communication without provision within it for an esthetic elaboration of the symbols which are used. In the spoken language the choice of words for their euphoneous character or for the rhythm of a syllabic progression becomes a natural part of dramatic and poetic speech. Decorative writing, the use of illuminated initials in manuscripts, and the arrangement of type on a page (Figs. 47–50) are all examples of the union of symbolic function with esthetic function in written communication. Often, in the combination of these

FIG. 48. *Chi rho monogram (XPI), from* The Book of Kells. *7th–8th cent. Trinity College Library, Dublin (Ms. 58, fol. 34r).*

FIGS. 49, 50. DENNIS WHEELER. *Posters for* Life *Magazine. 1964.*
(49) Banner of Leadership. *(50)* Fresh as Spring.

two functions, the concern for esthetic elaboration reduces the readability of the
message. In the reproduction of illuminated initials from The Book of Kells, an
early Celtic Biblical manuscript, the Greek letters Χ ρ ι , the first three letters of
the name of Christ, have been used as the basis for an intricate design. The design
is so complex that it all but eliminates the symbolic significance of the form. One
aspect of communication gives way to another. Contemporary examples of the
reduction of legibility to increase the decorative aspect of type are found in
Figures 49 and 50, both posters for the magazine *Life*. In Figure 49 the well-known
title has been cut and shifted to assume the shape of a stylized flag. The letters here
are out of their normal position, but still legible. In Figure 50 the letters "L" and
"I" are shifted and "F" and "E" are almost totally obscured as the designer uses
them to create the symbol of a flowering plant. Because the *Life* identification is so
well known, the designer can alter it considerably without losing the recognition
value of the symbol and its reference to the magazine.

Constantin Brancusi's marble head *Mlle. Pogany* (Fig. 51) is an example of
sculpture in which the esthetic relationships of the forms seem to dominate the
symbolic function of these forms. The carved marble object represents a human
female head, but because the repetition and continuity of flowing, curved lines was
of major concern to Brancusi, the recognition of the object as a head becomes more
difficult. In a manner similar to that employed by the designer of a beautifully
written word the artist reduces symbolic meaning for what might be called an

PL. 11. CAMILLE PISSARRO. *The Meadow and the Great Walnut Tree in Winter, Eragny.* 1885. Canvas, 23¼ x 38½".
Philadelphia Museum of Art (W. P. Wilstach Collection).

PL. 12. VINCENT VAN GOGH. *The Starry Night.* 1889. Canvas, 29 x 36¼" The Museum of Modern Art, New York (acquired through the Lillie P. Bliss Bequest).

PL. 13. REMBRANDT. *Portrait of a Young Man* (probably Titus). 1655. Canvas, 38 x 32½".
The Wadsworth Atheneum, Hartford.

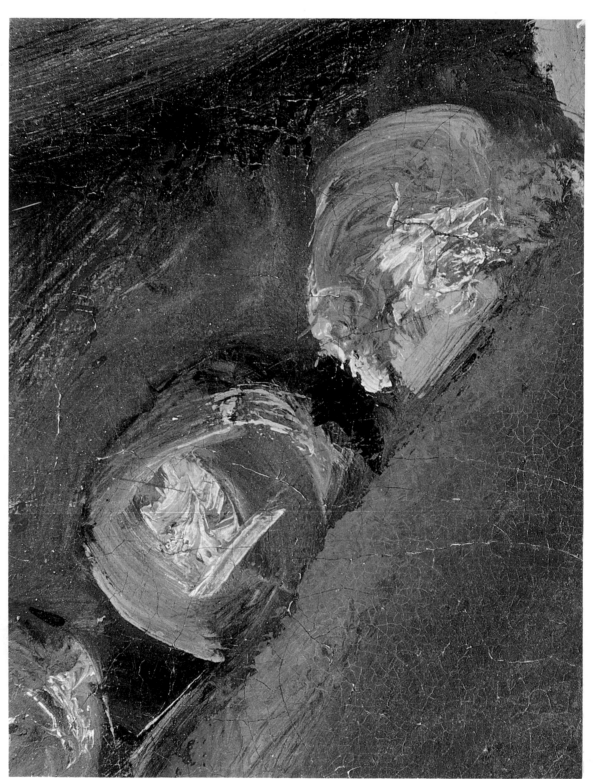

Pl. 14. Detail of Rembrandt portrait (Pl. 13).

FIG. 51. CONSTANTIN BRANCUSI. Mlle. Pogany. *1912. Marble on limestone base, height 17¹/₂".*
Philadelphia Museum of Art (The Louise and Walter Arensberg Collection).

esthetic effect. Yet it should not be assumed that there is a dichotomy between the esthetic concern and the symbolic concern of an artist. The very simplification of the natural details of the head of his subject so as to produce an elegant marble object enabled Brancusi to make a statement about the subject through the use of the material and the esthetic relationship of the forms.

The portrait of Mlle. Pogany can be "read" as a simplified human head; it can be "read" as an esthetically pleasing marble object, in which surface and form combine to produce a three-dimensional design; or, finally, it can be "read" as both symbol and object, the qualities of the object taking on a meaning directly related to the subject symbolized. Meaning in the visual arts may occur on any of these three levels or on all of them.

There are works of art which make no reference to subject matter of any sort. Often these art objects are characterized by an extremely sensitive exploitation of the potentials of color, form, or texture. In the common use of the word "meaning" it might be argued that these works are meaningless, even though they may produce an esthetic response within the viewer, but it is possible to conceive of works of art in this group as their own subject matter. They "speak" *of* themselves. Their meaning lies in the complex plastic relationships built into them. To understand them is to recognize the manner in which they have been constructed, to sense their order and the intellectual and emotional character of the person who produced them (Pl. 25, Fig. 62).

This discussion began with the question: "What can the artist communicate?" To sum up, art as communication has much that is common to all systems of communication; symbols and groups of symbols are combined in structured relationships to produce equivalents for human experience. The symbols that are developed are separate and distinct from the actual objects and experiences they represent. Often these symbols and their organization are based upon a previous tradition, but just as often they are the result of an individual artist's attempt to find the means of communicating those aspects of his experience which he feels cannot be expressed with the visual language of his heritage. Because of the new breadth of subject matter now a part of the environment in which men live, because of the relatively recent emphasis on subjective attitudes and responses to experience, there is a continuing search on the part of the artist for visual equivalents expressive of his inner world and of his consciousness of the world he perceives about him. Parallel with the artist's concern for the visual equivalent is his interest in the esthetic structure of his work. At times it is the symbolic meaning which dominates his art, at times the esthetic, but most often it is a fusion of the two.

As in the instance of verbal or written communication, there is a need for adequate preparation on the part of all parties to the intercourse; and for the observer of painting, sculpture, and architecture this means recognition of the problems of communication in the visual arts and active participation in the study of the new languages which appear as artists strive for an adequate expression of contemporary life.

THE VISUAL VOCABULARY :
The Plastic Elements

CHAPTER IV

W HEN A SCULPTOR begins to work with a mass of clay in his studio, he starts a process which may eventually result in the production of a work of art. The inert material is pulled and pushed into shape; pieces are added and removed; sculpture tools, hands, and fingers are used; and gradually the work approaches its final form. The forms are fixed; concavities, convexities, and open spaces all assume their places. Out of the soft, yielding, inanimate portion of earth a piece of sculpture develops. Shapelessness turns into ordered forms and spaces, chaos into meaning. Rarely does the sculptor, painter, or writer build a work of art as a child would build a tower of blocks, by placing one block upon the other so that each section sits firmly on the section under it and supports the section above. Instead, there is usually a period of trial-and-error operations which gradually produce a selected number of parts arranged in a specific order that is satisfying to the person organizing them. The writer chooses his words, constructs his sentences, arranges his paragraphs. The painter lays out his colors on the palette, paints forms in those colors on the surface of a canvas, combines those forms into larger groups of varying sizes and shapes. Each artist begins with the basic elements of his medium, and the final state of his work is dependent upon the nature of these elements.

In the visual arts the basic structural and expressive units are called the "plastic" elements.

THE PLASTIC ELEMENTS OF SCULPTURE

Sculpture is a three-dimensional art form. It is possible for a sculptor to imitate quite precisely the forms of things he finds in nature. The sculptor Donatello, who worked in Italy in the fifteenth century, appears to have approached sculpture in just this representational way. So does John Rogers, a nineteenth-century American. However, if we compare Donatello's *St. George* (Fig. 52) with Rogers's statuette entitled *"Wounded to the Rear," One More Shot* (Fig. 53), there are differences which obviously set them apart. Both of these statues represent human forms clothed in fabric; but if we study the *St. George*, there appears to be a concern for the disposition of the folds of cloth on the figure, which suggests that the sculptor wished to do more than imitate the appearance of a casual arrangement of the cloak. When seen from the back, the forms of the cloak in the *St. George* are

FIG. 52. DONATELLO. St. George. *c. 1417. Marble, height 6' 10¹/₄".*
Museo Nazionale, Florence.

FIG. 53. JOHN ROGERS. "Wounded to the Rear," One More Shot.
American Civil War period. Bronze, height 23¹/₂".
The Metropolitan Museum of Art, New York (Rogers Fund, 1917).

FIG. 54. *Rear view of Fig. 52.*　　　　　　FIG. 55. *Right side of Fig. 52.*

simplified into a strong diagonal plane (Fig. 54); the folds are indicated with an emphasis that repeats the diagonal. Seen from the front or the side, this statue seems contained in a relatively simple contour edge. Notice the sweeping curve which begins at the statue's left shoulder, continues down the arm to the elbow and through the drape of the cloak, and is then picked up by the diagonal line formed by the edge of the shield and carried down to the base. The figure's right side has a similar contour, which moves in a quieter arc from shoulder to arm to shield (Fig. 55). A study of the statue from its left side (Fig. 56) reveals the form of the cloak used once again to provide a simple, direct contour at the back, contrasting with a more active contour at the front edge, but even this complex movement seems to be unified into a strong diagonal.

Fig. 56. *Left side of Fig. 52.*

Obviously, the arrangement of the forms in the *St. George* is based on a deliberate, conscious design. Donatello's main concern was the creation of a religious image, but he also wished to create an esthetic object.

The statuette by Rogers is also concerned with representation. It is fair to say that representation is the sole intention of the sculptor who produced this piece. The forms of the clothing appear to follow no order other than the accident of a moment in time. One feels from the posture of the figures and the concern for naturalistic detail in figure and drapery that the sculptor wished the observer to forget that the statuette was a bronze equivalent for a real-life scene and to take it for life itself. There is nothing about "*Wounded to the Rear,*" *One More Shot* which directs the viewer to respond to it as a piece of sculpture.

Fig. 57. ELIE NADELMAN. Standing Female Nude. *c. 1909. Bronze, height 21³/₁".*
The Museum of Modern Art, New York (Aristide Maillol Fund).

Both Donatello and Rogers were limited in the way they could arrange the material which formed their sculpture. They may not have been fully cognizant of the limitations upon them, but the need for a relatively naturalistic form of representation restricted the disposition of the shapes, contours, and masses which, in total, comprise both pieces of sculpture. The human body has certain general characteristics of form which cannot be changed without suggesting grotesque distortion. There are proportions of head to body, of eye to head; there are positions natural to the torso, to the arms and legs; there are forms which are naturally concave, others which are convex. No sculptor may depart from these relationships and characteristic shapes, to any appreciable degree, and still maintain the integrity of a representational statue. Within these limitations, however, there is a possibility for arrangement which may be exploited by the artist. Like the choreographer who directs his dancers to take certain poses, the sculptor may arrange the position of torso, head, limbs, and drapery in a great variety of ways. He may simplify or selectively emphasize certain forms. But inevitably he is restricted by the necessity for producing an object which appears to be an accurate, form-for-form equivalent of a human being.

Should a sculptor decide that the esthetic relationships in his work will be his primary concern, he is released from the necessity for arranging the forms and spaces of his sculpture in a manner that approximates the forms and spaces found in natural objects. He may place concave and convex contours where he feels they will produce the most satisfying esthetic result. He may make his forms angular or rounded; he may finish them to a smooth, light-reflecting surface or leave rough surfaces still showing the marks of the tools used to fashion them. If the sculptor feels that two forms should be separated by a space, or that one should be placed above and to the right of another, he can arrange them in that position. Often a sculptor will base his work on natural objects, using his subject as a point of departure for the statue but altering the natural arrangement of forms and spaces so that they satisfy his esthetic sensibilities. The nude by the American sculptor Elie Nadelman (Fig. 57) is an example of just this kind of sculpture. If Nadelman's figure is compared with Donatello's *St. George*, Nadelman's greater concern for the esthetic relationships is obvious. Nadelman consciously treats the female figure as a group of simplified spherical forms. Each portion of the statue becomes a part of a flowing sequence of curvilinear masses and silhouetted edges. Though the difference between the forms of an actual female figure and those produced by the artist are not dramatically different, the sculptor's changes do give a quality that is based upon the repetition and variation of curved forms, rather than on the fact that the subject is a nude female figure.

Henry Moore, a contemporary English sculptor, also uses the female figure as the subject matter for his statue *Reclining Figure, Internal-External Forms* (Fig. 58). Concern for sheer esthetic relationships is even more obvious here than in the work by Nadelman, and as a result the naturalistic representational aspect of the statue is reduced. Moore produced an enveloping hollow shell reminiscent of some of the forms to be found in the female figure. Within the space of the shell he placed another, more linear mass which also derives from human forms. The outer shell is pierced by openings permitting the viewer to look into the somewhat mysterious inner recesses which contain the enfolded figure. The openings in the exterior affect the shape and the disposition of the solid parts of this envelope. Open spaces and

Fig. 58. Henry Moore. Reclining Figure, Internal-External Forms. *1951.*
Bronze, length 21". Museum of Fine Arts, Montreal.

solid forms are interrelated, each affecting the shape and disposition of the other, and it is obvious that it is this organization of open and closed form, inner and outer space, which dominates the conception of this work, and not the demands of representation.

No matter what the intent of the sculptor, he begins with the same basic elements, which must be arranged to achieve those ends. *Form* is one of these elements. He may produce solid forms of varied sizes and shapes ; they may be many or few ; they may be clustered into a tightly grouped mass or separated from one another by open space. The decisions which affect the quality, the number, and the arrangement of the forms are basic to the final appearance of the sculpture. Form, however, cannot be controlled without an awareness of *space*.

Space is an element that is difficult to illustrate unless an actual three-dimensional object is present. The following diagrams may be of some help. Diagram 8 represents four thin cylinders standing upright upon a flat, square field. The cylinders vary in height, and the distances between them are irregular. The cylinders are the vertical forms in this three-dimensional arrangement.

The Visual Dialogue

Diagram 9 represents an overhead view of Diagram 8. The cylinder forms are seen as circles. Each one of these circles is at a measurable distance from every other circle and from the edges of the square on which they are placed, and each one forms an angle with any other two (see dotted lines). These distances and angles describe the space between the forms. When this group of three-dimensional forms is seen from the side, as in Diagram 8, it is possible to sense a spatial relationship between them which results from their varying heights (see shaded area). The

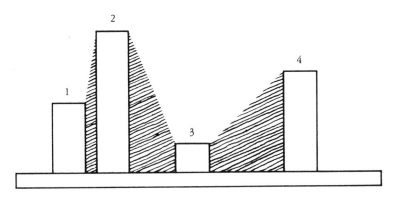

DIAG. 8. *View from the south.*

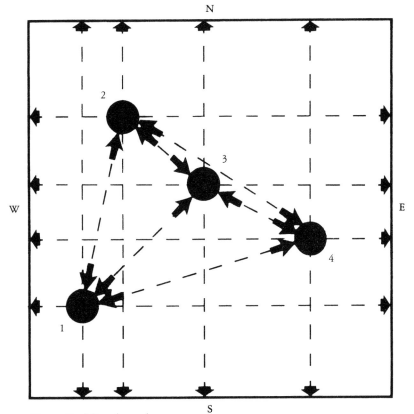

DIAG. 9. *View from above.*

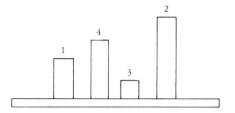

DIAG. 10. *View from the east.*

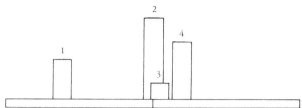

DIAG. 11. *View from the southeast.*

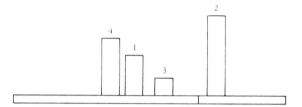

DIAG. 12. *View from the east-northeast.*

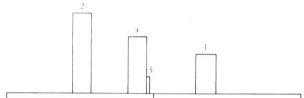

DIAG. 13. *View from the southwest.*

arrangement indicated in these drawings will give the viewer a variety of *apparent* form-space relationships when seen from different points of view (Diags. 10–13). Shifting the position of the forms can result in an infinite range of different spatial relationships.

When the forms used in a three-dimensional composition are more complex than simple cylinders, the variation in shape has a stronger effect on the shape of the space between them. This interaction of form and space can become so complex and interrelated that it is impossible to discuss form and space as separate entities. Imagine Émile Antoine Bourdelle as he was working on the clay model for his *Hercules* (Fig. 59). The forms of his sculpture are directly controlled by the forms and proportions of the human body, but had he raised the left arm a bit, the size and shape of the space between the body, the left leg, the arm, and the bow would have changed. Similarly, changes in the forms and the positions of the legs and in the forms of the rock would have altered the shape and size of the space bounded

FIG. 59. ÉMILE ANTOINE BOURDELLE. Hercules (The Archer). *1908–09. The Wadsworth Atheneum, Hartford (Keney Fund).*

by these elements. The decisions Bourdelle made that resulted in this statue had to include those which affected the open spaces between the forms. In Moore's composition (Fig. 58) the artist, unconcerned with the representational function of his sculpture, has integrated forms and spaces into a complex structure. Though not so important as the forms, the inner space of the outer shell and the spaces between the forms of the outer and inner sculptural elements play a major role in the esthetic order that Moore has conceived.

Form and space are the most important of the plastic elements in sculpture, but there are others. The surface quality of the sculptor's material can have a real importance. The *texture* of the material may be controlled to become a significant part of the over-all design. Texture may be produced by working the material with tools, or by smoothing and polishing it. If the basic material is soft, the act of pushing and pulling it into its final shape, the caress of the artist's hands, or the slash of his knife will produce tactile surfaces which must be subjected to a considered judgment before they are allowed to remain as a part of the completed work.

The small figure by Medardo Rosso called *The Bookmaker* (Fig. 60) is made of wax. Rosso was interested in the play of light over his work. He found the soft, reflective surfaces of wax an ideal material for the luminous effects he wished to achieve and developed a method of working wax over a plaster core. The surface of the wax figure retains the evidence of the way the material was manipulated with fingers and warm instruments. Hollows and built-up forms suggest the surfaces produced by dripping candles as much as they do the image of a figure.

FIG. 60. MEDARDO ROSSO. The Bookmaker. *1894. Wax over plaster, height 17⁷/₈". The Museum of Modern Art, New York (Acquired through the Lillie P. Bliss Bequest).*

FIG. 61. RICHARD LIPPOLD.
Variation Number 7: Full Moon.
*1940–50. Brass rods, nickel-chromium
and stainless-steel wire, height 10".
The Museum of Modern Art, New York.*

The sculptor uses the element of texture even when he seems to neglect it. The thin wires that form Richard Lippold's construction *Variation Number 7: Full Moon* (Fig. 61) would seem to have a negligible texture, and yet it is due to their polished surfaces that these wires reflect the light as they do. Had the surface of the wire been coated so that it was rough and nonreflective, the resultant work would have had an entirely different character.

Form, space, and texture in any single piece of sculpture are directly related to the *material* employed in the construction of the work, and in sculpture the material must be considered one of the plastic elements. When the artist uses clay, plaster, or wax as his original material, he often intends the completed piece to be produced by casting the original model in some more permanent material. He designs the forms, spatial organization, and surfaces with the anticipation that the final casting will be in bronze, brass, or perhaps concrete or some other material. Other materials, such as stone, wood, or welded metals, permit the sculptor to work directly to the completed piece, without a preliminary step. In this case the strength of the material, its ductility, hardness, grain, and the surface qualities that may be given it are necessary considerations in choosing the material.

Linked to the material chosen for a piece of sculpture is another plastic element, *color*. In most instances the color of sculpture is a function of the material selected and the variations produced in it by the application of waxes, stains, and varnishes on wood sculpture, for example, or acids and heat on metal. These finishes, or *patinas*, bring out the characteristics of the material, enhancing the depth of shadowed areas, highlighting those sections which take the light.

Color may be used as a purely decorative element, as in the sculptured metal screen by Harry Bertoia (Pl. 18), in which a combination of brass, copper, and nickel have been used to coat a steel framework with a rich variation of warm tones. *Overture in Black and White,* by John Clague, is a work in which the painted surfaces of the construction actually seem to contradict the forms themselves, so that there is an esthetic conflict between actual form and painted form (Fig. 62). George Sugarman is a sculptor who uses bright color to paint the sections of his constructions in laminated wood. The color is used to isolate each part of the work, with the result that in shape and color the individual segments are joined in a progression of contrasts (Pl. 19).

Fig. 62, John Clague. Overture in Black and White. *c. 1964.*
Fiberglass and steel, 56 × 68 × 42". Grippi and Waddell Gallery, New York.

There are well-established historical precedents for the use of color for naturalistic representation in sculpture. For example, the late-Gothic *Virgin and Child* (Pl. 20) is a painted wooden piece in which the carved forms have been colored to approximate the appearance of cloth and flesh. In contemporary work color is employed for the same purpose in Frank Gallo's *Bikini Girl,* which is constructed of polyester resin (Pl. 21).

Another basic constituent of sculpture is *line.* When applied to the work of the sculptor, "line" can have a number of meanings. It can mean an incised line, a mark scribed into the surface of a form, much as a line is drawn by a pencil on a sheet of paper, but it is also possible to consider line as part of the element of form. When the edge of a form is seen in silhouette, its shape may be considered a linear element, so that one might speak of the curved line produced by the form of the thigh in the figure by Elie Nadelman (Fig. 57). Then, too, when a form has a sharp edge, that edge may be regarded as a linear element. The head by Brancusi has a curved form derived from the eyelashes of the subject (Fig. 51). This form comes to a hard, sharp, curved edge. Its lower surface is in shadow, while the upper plane reflects the light. The edge produced by the change in plane is linear, and it repeats similar linear elements in the work resulting from other changes in planes, as well as the obvious curved silhouette of the entire piece.

These six—form, space, texture, material, color, and line—are the elements which concern the sculptor as he works. He thinks in terms of these basic components. If he is working on a portrait bust which is to approximate the physical forms of his model, he must think, "How shall I shape the clay to construct an equivalent for the physical shape and the nonphysical personality of my sitter?" Or, carving a large piece of wood, he may ask, "What forms, what spaces will best utilize the living pattern of grain? Shall I leave the marks of the chisel, or will polishing the wood to a high luster enhance its appearance?" Decisions such as these are a part of the creative process. They are made continually during the progress of the work, and in total they are the work.

THE PLASTIC ELEMENTS OF ARCHITECTURE

Much of what has been said about the nature of sculpture could be applied to architecture, and both share the plastic elements of form, space, texture, material, line, and color. Both are three-dimensional art forms ; both are concerned with the organization of forms in space. There are, in fact, many examples of architecture which may be considered as monumental pieces of sculpture. If a division is to be made between these two art forms, it may be defined best by recognizing two aspects of architecture which do not find a parallel in sculpture.

First, architecture is a *functional art.* A building is erected to fulfill some practical purpose. It may be argued that sculpture also functions for a purpose, but the purpose of the sculptor's art is restricted to symbolic communication and the evocation of an esthetic response. The architect may wish to include these two functions in his work, but he must also concern himself with the problems of providing a sheltered space for some specific social function.

Second, architecture is a *structural art.* The art object designed by the architect is always large enough to require a structural system to keep it erect. It is possible to think of sculpture without concern for the way in which the forms are held

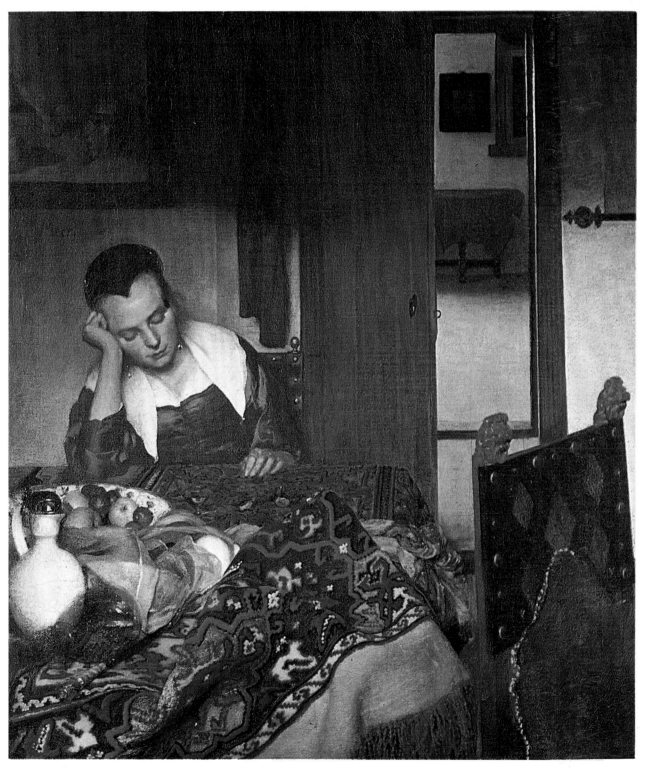

PL. 15. VERMEER. *Girl Asleep.* c. 1656. Canvas, 34½ x 30⅛″. The Metropolitan Museum of Art, New York (Bequest of Benjamin Altman, 1913).

PL. 16. BRONZINO. *Portrait of a Young Man* (possibly Guidobaldo II, Duke of Urbino). 1530–32. Panel, 37⅝ x 29½". The Metropolitan Museum of Art, New York (The H. O. Havemeyer Collection, Bequest of Mrs. H. O. Havemeyer, 1929).

PL. 17. *Bahram Gur in the Turquoise Palace on Wednesday.* Persian miniature,
Herat school, 16th cent. The Metropolitan Museum of Art, New York.

PL. 18. HARRY BERTOIA. *Gilded Screen.* 1958. Plated metal, 9 x 11'. Yale University Art Gallery, New Haven (Gift of International Business Machines Corporation).

together. In architecture the method used to hold the separate elements together is an integral part of the design. For this reason the materials used by the architect, the strength of these materials, and the way they are joined to keep the building erect become a primary concern in the conception of an architectural design.

Ideally, function, structure, and materials in architecture should be so interrelated that they become a tightly woven fabric which gives the building its form, space, and textural variation. This ideal condition rarely occurs. There are often social and economic factors which have an effect on architectural design, requiring the architect to compromise ideal solutions for practical ones. The painter and the sculptor are, for the most part, removed from the pressures of cost in the completion of their work, but the architect seldom is. Some person or group must pay for the erection of the architect's work of art, and it is a rare client who will permit the artist to do whatever he wishes without regard for cost or the client's personal taste. A critical assessment of a building would be unrealistic if the architect–client relationship were disregarded.

SPACE IN ARCHITECTURE.   A building may be perceived from either the outside or the inside. When seen from without, a simple colonial house gives the appearance of a modified cube (Fig. 63). An observer who looks at this building from the street has no accurate idea of the layout of the interior rooms. For him the building exists as a solid form pierced by window and door openings. Once inside,

FIG. 63. *The Towne House, relocated from Charlton, Mass., to Old Sturbridge Village, Sturbridge, Mass. 1787.*

FIG. 64. *Dining room of the Towne House, Fig. 63.*

he is no longer able to react to the exterior, sculptural appearance of the building ; the house becomes a volume of space created by the placement of walls, floors, and ceilings (Fig. 64). The visitor, glancing around the entrance hall, can sense the size and proportions of this space. Doors on either side of the hallway allow him to enter other spaces, each one somewhat different from the others in size and proportion. Windows permit him to look out into the surrounding environment. These connected spaces exist between the limits of the exterior and interior walls that surround them, and though they fill the house, cutting it into many different volumes, each one can be seen and understood only when the viewer stands within it.

In the colonial house there is a certain similarity between the forms of the exterior of a building and the spaces of the interior. For the most part, both aspects of the building are rectangular, and the size of the exterior gives some suggestion of the interior dimensions. An example of a building that seems to integrate form and space to the point at which they are almost indistinguishable is the Glass House, designed by Philip Johnson as his residence (Figs. 65, 66). The walls of glass do not act to isolate its exterior from its interior space. The transparent walls give the viewer a hint of the rectangular form of the building as the reflections in the glass delay his perception of the interior. The flat plane of the roof and the supporting columns also work to define the form, but it is the interior volume which dominates the conception of this structure. The guest house adjacent to this is also the work of

FIGS. 65, 66. PHILIP JOHNSON. *Glass House,*
exterior and interior, New Canaan, Conn. 1949.

FIGS. 67, 68. PHILIP JOHNSON.
Guest House, exterior and interior,
New Canaan, Conn. 1953.

Johnson, and it is in marked contrast to the transparent glass block of the first house (Figs. 67, 68). It is opaque. The relatively small openings which pierce its sides only heighten the sense of the opacity of its exterior mass. The interior of the guest house gives further evidence of the desire of the architect to isolate form and space in this design. Within the cubelike exterior shape Johnson has constructed a series of canopied vaults, creating a rounded space within the cube, a surprise to the visitor who anticipates an interior which reflects the exterior forms.

Space in architecture is created and defined by the shape, the position, and the materials of the forms employed by the architect. Opaque planes set at right angles to one another to form a box will produce an interior space that is cubelike. The effect of this space will be directly related to the volume enclosed by the opaque planes. A small spatial volume with low ceilings will affect the person within it in a manner entirely different from a space of similar proportions but enlarged dimensions. If the planes used by the architect are of glass, the enclosed space will differ from the apparent space felt by an observer, and both of these spatial volumes may be controlled by the architect's design.

Quite obviously the shape of the forms used by the architect will shape the space. Even the flat, two-dimensional photograph of the interior of the Trans World Flight Center at Kennedy International Airport in New York, by the architect Eero Saarinen, conveys the sense of an enclosed space which flows through the building, shaped by the flowing forms of concrete into a dynamic series of connected curved volumes (Fig. 69).

FIG. 69. EERO SAARINEN. *Trans World Flight Center, interior, Kennedy International Airport, N.Y. Opened May 28, 1962.*

Fig. 70. *Painted tepee. Plains Indian (probably Cheyenne).*

Fig. 71. Ludwig Mies van der Rohe. *Seagram Building, New York. 1956–58.*

94

FIG. 72. EERO SAARINEN. *Trans World Flight Center, exterior,
Kennedy International Airport, N.Y. Opened May 28, 1962.*

FORM IN ARCHITECTURE.   Many of the forms in architecture derive from
the materials employed and the structural system selected by the architect. The
simple conical form of the tents of the American Plains Indian is created by stacked
poles covered by skins or fabric (Fig. 70). In a similar way the tall steel-and-glass
office buildings of the contemporary city owe much of their appearance to the
nature of their construction. The severe rectangularity of the Seagram Building by
Mies van der Rohe, in New York City, results from the fact that the architect has
used relatively short steel beams connected into a vertical and horizontal web, or
cage (Fig. 71). The buildings seen behind and beside the Seagram Building are
constructed in a similar manner, and though they are sheathed in stone, brick, and
concrete, they display the same boxlike forms. Contrast these buildings with the
TWA terminal (Fig. 72). The forms of the exterior of this building repeat the
flowing movement of those within it. They result from the use of reinforced
concrete, which was poured into wooden forms much as batter is poured into a
muffin tin. The fluid concrete filled the forms and, when rigid, produced a group of
soaring shells which remained when the supporting forms were removed. These
three examples all demonstrate the use of material and structure as a prime influence
on form in architecture.

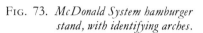

FIG. 73. *McDonald System hamburger stand, with identifying arches.*

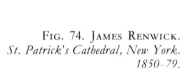

FIG. 74. JAMES RENWICK.
*St. Patrick's Cathedral, New York.
1850–79.*

It is possible to shape the materials of the builder into forms which deny their inherent characteristics or the structural system of the building. An obvious example is to be found in the roadside restaurant with two nonstructural but very prominent arches as a part of its design (Fig. 73). Esthetically pleasing examples may be found, including many of the eclectic buildings in imitation of early historical styles of architecture. St. Patrick's Cathedral in New York City (Fig. 74) is a relatively modern building constructed from 1850 to 1879 on a metal frame. The architect wished to create the impression that the building was entirely constructed of stone, like the Gothic church of St. Ouen in Rouen (Fig. 75). The forms of St. Patrick's Cathedral were designed with little or no concern for their structural function, and even though stone was employed on the exterior surfaces, some of the interior vaults have plaster surfaces in imitation of stone. In this instance both form and space, as conceived by the architects, were unrelated to material and structure. Instead, they resulted from a desire to create an architectural illusion to satisfy the esthetic taste of those who saw and used this building.

FIG. 75. *Church of St. Ouen, Rouen. Begun 1318.*

FIGS. 76, 77. FRANK LLOYD WRIGHT. *Taliesin West,*
two details, Phoenix, Ariz. Begun 1938. (See also Pl. 22.)

The Visual Dialogue

Texture in Architecture.   The use of texture is no less important in architecture than in sculpture. Brick and wood may be used so that patterns are produced by the methods of erecting walls and partitions, or the material itself may provide a surface which may be exploited by the designer. Certain materials may be preferred by an architect who wishes to integrate the design of his building with the site on which it is constructed. An extraordinary example of this approach to the esthetics of architecture is the impressive complex of buildings designed by Frank Lloyd Wright at Taliesin West, near Phoenix, Arizona (Pl. 22). Constructed of local stone and wood, the forms of these buildings seem almost to grow out of the desert which surrounds them (Figs. 76, 77). Forms and textures of building and site share a common quality in the sun and heat of the desert. Contrast this intimacy of texture and form with the severe separation of building and land to be found in the Savoye House, by the architect Le Corbusier, who used flat concrete, glass, and steel to isolate his work from its natural surroundings. Le Corbusier's building (Fig. 78) could be placed in many different sites without losing its essential character, for it seems to be designed as a separate and distinct unit without regard for the appearance of the land about it. The architectural approaches of Wright and Le Corbusier reflect two major esthetic attitudes in contemporary building, and in each instance the textures of the materials used in construction are important considerations in the work.

Fig. 78. Le Corbusier. *Savoye House, Poissy-sur-Seine. 1929–30.*

LINE AND COLOR IN ARCHITECTURE.   Line and color are secondary elements in architecture, as they are in sculpture. Line exists for the architect as the silhouette of forms (Fig. 79)—as the edge created by a change of plane or at the juncture of two or more planes. It is also possible to consider the axis of a form or a spatial volume as having a linear quality, so that the Seagram Building can be described as having a strong vertical line, meaning a vertical axis that is emphasized. One might also refer to the vertical lines created by the forms of the metal elements, which produce the regular patterns on the surface of the same building.

The role of color in architecture often seems similar to that played by texture. The materials used in building have their own integral color. The gray of concrete, the red of brick, or the great variety of colors in wood and stone may be used to integrate the building with its site or to separate it. The protective film that paint provides for certain structural materials offers the architect an unlimited choice of applied colors for both the interior and the exterior of his buildings. There are expressive and functional aspects to the selection and application of color in architecture, and often these factors can be an important consideration in the design. In the past history of architecture it seems fair to say that color has played a minor role in the design of buildings, but with the new developments in the treatment of metals to give them permanent, integral color, with the advances made in plastics, and with the deeper understanding of the psychological function of color, it is possible that this element will become more significant in architectural design.

THE PLASTIC ELEMENTS
OF TWO-DIMENSIONAL ART

It is possible to walk about a building. The space is real, the forms actual. The wood or bronze of a statue exists in space, casts shadows, and offers itself to be touched. A painting or drawing, on the other hand, exists in a world without depth. Two-dimensional art actually stops at the back of the frame, and it is this essential difference which affects the plastic means of the painter and contrasts with those of his counterparts in the three-dimensional arts.

The painter, the draftsman, and the printmaker all begin with color as their basic plastic element. Color is a minor part of the vocabulary of the three-dimensional artist, but in the arts of two dimensions it becomes the means for the development of all the other elements. Two-dimensional form cannot exist without color; even a black form on a white background is dependent upon the contrast between white and black for its existence. No form can be produced unless it is in some color. No form can be seen unless it is on some color.

The artist who works in two dimensions begins by making marks on a flat surface. This surface is his *space*, the world in which he constructs the plastic order which is his work. Limited by the size and proportions of the two-dimensional plane, the painter arranges his forms so that they occupy positions in this space which satisfy the esthetic and expressive demands of his plastic concept. He has the choice of filling the space or leaving it empty. He may vary the size of his forms and the spaces between them. He may vary their shape and, of course, their color. All this activity occurs on the surface of the picture plane. There is little or no extension from the surface of that plane, nor is there usually a penetration through it.

FIG. 79. FRANK LLOYD WRIGHT. *Kaufmann House (Falling Water), Bear Run, Pa. 1936–39.*

FIG. 80. REMBRANDT. Old Woman Cutting Her Nails. *1648.*
Canvas, 49⁵/₈×40¹/₈″. The Metropolitan Museum of Art, New York
(Bequest of Benjamin Altman, 1913).

Certain contemporary painters have attempted to extend the limitations of the two-dimensional arts by adding three-dimensional elements to the surface plane. Precedents for this enrichment of the surface can be found in many periods of the history of art. Gothic painters often embossed the gold backgrounds and details of their panels (Pl. 23), and the works of painters such as Rembrandt (Figs. 80, 81) and Daumier (Pl. 24) exhibit the use of thick paint that protrudes from the plane of the painting. Vincent Van Gogh, among others, also used the *impasto* surface (Fig. 82). Early in the twentieth century the elaboration of the surface was extended even further by combining paint with other materials—painted paper, cloth, wood—which were attached to the surface of the canvas, in works called "collages" (Figs. 83, 84 ; Pl. 25). Contemporary painters such as Burri and Rauschenberg have extended even these innovations to produce works which approach the depth of sculpture (Pls. 26, 27). Yet even these works have relatively little depth and depend primarily upon color to create the form and space relationships.

Fig. 81. *Detail of Fig. 80.*

Fig. 82. VINCENT VAN GOGH. Sunflowers. *1887. Canvas, 17×24″.*
The Metropolitan Museum of Art, New York (Rogers Fund, 1949).

FIG. 83. JUAN GRIS. Breakfast. *1814. Pasted paper, crayon, and oil on canvas,*
31⁷/₈×23¹/₂". The Museum of Modern Art, New York
(Acquired through the Lillie P. Bliss Bequest).

PL. 19. GEORGE SUGARMAN.
C Change. 1965. Laminated
wood, height 9′ 2″. Albert
A. List Collection, New York.

PL. 20. *Virgin and Child*. c. 1500. Polychromed wood, height 10¼".
The Metropolitan Museum of Art, New York.

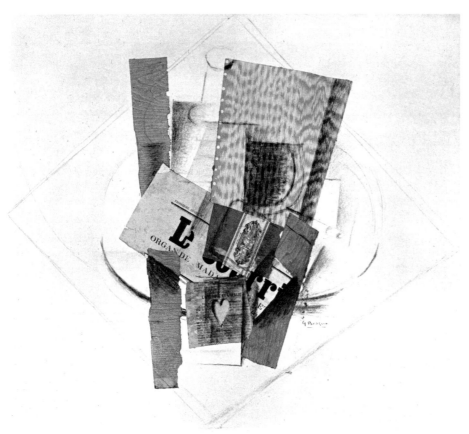

When discussing two-dimensional art, it is important to distinguish between the actual plastic elements employed by the painter and the illusions he can produce by using these elements. Forms and the spaces around them on a canvas, though actually flat, can appear to be three-dimensional. A viewer may respond to a painting as though certain forms were in front of others, as though an actual depth existed between parts of the work. He may refer to the "space" of a painting and really mean the "illusion of space." Similarly, he may discuss opaque and transparent forms, surface texture, or light and shade, and all these elements may be illusionary rather than actual. (Chapter VI discusses the illusion of the third dimension.)

The two-dimensional arts, then, have the plastic elements of *color, form,* and *space.* To these may be added the *texture* of an impasto surface or the surfaces of collage segments and finally the element that is basic to all forms of drawing—*line.* Line, like form, is the result of a mark produced by some instrument on the surface of the picture plane. We might say that a line is actually a form so long in proportion to its width that we tend to overlook the dimension of width and assume that the element has only the one dimension of length.

It is difficult to isolate the individual plastic elements in the works of most painters. Form and space cannot be separated from color. Line and form are often the same thing. The impasto of the brush stroke may be texture, form, and color simultaneously. The beginning student in painting and design is often given a specific problem intended to deal with one or two of these elements at a time, but it does not take long for him to realize that art results from their interaction, from their interdependence, rather than from their operation as independent parts of the whole.

For the painter, the sculptor, or the architect, the plastic elements are the means to his ends. His choice of these elements, his decisions on their disposition and interaction, can produce art or chaos. The observer who is unaware of their existence can find meaning in some art, but it is a meaning which stops at the level of *what* the work is or *what* it represents. Often, perhaps most often, the symbolic meaning, the representational equivalence in a work of art is so insistent, so obvious, that the observer fails to notice the means by which it was produced. Sometimes this lack of awareness is unimportant, for there are works of art which exist solely to project an image. On the other hand, many paintings, pieces of sculpture, and even buildings offer a viewer an opportunity to reach to the *how* of their meaning, as well as the more obvious aspects of the communication; and in many cases the *how*, the organization of the plastic elements, is the prime reason for the existence of the art object. Even when the structural organization plays an auxiliary part in the totality of the art object, response to it can add significantly to the esthetic experience.

THE VISUAL LANGUAGE :
Esthetic Organization of Painting

CHAPTER V

THE PLASTIC ELEMENTS of the visual arts are the basic components used by an artist to construct each of his works, but the way in which he organizes these elements distinguishes one art object from another. A painter may, in one instance, combine color, form, texture, and line to produce a representational image; in another he may combine these same elements in an entirely different way to express his subjective response to a personal experience. Basic to every art object is a central intention, a focus, which requires the artist to make decisions about the number and the kind of elements he will use and the way they will be arranged.

Ideally, every element in a work of art should be an essential component of the artist's intended representational, functional, expressive, or esthetic meaning. It is this unified combination of selected elements which gives the work its meaning, and an observer who approaches a work of art must be able to recognize that the elements are unified before he can understand or appreciate their significance. In art, unity and meaning are closely related. The appearance of a work of art rarely results from a purely expressionistic or representational intention on the part of the artist. Most often it is possible to recognize aspects of an art object which take their form from the desire of the artist to give his work an esthetic order. Frequently it is difficult to separate this order from the total content of the work. The expressive meaning of a blue form in a painting is achieved by its position on the canvas, by the particular color and shape of the form, and by the interaction between this part of the painting and the other parts that surround it. This meaning may also be determined by the identification that the viewer may make between the blue form and objects in nature. The blue form may be a part of a pattern of color or of forms, which can reveal itself to those who are aware that such a pattern may exist, and the content of the painting will be intensified or broadened when the viewer can recognize the multiple functions played by the elements in it.

In many art objects the expressive or descriptive aspects of the elements are restricted. In some, these elements are employed solely as parts of an esthetically satisfying unity. What can stimulate a viewer to respond to the appearance of a vase? The vase is not a symbol. It does not describe or express an experience of anything seen in nature. The viewer's response to the vase must depend upon the forms, the color, and the surface of the object and upon the way these elements relate to each other. Imagine a potter at work at his wheel. He has before him a spinning,

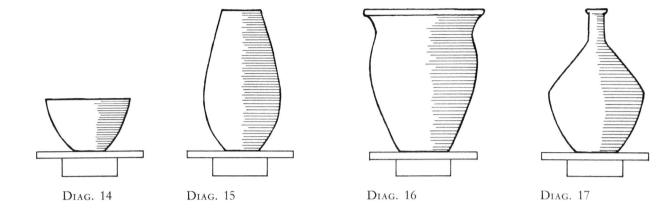

DIAG. 14   DIAG. 15   DIAG. 16   DIAG. 17

inert mass of clay. If he builds the clay up to the shape shown in Diagram 14 and he wishes to produce a vase three times the height of the mass he has built, how should he form it? Diagrams 15, 16, and 17 are possible solutions. It is not necessary here to agree on one of these solutions in preference to the others. It is important to realize that one of them, or rather one of many possible solutions, will be chosen. After that choice has been made, other choices will be necessary before the vase is complete; for example the color and the surface treatment must be selected.

The artist continually makes choices from among many possibilities as he works. Once the art object has been started, some of his choices follow as a result of his initial decisions. Forms and colors in the work suggest other forms, other colors, to a painter; the shapes and surfaces in a piece of sculpture suggest related treatments to the sculptor. The esthetic order sought by the ceramist, the sculptor, the painter, or the architect can be developed in many ways that are basic to all the visual arts. Young art students are introduced to these methods in the early phases of their training, and it will be useful for those who wish to understand the visual arts to acquaint themselves with a number of the ways employed to organize art objects. However, it should be understood that the skillful plastic organization of a work of art does not in itself ensure the production of a masterpiece, any more than the work of a skilled grammarian necessarily produces a great novel. Often the person who defies the traditional esthetic form or who creates new forms of order is the one who produces the extraordinary work of art. A slavish adherence to established principles can result in a dull, academic exercise. Despite this possibility, it is still valuable to understand certain basic organizational principles, so that even those works of art which appear to be a reaction to those principles can be seen in contrast to them.

UNITY AND VARIETY

Esthetic unity is achieved when the parts of an art object fit together in some identifiable order. The order, or organization, of the elements may appear to be simple or it may be highly complex; it may be based upon one or several characteristic qualities in the elements.

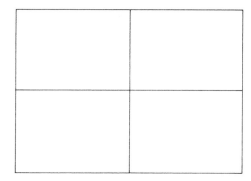

DIAG. 18

Perhaps the simplest method for creating unity within a work of art is by repeated use of similar or identical elements.

In Diagram 18 the large rectangle has been divided into four similar areas. This is a design in which there are many repeated elements. All the forms are rectangles, and all the rectangles are identical in size and shape. Their color is the same. They are placed so that their long and short axes are parallel. This extensive repetition produces a unified design, but though the similarity between the several elements is immediately recognizable, the design has little interest for most viewers. Yet the composition is undeniably unified. If the observer seeks meaning (and meaning in the visual arts derives from esthetic order), why does Diagram 18 seem so dull ? Psychologists tell us that the need to understand, to find meaning in the world about us, is coupled with a need for stimulation and involvement. The individual needs to be challenged ; he needs problems to solve, mountains to cross. He needs a sense of participation in his environment.

> The "will to live," often said to be the great inclusive motive of all living creatures, is in human beings not simply the will to stay alive but rather the will to live in active relations with the environment. Being equipped with sense organs and motor organs and a well developed brain, the human individual has a fundamental inclination to deal with environment. This motive is not primarily directed toward serving the organic needs and meeting the emergencies of life, but toward knowing objects and persons, doing things to them, and participating in what is going on in the environment. Just because this objective tendency is so all persuasive it is often overlooked and omitted from a list of fundamental motives, where it certainly belongs. It shows itself in the general tendencies to explore and manipulate the environment, and in a great variety of more specific interests.[1]

The artist recognizes the need to involve the observer by presenting him with a work that is ordered and seems comprehensible, but at the same time the artist understands that the observer cannot be bored. A work of art must provide

---

[1] Robert Woodworth and Donald Marquis, *Psychology,* 5th ed., Holt, Rinehart and Winston, Inc., New York, 1947, p. 323.

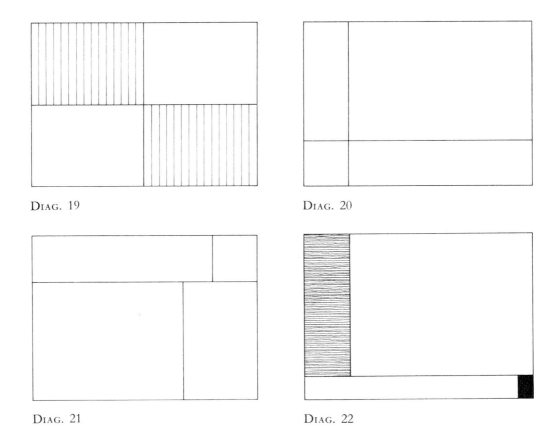

DIAG. 19

DIAG. 20

DIAG. 21

DIAG. 22

enough of a challenge to maintain the interest of those who stop to view it. It must have unity, but it must also have within this unity a complexity, a challenging difficulty, to involve the viewer in a search for a meaning that he senses must be there in the work. Both of these attributes, unity and complexity, or, as it is often called, variety, are essential to any work of art, and the measure of an art object is often the result of the skill of an artist who combines the elements of his work into a unified whole with the imagination that adds variations to and within the basic unity.

In Diagram 18 a more pleasing composition would result if some of the elements were unified and others were used to provide variety.

The rectangle in Diagram 19 is the same as the rectangle in Diagram 18. The four forms within the larger one are identical with those in the previous drawing, but the color of two of the areas has been changed. This design is not exceptionally exciting, but even a variation as simple as this adds more interest to the original composition.

Diagram 20 demonstrates another variation on the original design. Again four small rectangular forms are drawn. Unity is retained by repetition of rectangularity in the forms and by repetition of color, but the rectangles are no longer of identical proportions and size. Their major axis has been shifted, too, adding still another variation to the design. Diagrams 21 and 22 demonstrate two other ways of varying the basic scheme. In each one there remains enough similarity in the character of

The Visual Dialogue

the four separate forms to give a sense of unity, but at the same time each drawing exhibits a variation or a number of variations which introduce a certain added degree of complexity.

Obviously it is possible to combine a number of these variations in one design. The painting *Composition in White, Black, and Red* by Piet Mondrian (Pl. 28) is an excellent example of just this kind of play with similar and dissimilar characteristics. Using a minimum of means, the artist has devised a composition in which the space of his canvas is divided into rectangular areas. Careful examination of the painting will show that areas which seem identical, including the width of the lines, have been subtly varied. The red long rectangle at the bottom of the canvas and the area of black at the top contrast with the other white rectangular forms separated by the black lines.

The apparent simplicity of this painting is misleading, for it is a carefully and painstakingly controlled composition. The precise size, shape, color, and position of the elements on the surface of the canvas are those which the artist felt were the optimum choices for the creation of the greatest esthetic effect. It is the precision of the decisions that makes this painting complex, so that a seemingly simple composition can, in fact, result from a complex series of interrelated and interdependent choices.

The paintings of Josef Albers are superficially even simpler than those by Mondrian. The example of Albers's work in Plate 63, *Study for an Early Diary*, is composed of three square forms aligned on a vertical axis. Each of the forms is painted in a relatively flat single color. Actually it is incorrect to describe this painting as having three squares, for only the center form is a square. The other two forms are more accurately described as square "doughnut" shapes. This distinction is important, because the composition of this painting is based upon the effects produced by the interaction of color areas enclosed by other areas of color. By surrounding the blue center square with orange and the orange area with pink, Albers produced a brilliant, rather mysterious color experience. The painting seems to radiate light, and the flat forms appear to shift in space, moving toward the observer and then away from him.

The complexity in this painting depends upon the precise selection of the colors, the arrangement of those colors, and the size of the color areas. The shape of the forms used by Albers is restricted, the number of the forms is severely limited, and the application of the paint to the surface of the canvas is simple and direct ; but even with these limited means the possible combinations and variations of color and form open to the artist are overwhelming in number.

An adequate response to paintings of this type requires a highly discriminating sensitivity to the interaction of color. For those who can recognize the differences between very similar hues and values of color and the way color areas appear to change when related to other areas of color, this form of painting can be the basis for a satisfying esthetic experience.

Plate 29 is a painting by Peter Paul Rubens, dated in the seventeenth century. Though an initial glance at this painting may give the viewer the feeling that it is very much like a photograph, a more careful study will disclose important differences between the mechanical system of photographic representation and the work this artist has produced. Rubens was extremely careful about the organization of his work. Wherever possible he has repeated curved lines and curved forms so that

DIAG. 23. *Compositional analysis of Rubens's* Tiger Hunt *(Fig. 85, Pl. 29)*.

a basic unity is achieved. Note the repetition of the curve in the back of the tiger as it continues through the body of the attacked rider. This curve is echoed by the movement of the breastplate of the rider at the right. It is picked up and repeated innumerable times throughout the rest of the painting. Even the arms of the figure fighting with the lion have been stylized into curved muscular forms (Fig. 85, Diag. 23).

This composition is purposefully organized. In that respect it is similar to the Mondrian. It differs from the more contemporary painting in that here the basic design has been used as a skeleton for the arrangement of human and animal forms, whereas in the work by Mondrian the skeleton and the finished forms are one. In both cases, however, the repetition of qualities in the elements has been used as one of the basic means for the unification of the work.

UNITY THROUGH CONTRAST.   Unity may also be found where seemingly it should be absent—in contrast. If the repetition of similar qualities in the plastic elements produces unity, contrast might be thought to be an ideal way of creating

FIG. 85. PETER PAUL RUBENS. Tiger Hunt. *c. 1616. Panel, 38 × 48³/₄".*
The Wadsworth Atheneum, Hartford. (See also Pl. 29.)

chaos. Contrast may be defined as a relationship between extremes, an expression of differences. This definition in itself hints at the unity of contrast. In the statement that contrast is a *relationship* an assumption must be made that there is a connection between the contrasting parts; they are joined as extremes of the same or similar characteristic qualities. Black and white are bound together, as are green and red, empty and full, or up and down. In each instance the presentation of one half of a polar couple calls forth its opposite number. Each part of the combination seems to need the other to reach completion, a state of equilibrium. The union which results from the combination of two opposite elements is a demonstration of a resolution of forces. It is a unity that most people can sense immediately. Often it is referred to as a "sense of balance."

Many writers on art, including those who are trained as psychologists, consider balance a requisite for a satisfactory esthetic composition. No one is absolutely sure why balance should be an essential factor, but apparently it is.

The simplest form of balance is achieved by duplicating on one side the forces in operation on the other side of a fulcrum, as in placing two children of equal weight

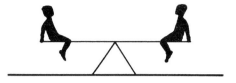 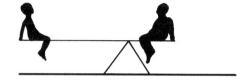

DIAG. 24   DIAG. 25

at equal distances from the center of a seesaw. This kind of balance, in which one side is identical to the other, is called "formal" (Diag. 24). It is an extremely limiting method of creating equilibrium. An artist who uses it must be prepared to repeat all elements on each side of the center line. A state of equilibrium may be accomplished without this restrictive requirement. Two children of different weights may balance themselves on their seesaw by adjusting the distance between themselves and the center of the board, so that the heavier one is closer to the fulcrum. A similar adjustment may be made to achieve balance in other circumstances. This kind of balance, in which unequal elements are resolved, is called "informal" (Diag. 25). Dissimilar elements may be combined to equal other combinations of dissimilar elements. In the case of the seesaw, weights and distances are combined so that their product is equal, even though the individual parts are different. However, the elements need not be restricted to two only. As our visual interpretation of balance changes from actual physical weight to other kinds of "weight,"

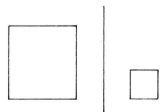

DIAG. 26. *When forms are identical in shape and color, size affects visual weight.*

DIAG. 27. *When forms are identical in shape and size, color affects visual weight.*

DIAG. 28. *Shape can affect visual weight, though mass and color may be similar.*

116

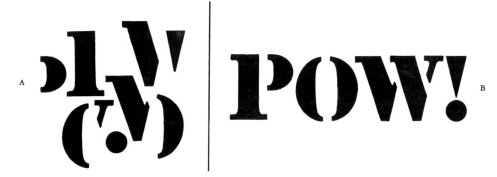

DIAG. 29. *The symbolic content of a form or group of forms can add visual weight to an area. Because the forms in* B *are grouped to read as a word, their visual weight is affected.*

such as the "weight" of colors, the "weight" of textures, or even the "weight" of ideas, it is possible to perceive rather complex combinations of elements as equaling other combinations and therefore in balance with them (Diags. 26–29).

As has been noted, there is little disagreement on the necessity for balance in art. However, once the composition of a work of art becomes complex and many different colors and irregular shapes are introduced, it is impossible to arrive at a balanced composition by a mechanical method. Balance in the visual arts is a function of *visual weights*. The apparent weight of an element in a composition may vary as its color is changed, its shape is altered, or its texture or size is varied. Its position on the sheet of paper or the canvas is a critical factor in this system. Elements may vary in weight as they are moved from the bottom to the top or from side to side of a composition (Diag. 30). Even the symbolic significance of an element may influence its effect on the balance of a composition. For instance, a gray rectangular form will have a certain weight in a composition, depending on its size, shape,

DIAG. 30. *Visual weight can be affected by the position of the form in relation to the edges of the space being composed.*

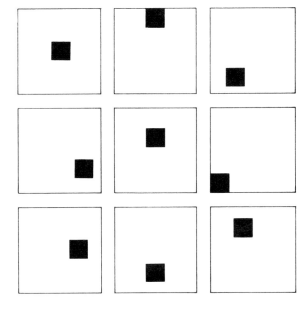

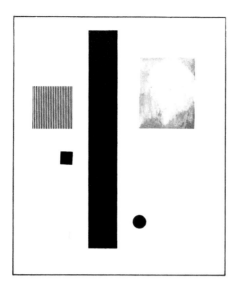

DIAG. 31

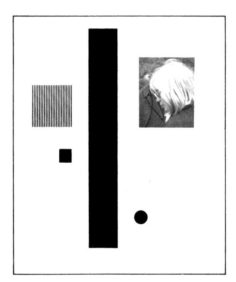

DIAG. 32

position, color, and surface variation. When a photograph of about the same tonality is substituted for the rectangle, the visual weight increases, because the image of the photograph gives an added level of meaning to the form it fills (Diags. 31, 32).

Obviously the complexity of even such an apparently simple composition as the Mondrian painting requires more than a mechanical placement of elements to arrive at a state of equilibrium, so that even though everyone may agree about the necessity for a balanced composition, the most that may be said about its achievement is that the artist arrives at it intuitively and the viewer must use his intuition in responding to it. With so many variables affecting the weight of his elements, no artist can consciously control all the significant factors that must be resolved in the balance of a work of art. Nevertheless, because he needs a feeling of equilibrium when he studies his work, he organizes the elements in it to satisfy this need.

Another use of contrast as the basis for the organization of painting is to be found in the work of "optical" artists such as Richard Anuszkiewicz and Bridget

Riley. Anuszkiewicz was a student of Josef Albers and, like Albers, he concerns himself with problems of color interaction. His paintings are composed of simple geometric forms, usually divided into small areas. By restricting the light-and-dark (value) contrast of his colors and exploiting the contrast between hues through the use of such combinations as red and green, orange and blue, or violet and yellow, Anuszkiewicz produces paintings which shimmer and vibrate in a manner suggesting the brilliance of flickering neon light (Pl. 61). A discussion of "value" and "hue" is given in Appendix IV.

Bridget Riley, an English painter, uses the same compositional device in the illustration shown here (Fig. 86). The narrow, contrasting curved forms produce a startling illusion of vibrating and shifting planes. The use of black and white permits this artist to produce the greatest possible contrast between contiguous areas.

Both of these paintings depend upon the effect produced by a pattern of contrasting color forms. The optical illusions created result from the response of

Fig. 86. Bridget Riley. Current. *1964. Synthetic polymer paint on composition board, 58³/₈ × 57⁷/₈″. The Museum of Modern Art, New York (Philip C. Johnson Fund).*

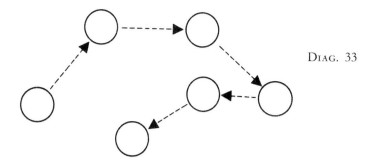

the human eye to the excitation produced by the agitating patterns. These paintings are unified in the sense that each color form becomes a part of the interacting matrix. Variety in the composition does not depend upon changes in the shape, size, color, or placement of forms, as it did in previous examples of painting illustrated here. Instead, it comes from *optical* shifts and movements on the part of the observer.

The use of color contrast to produce vibration is not, in itself, an innovation. The impressionists used this device, but in impressionist painting the vibration of areas was employed as a means for the representation of light and shadow in nature. In these paintings it became a means for the esthetic organization and the production of an image to which the observer responds as the essential meaning of the work. Paintings such as those by Riley and Anuszkiewicz have been grouped into a category identified as "optical," or "op," art. Actually all paintings are in a sense optical, for they all depend upon the function and the limitations of the eye for the perceptual response of an observer. However, "optical" painting does differ from earlier types of painting in that the organization of "op" works is almost totally dependent upon the creation of a pattern of contrasting, interacting color forms.

The observer, like the artist, needs a world in balance, and he, too, is satisfied by a recognition of forces in equilibrium. However, unless he realizes that balance may be effected by the operation of many plastic elements, he is likely to respond only to those obvious visual weights which have become important to him. Given enough time, however, even an untrained observer can learn to recognize the significance of many of the plastic elements in a balanced composition.

UNITY THROUGH MOVEMENT AND CONTINUITY.   In Diagram 33 the reader is given a prescribed path to follow, which moves from separate element to separate element and ties them all together by virtue of a continuous visual sign. The observer is given a series of visual orders which moves him in a step-by-step awareness from part to part—now up, now to the right, then down, and back again. No matter how complex the path, no matter how devious the route, if he can follow it, the observer is able to sense a continuity between individual elements, because they are connected by a ribbon of linear movement.

In his desire to unify many different elements in a composition, the artist can make use of this sort of linear connection. He can establish a more or less continuous linear path which ties the separate elements into a large understandable unit. This unit may be very simple—a geometric form such as a triangle or a circle—or it may be developed into a highly complex movement of mazelike appearance.

The *Madonna del Gardellino* by Raphael uses this device. It groups the major elements of the painting into a triangular structure (Fig. 87 ; Diag. 34).

FIG. 87. RAPHAEL. Madonna del Gardellino. *1505. Panel, 42 × 29¹/₂". Uffizi Galleries, Florence.*

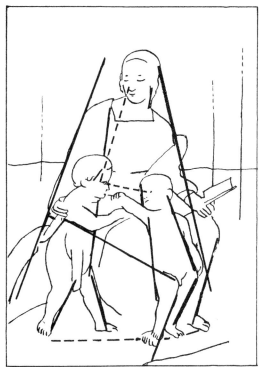

DIAG. 34. *Compositional analysis of Raphael's* Madonna del Gardellino *(Fig. 87).*

121

The three figures, the two infants and the female figure, are placed so that they are contained within the space of the triangle. This simple geometric form is easily recognized and provides the unifying basis for the entire composition. Notice, too, that this large triangle sets the pattern for the introduction of many subsidiary triangular motifs, which the artist repeated in the position of the children's legs and in the movements in the drapery. Here is an instance of unity by repetition reinforcing unity by continuity.

Repetition, balance, and movement, or continuity, are often found in combination as unifying methods in a single work of art. It is rare that an artist depends on only one of them to establish the design of his work. In his desire to integrate his work the artist uses whatever seems to him effective for his purpose. He may make the individual choices consciously, but often he may make them as a part of a series of intuitive decisions as he works at his object, trying to complete it, changing element after element until each feels right and all go together.

ESTHETIC ORGANIZATION IN PAINTING

Repetition, balance, and continuity are used in all the visual arts as methods of organization, but each art form requires a slightly different application of the organizational means.

Painting can be understood as a flat, two-dimensional arrangement of colored forms, or it may be regarded as an illusionistic device which presents an equivalent for three-dimensional form and space on a two-dimensional surface. In either case the methods of esthetic organization can be applied to arrive at a unified composition.

If the painting is considered in its actual two-dimensional context, the area to be organized is that bounded by the sides of the canvas. It is a flat, two-dimensional plane of measured length and width (Diag. 35).

This frontal plane is called the "picture plane." When the artist concerns himself with the organization of the picture plane, he thinks in terms of flat shapes, which may vary in size, shape, color, and pattern. These shapes may be arranged on the surface of the picture plane in an infinite variety of positions. No indication of depth in the painting is considered in picture-plane organization. It is as though the artist worked with a group of cut-paper forms which were never permitted to overlap.

Pablo Picasso's painting *Still Life with Fishes* (Pl. 30) can be analyzed as a picture-plane composition which utilizes a number of the organizational methods described in this chapter.

DIAG. 35

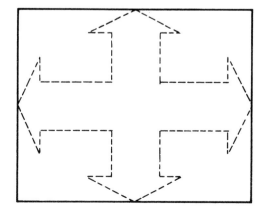

PL. 21. FRANK GALLO. *Bikini Girl*. 1964. Polyester resin, height 36″. Graham Gallery, New York.

Pl. 22. Frank Lloyd Wright. Taliesin West, Phoenix, Ariz. Begun 1938.

Pl. 23. GENTILE DA FABRIANO. *The Adoration of the Magi.* 1423. Panel, 9' 10⅛" x 9' 3". The Uffizi Gallery, Florence.

PL. 24. HONORÉ DAUMIER. *Two Sculptors* (*L'Atelier du Sculpteur*). c. 1870. Panel, 11 x 14". The Phillips Collection, Washington, D.C.

PL. 25. KURT SCHWITTERS. *Cherry Picture.* 1921. Collage on painted cardboard, 36⅛″ x 27¾″.
The Museum of Modern Art, New York (Mr. and Mrs. A. Atwater Kent, Jr. Fund).

PL. 26. ALBERTO BURRI. *Nero Plastica La 3*. 1963. Plastic with oil on canvas, 80 x 77⅜".
Marlborough-Gerson Gallery, New York.

Pl. 27. ROBERT RAUSCHENBERG. *Canyon*. 1959. Canvas with assemblage, 86½ x 70½ x 23″.
Collection Mrs. Ileana Sonnabend, Paris.

PL. 28. PIET MONDRIAN. *Composition in White, Black, and Red.* 1936. Canvas, 40¼ x 41″.
The Museum of Modern Art, New York (Gift of the Advisory Committee).

There is repetition of the shape of the forms. With few exceptions they are constructed out of triangular sections with straight edges. A number of curved forms are introduced, notably in the railing at the left. These curves are also repeated in the bottom of the drape at the right and in the tail of the lower fish. Triangular forms dominate the composition, but curves in a subordinate grouping help to unify the design. Color, too, is found in a repetitive distribution. Black forms and green, yellow, blue, and orange forms are placed in a complex interrelation. Sizes of the areas vary greatly, as do the intervals between them, introducing a significant factor of variety within the basically unified composition. A number of edges are disposed so that there is a continuous movement along them. Sometimes this occurs without a break, as in the edge at the top left, which combines the black, green, and orange forms in a diagonal that echoes the major diagonal movement of the black form at the right edge of the table. Another movement continues the vertical edge of the right table leg into the form of the curtain. To the left there is still another vertical movement along the edge of the table, but this time it is not continuous but, after a space, is picked up directly above to extend the vertical movement.

A more extended structural analysis of this painting would show the same methods of organization applied to smaller details. However, it must be emphasized that an analysis such as the one above comes after the fact of the painting. It is doubtful that Picasso consciously planned all the relationships he organized in this painting; many must have been intuitively felt. Nevertheless, the finished work does take on much of its character from the interrelated plastic elements on the picture plane.

In contrast to the flattened picture-plane emphasis of this Picasso, Canaletto's painting *View of Venice, Piazza and Piazzetta San Marco* seems to deny the existence of a picture plane (Fig. 88). It is as though the artist wished to eliminate the front surface of the painting to make the viewer believe that an actual three-dimensional space existed behind the picture frame. Linear perspective (see Chapter VI) is used here to represent the deep space, but at the same time the converging diagonal lines of the buildings produce a linear continuity which connects the many separate forms into a few basic movements on the picture plane (Diag. 36). Vertical repetitions are also a unifying factor, as are the repeated curved forms in the arcades and umbrellas. Here, then, is a painting in which the organization of the picture plane seems to be disregarded, and yet that organization does exist, though it is not so complex as in the later painting by Picasso.

To assume that Canaletto was primarily concerned with the picture-plane composition would be to deny the obvious pictorial emphasis in this painting. The painter has produced an illusionary space representing two great squares in the city of Venice. However, the pictorial intention does not eliminate the need for esthetic organization in the painting. The illusionary space and the forms filling that space may be organized much as a choreographer or a director would organize the human and constructed forms which fill a stage. If the artist paints as though there were no picture plane, he may apply the methods of esthetic organization to the *pictorial* elements rather than to the *plastic* elements. He can arrange buildings, walks, trees, and people, rather than forms, lines, and colors.

Imagine the space in the Canaletto painting without the figures in it. If the artist had wished to, he might have painted figures so that they appeared to stand

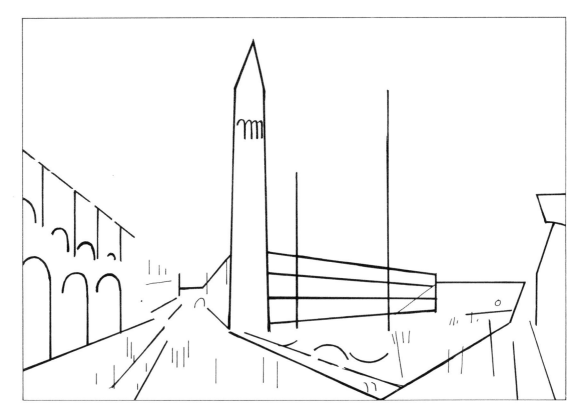

DIAG. 36. *Compositional analysis of Canaletto's* View of Venice, Piazza and Piazzetta San Marco *(Fig. 88)*.

at any spot within the illusionary space of the two squares. All the figures could have been lined up, evenly spaced, along the front of the pictorial space, leaving the rest of the square empty. They could all have been grouped at the left or at the far right. Instead, the painter has arranged them in groups of various sizes and then arranged the groups in groups. Grouping is another form of linear continuity, and it is used rather frequently by painters in organizing a pictorial space.

Note, too, that the space created by the painter varies in depth, receding far back at the left-center but blocked by the mass of the building and the enclosed area of the Piazza at the right. The speed of the movement back seems to shift also, moving quickly at the left and more slowly at the right.

It might be argued that the composition of this painting was an *automatic* result of the arrangement of the buildings and spaces in the actual subject matter—that the artist did no more than record what he saw. Even if this were true, the artist could have placed himself anywhere in the Piazza to draw the forms and space there. His *choice* of observation point would be an important way in which he might arrange the elements of his composition. The fact is that this painting is not the simple result of the work of a painter who set up his easel in the Piazza San Marco and began to paint. It is the result of a careful construction of space based upon a perspective system of drawing, in which the receding, converging diagonals of the forms are organized as the artist wished them. (See Chapter VI for discussion of perspective.) The detailed rendering of forms, textures, and light in this painting depends on the skill of the artist. No camera, unless fitted with a special lens, could have pro-

FIG. 88. CANALETTO. View of Venice, Piazza and Piazzetta San Marco. *c. 1730.*
Canvas, 26 × 40¹/₂". The Wadsworth Atheneum, Hartford.

duced an image comparable to that produced by Canaletto in this work. Had the
camera or the eyes of a human observer been pointed down to the Piazzetta and
the ships moored at the Grand Canal on the left, the deep space to the right would
not appear as it does. If the camera had been turned to the right, pointing into the
Piazza, the space of the Piazzetta could not have been seen. The painting is actually
composed of two separate views, though these views have been combined to
conform to perspective rules.[2]

Divide the painting along the vertical axis of the bell tower, and two distinct
scenes, correctly organized according to linear perspective, are produced. That they
have been united into one painting suggests that the composition is a deliberate
organization based upon the artist's wish, rather than the result of an accurate
transcription of a scene observed from a single viewpoint.

Esthetic organization in painting may take place either on the picture plane
or in the illusionary space that an artist can suggest behind the flat surface of the
painting. Whether the organization is two-dimensional or in the illusion of a
third dimension, it unifies the elements employed by the painter into a coherent,
interrelated structure. Repetition, continuity, and the balance of visual weights
may serve to achieve unity, just as they may serve to give variation or complexity.

---

[2] It is known that Canaletto, during this period of his life, used an instrument *(camera ottica)*
to assist him in drawing perspective images. It is possible that this instrument was used in the
production of this painting. However, it would have required a combination of several views
through the instrument to achieve the results seen in this painting.

THE MEDIUM AND ESTHETIC ORGANIZATION

In the visual arts, as in all the arts, the artist must manipulate material or utilize a process or group of processes to produce his finished work. The colors in a painting result from the application of colored materials to a surface. The viewer may see a red area which is an integral part of an ordered esthetic relationship, but the artist had to manipulate *paint* to produce the area. Because paint has certain physical properties, the artist must master the craftsmanlike control of those properties to achieve the esthetic results required in any one particular art object.

Though it is possible to discuss a work of art in terms of its plastic elements, the viewer must remember that these elements are products of, and therefore affected by, the medium used to produce them.

Ideally the manipulation of a medium should be an integral part of the esthetic unit produced by the artist. In fact, however, many works of art are demonstrations of an extraordinary technical virtuosity, in which the exploitation of the medium overshadows the content of the work.

There is a great difference between the effect produced by an artist and the means used to produce that effect. The shimmering brilliance of an area of color in a Monet still life (Pl. 48) is the result of an application of small areas of oil paint, mixed on a palette or taken directly from the tube, and applied by a stiff brush to the surface of a canvas fabric stretched tightly over a wooden frame. The visual effect produced by Monet was the result of the choice of color and the size and disposition of the color areas, but it was also affected by the texture and viscosity of the paint, the flexibility of the brushes, and the surface of the canvas support. Similarly, the quality of the red area in the water color *From the Bridge,* by John Marin, is partially due to the physical properties of the medium employed (Pl. 31).

Oil paint similar to that used by Monet can be employed to produce a great many different surface and color effects. For this reason oil has been a popular medium since its introduction. It may be thinned into a transparent film and applied in successive layers, as in the work of El Greco. In *St. John's Vision of the Mysteries of the Apocalypse* (Pl. 32) the artist began to work on a canvas tinted with a dark color. The light areas in the painting were created by laying layers of white, transparent paint, one over the other, until the desired degree of lightness was reached. Finally, the local hues were introduced by the use of additional glazes of thinned paint.

Edouard Manet, in the nineteenth century, applied his oil paint directly on a white canvas in vigorous brush strokes which were meant to be seen. *Boating,* by this artist, is painted without the use of glazed overlays. Each color placed on the canvas was mixed in the hue and value the artist wished and then transferred directly from the palette to the surface of the painting (Pl. 33).

Another example of direct painting is to be seen in the work of Chaim Soutine. His *Portrait of Kisling* has a sense of immediacy and vitality deriving in part from the thick paint surface (*impasto*) employed in the painting (Pl. 34).

Each painting medium offers the artist a great number of possibilities for the production of color and surface effects. Decisions as to the kind and number of technical variations to be used in a single work of art depend upon the artist's personal style and his esthetic and expressive intentions. (See Appendix III.)

In the painting *Violin and Pipe with the Word "Polka"* (Pl. 35), by Georges Braque, the artist applied oil paint to the canvas in relatively flat areas. The gray-green forms have a painted pattern applied to them; diamonds, circles, and broken lines in diagonal movements provide a contrast to the flat areas and, at the same time, repeat the diagonal and curved forms found throughout the composition. Additional variety is introduced by mixing sand with the paint, so that certain areas of the painting differ in surface texture. The rough surface tends to modulate the light which falls on the flatly painted surfaces, producing a subtle variation in the color. The degree of roughness is controlled within specific areas, so that the smoother surfaces, like the white forms, contrast with the more obviously textured blacks in the center of the composition. Besides adding sand to the paint, Braque combed the thick film of brown paint covering those forms based on the table top and legs, so that the wavy lines were incised into the paint surface. Within this painting the paint substance has been used in several ways, and yet the over-all effect is one of an ordered composition, because the artist has used the technical variations as part of an over-all compositional plan.

Drawing and printmaking techniques offer the artist possibilities for exploitation of the medium similar to those found in painting.

At one time in the history of art the definition of a drawing was a simple matter. All artists made studies in preparation for work to be finished in more complex media. A drawing was a part of this preparation. The artist employed an instrument or material that produced essentially linear effects, such as chalk, silverpoint, pen, or brush and ink. By using an uncomplicated means for the recording of natural phenomena or for making studies of his work, the painter or the sculptor could prepare the organization of his material and try out tentative ideas for important projects (Fig. 89). The drawing process was much simpler than the process of

FIG. 89. MICHELANGELO.
Studies for the Libyan Sibyl. *c. 1508.*
Red chalk, $11^3/8 \times 8^1/4$".
The Metropolitan Museum of Art, New York
(Purchase, 1924, Joseph Pulitzer Bequest).

135

Fig. 90. KIMON NICOLAÏDES.
Study for a painting in progress. c. 1930–37.
Pencil on transparent paper, 10³/₄ × 8¹/₄".
Collection Mamie Harmon, New York.

Fig. 91. EDWARD CORBETT.
Number 18. *1952. Chalk, 23¹/₄ × 18¹/₄".*
Collection Mrs. John D. Rockefeller III,
New York.

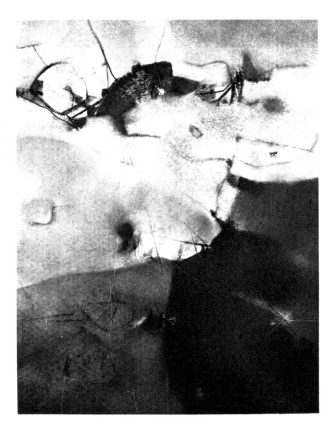

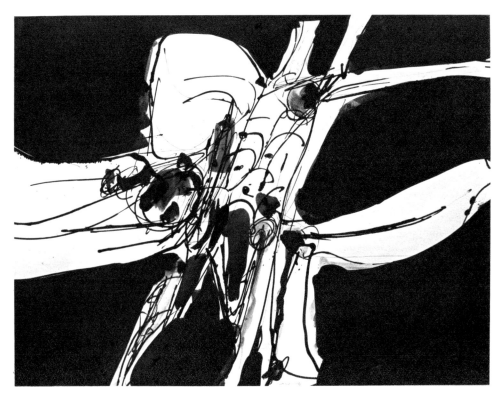

FIG. 92. CARMEN CICERO. *Untitled. 1955. Pencil, brush, and pen, 18*^{15}/$_{16}$×25".
The Museum of Modern Art, New York.

painting or carving stone. Rapid studies could be made of anatomy or drapery. Nature could be recorded easily by working out of doors without the necessity of carrying complicated paraphernalia to the site. Drawings were valuable to the artist, but they were rarely considered an end in themselves. At times rapidly executed and intimate, they often gave the impression of just having left the hand of the executor.

Many contemporary artists continue to draw for reasons much the same as those which motivated their predecessors, but there is a large body of recent drawing which seems to be produced as an esthetic end in itself. In many instances the line between drawing and painting has become fuzzy and indistinct. Exhibition committees faced with the problem of defining a drawing usually resort to general definitions, which limit the requirements for a drawing to those works in one color (or perhaps two) presented on a paper surface. Definitions this broad permit the inclusion of works as varied as the pencil study by Kimon Nicolaïdes (Fig. 90), Edward Corbett's chalk composition (Fig. 91), and Carmen Cicero's work in pencil, brush, and pen (Fig. 92).

Common to all these drawings is a rather direct use of the medium. In each the marks produced on the surface of the paper still retain the identity of the drawing instrument or material that was used.

The drawn lines in the study by Nicolaïdes were produced by grains of graphite deposited on the surface of a sheet of paper as a pencil was pressed against it. The granular line varies in value as the pressure of the artist's hand increased or decreased. Changes in value were also created as lines were brought closer together, overlapped, or rubbed to produce a uniform tone. Cicero's drawing was made by a

FIG. 93. OSKAR KOKOSCHKA.
Portrait of Olda. *1938. Blue crayon,
$17^3/_{16} \times 13^{13}/_{16}''$.*
*Allen Memorial Art Museum,
Oberlin College, Oberlin, Ohio
(R. T. Miller, Jr., Fund).*

variety of linear strokes on the surface of the paper. Pen and brushes were used to vary the thickness of the line, but the color of the marks is consistently black, without any tonal variation. The Corbett drawing, like the Nicolaïdes, was produced by a material that deposits a granular mark on the paper's surface, but in this instance the medium was chalk, rather than pencil. Chalk has a greater tendency to smear and smudge. By carefully controlling this characteristic, the artist was able to produce a variety of tonal areas, as well as sharp, incisive lines, which contrast with the softer tones. (See Appendix I for a description of drawing media.)

Often the fragmentary or spontaneous nature of a drawing results in a work which is somewhat limited in formal structure but has an undeniable esthetic appeal. Oskar Kokoschka's crayon drawing *Portrait of Olda* (Fig. 93) has this quality. Here the nervous energy and fluid movement of the line offer the viewer the pleasure of empathizing with the artist as he produced the work in an excited dance of crayon across paper. One responds to the vitality and the virtuosity of the act, almost as one would respond to the movement of a dancer. But even as the line provides the viewer with visual excitement, the consistency of its rhythm creates a unifying focus and gives the work a coherent quality.

Printmaking offers the artist a medium which combines some of the properties of painting with those of drawing. Early prints were important to artists because they reproduced the form and substance of an original drawing. *The Battle of the Nudes,* by the Renaissance Italian Antonio Pollaiuolo (Fig. 94), is an early engraving which demonstrates the artist's interest in the representation of the male figure in action. A comparison between the engraving and a painting by the same artist, in collaboration with his brother, *The Martyrdom of St. Sebastian* (Fig. 95), suggests a similarity of interest in both. Compositionally the two works share a common

The Visual Dialogue

Fig. 94. Antonio Pollaiuolo. The Battle of the Nudes. *c. 1465.*
Engraving. Uffizi Galleries, Florence.

FIG. 95. ANTONIO *and* PIERO POLLAIUOLO. The Martyrdom of St. Sebastian. *1475.*
Panel, 9′ 9″ × 6′ 7¹/₂″. National Gallery, London.

emphasis on outlined forms with hard edges and curvilinear and diagonal movements, and though the painting deals with a Christian subject, it obviously becomes a vehicle for the representation of the male figure.

An engraving like *The Battle of the Nudes* is produced by cutting grooves or lines into the polished surface of a flat metal plate. Ink is then deposited into these grooves, and the surface of the plate is wiped clean. A sheet of paper is placed over the engraved surface, and pressure is applied to the sandwich of metal and paper. The ink in the grooves is forced into the fibers of the paper, and when the sheet is removed, a mirror image of the plate has been impressed upon it. By the use of this process multiple imprints may be made from the same plate.

Prints are not to be confused with *reproductions*. A reproduction is a *copy* of an original work produced by one or another more or less mechanical process. The artist rarely has control over the quality of a print and is often unaware of its existence. On the other hand, each print is considered an original work of art and is usually signed by the artist to indicate that the quality is approved by him and that it is an authentic impression. The artist often prints his own editions or has control over the printing process performed by a trained craftsman.[3]

Present-day printmakers are concerned with the print as a separate and distinct art form. Contemporary printmaking techniques permit the artist to employ a wide range of coloristic and textural effects rivaling, but not imitating, the expressive and esthetic potential of painting. Like the several painting media, each print process can have an influence on the esthetic organization of the art object. (For a description of printmaking processes, see Appendix II.)

Two prints by Gabor Peterdi suggest the flexibility of etching as it is used today. Both prints were executed by a process technically similar to that used by Pollaiuolo. *Cathedral* (Fig. 96) is an etching and engraving. Though the subject matter and the style differ from Pollaiuolo's engraving, the effects in both works are the result of a complex of many small lines. The etching process permits the artist to produce lines which are more spontaneous and direct than those possible in engraving, and the Peterdi print uses the freely drawn line as an integral part of the style. Within the mesh of etched lines one may find engraved lines used to darken and reinforce certain areas, helping to produce soft, curving movements within the composition.

The color etching and engraving (Pl. 36) by Peterdi, is technically more complex than the previous example. Instead of a completely linear treatment this print has large areas of relatively solid forms combined with inscribed line. Color is used here as an added esthetic element.

The effect of the process on the esthetic organization of a print is illustrated rather obviously when a comparison is made between a print produced by etching or engraving and one made by cutting a wood block. *Self Portrait* (Fig. 97) is a woodcut by Antonio Frasconi, a contemporary American. Prints in this medium

---

[3] To guard against the sale of reproduction as original prints, the Print Council of America, in 1964, issued the following definition of an original print of today (not necessarily applicable to prints made before 1930): "(1) The artist alone has created the master image in or upon the plate, stone, wood block, or other material, for the purpose of creating the print; (2) the print is made from the said material, by the artist or pursuant to his directions; (3) the finished print is approved by the artist." Many prints are available without the artist's signature. Usually such prints are considered less valuable than signed impressions.

Fig. 96. Gabor Peterdi. Cathedral. *1958. Etching and engraving, 31³/₄ × 22⁵/₈″.*
Print Council of America, American Prints Today—1959 *(exhibition catalogue)*.

are printed from flat wooden boards cut and gouged so that the areas to be left white in the print are removed. Because the wood block is a relatively soft material, the artist cannot produce extremely fine detail. Most woodcut artists tend to rely upon large, flat areas as a major stylistic device in their prints. When black lines are used, as in the Frasconi print, they must, of necessity, be rather heavy. The edges of forms in woodcuts often exhibit a characteristic angular quality, which results from the cutting process as the knife slices through the resistant surface of the block.

In the print media, as in drawing and painting, the medium can provide a strong influence on the final appearance of a work, but unity and variety remain the cardinal requirements for the esthetic organization of the two-dimensional arts. The rather obvious character of this statement and its simplicity should not be interpreted to mean that the construction of a work of art is, in itself, simple. The difference between the work of an artist and the work of a novice student is to be found in *how* they unify their work, *what kind* of variety is employed, and *how much* technical facility enters into the results. To say that an object has repetition, continuity, and contrast, or that it exploits the medium, is not to say that it is a satisfying work of art. It is the nature of the work of art that it results from a great many decisions, and the final appearance of the work depends upon the sensitivity, intelligence, knowledge, skill, and character or personality of the decision maker.

FIG. 97. ANTONIO FRASCONI. Self Portrait. *1951. Woodcut, 21⁷/₈ × 6¹¹/₁₆″.* *The Museum of Modern Art, New York (Inter-American Fund).*

143

THE VISUAL LANGUAGE:
The Representation of the Third Dimension

CHAPTER VI

OBJECTS IN THE REAL WORLD may be touched; they may be seen from front, side, or back; often it is possible to see them under different conditions of light. When these same objects and the space they occupy are to be represented on the flat plane of a painting or a drawing, the artist finds it impossible to include in the representation all he can perceive about them. Even the representation of the simplest solids produces problems which suggest the restrictions placed upon the artist who works in the two-dimensional arts.

What is a cube as perceived by an observer? It is a solid that is square in cross section; it has six sides, each shaped as a square, each in a different plane. Each side is parallel to one other side and at right angles to the four remaining sides. All this information an observer may state about the cube, based upon his perception of it. How is it possible for a painter to represent this information? If emphasis is placed on a form of representation that emphasizes the shape, it will be necessary to begin with a square.

Diagram 37 represents the square form. The sides are equal and the angles are 90 degrees. But only one of the six sides is shown.

Diagram 38 represents six sides, but the orientation of the sides does not correspond to the described perception of them.

Diagram 39 does not seem to answer the requirements of the representation with any more satisfactory solution.

So long as the artist wishes to retain an accurate representation of shape relative to the perception of the cube, he is faced with the obvious limitations that exist in the previous three figures. What happens if a variation in the shape is permitted, granted that at certain times the square shape of the sides of the cube does not look square? At times the sides may look like single lines or edges (Diag. 40).

Even with this change it is still impossible to represent the sixth side. If the sides are represented as forms approximating rhomboids, what then? Diagram 41 more closely fits the image most people would accept as a satisfactory representation of a cube, but only three sides are shown, and they show a considerable degree of variation from the perceived orientation of the sides in our initial description. Even the assumption that the cube is transparent, as in Diagram 42 (surely a specialized case), does not give total satisfaction to our perceptions. (Notice that color and light conditions have not been introduced here, for these two factors cause even more complications.)

144

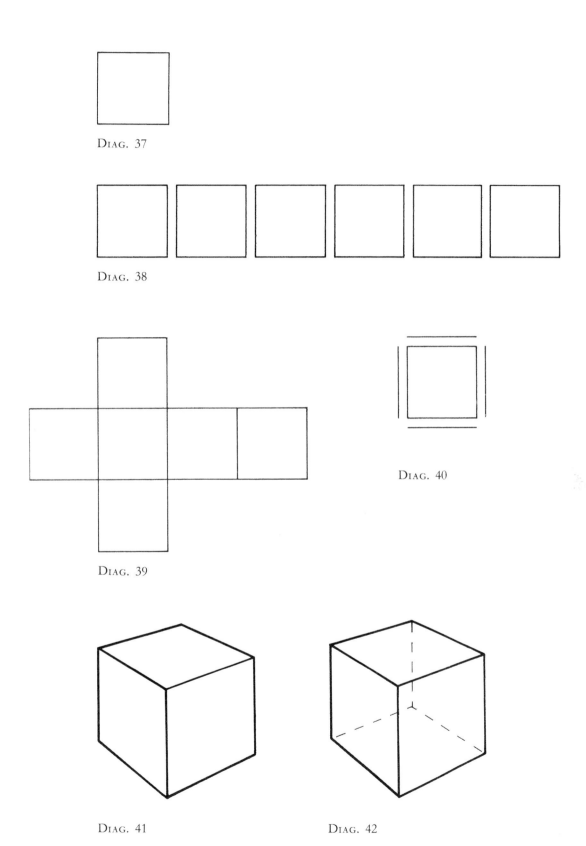

Diag. 37

Diag. 38

Diag. 39

Diag. 40

Diag. 41

Diag. 42

FIG. 98. *Main street of Dodge City, set for the television series* Gunsmoke. *Hollywood.*

The problems in the representation of the simple three-dimensional cube on a two-dimensional surface indicate the problems that confront any artist in the representation of the infinitely greater complexities of human form, landscape, and interiors. It cannot be stressed too often that it is impossible for an artist to represent all he perceives of a single scene in the three-dimensional world on any one two-dimensional surface.

The question might be asked: "Why does Diagram 41 seem so satisfying as a representation of a cube?" The answer is not known with certainty, but studies in the area of perception suggest that the limited amount of information conveyed by Diagram 41 communicates to the observer that there is more to the figure than he can see. Though he can see only three sides, he deduces that there are three other sides which cannot be seen. A photograph gives information in a manner quite similar to that adopted in Diagram 41.

From a photograph showing only two sides of a building the assumption is made that the other two sides are there too. Sometimes that assumption is proved wrong, and the observer discovers that he has been fooled, as in the case of a false-front movie set, which is revealed to be nothing but a façade (Fig. 98).

Many people today believe that the photographic image is the "real," most truthful, and accurate way of picturing the three-dimensional world on a two-dimensional surface. This notion is not common to all times and all cultures. In fact, psychologists and anthropologists, including Carl Jung and Melville J. Herskovits,

Pl. 29. PETER PAUL RUBENS. *Tiger Hunt.* c. 1616. Panel, 38 x 48¾″. The Wadsworth Atheneum, Hartford.

PL. 30. PABLO PICASSO. *Still Life with Fishes.* 1922–23. Canvas, 51 x 38½".
Collection Mrs. Albert D. Lasker, New York.

have reported that primitive men often cannot identify human images in photographs. Photographic symbolic forms have been commonly recognized as accurate equivalents of natural forms only in Western art. Certain tribal groups make drawings that represent both sides of an animal in full view at the same time, something the photograph does not do (Fig. 99). Even within the culture of the Western world, nonphotographic representation is often used to communicate information that cannot be shown in a photographic image. Maps and building plans fall within this category, as do cartoon drawings and diagrams (Figs. 100–103). If photographic representation is conceptualized by the average person as the kind of image seen in the common snapshot of people, places, and things, then even certain present-day photographs made with unusual lenses and with unusual lighting conditions do not fit into the conceptualization.

FIG. 99. *Haida motif representing a bear.*
Franz Boas, Primitive Art, *Instituttet for*
Sammenlignende Kulturforskning, series B, VIII,
Oslo, Leipzig, Paris, London,
and Cambridge, Mass., 1927, fig. 222.

FIG. 100. *Rand McNally road map*
of New York State, detail.

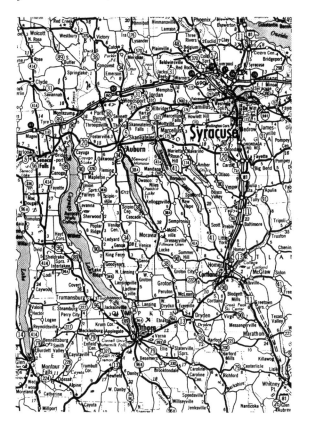

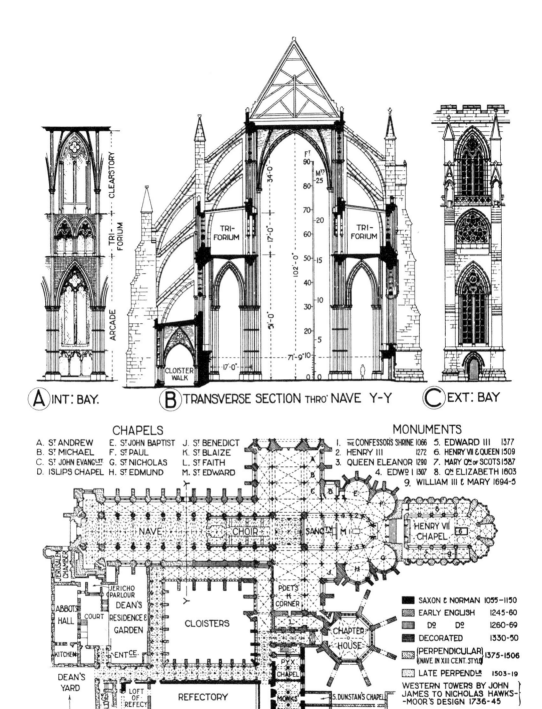

FIG. 101. *Westminster Abbey, London, section and plan.*
Banister Fletcher, A History of Architecture...,
Charlers Scribner's Sons, New York, 1963, p. 424.

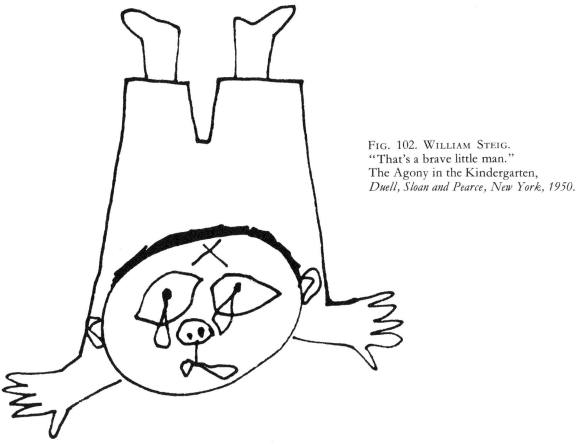

Fig. 102. William Steig.
"That's a brave little man."
The Agony in the Kindergarten,
Duell, Sloan and Pearce, New York, 1950.

Fig. 103. *Illustrated parts catalogue drawing.*
George Magnan, Visual Art for Industry, *Reinhold Publishing Corporation,*
New York, 1961, p. 77.

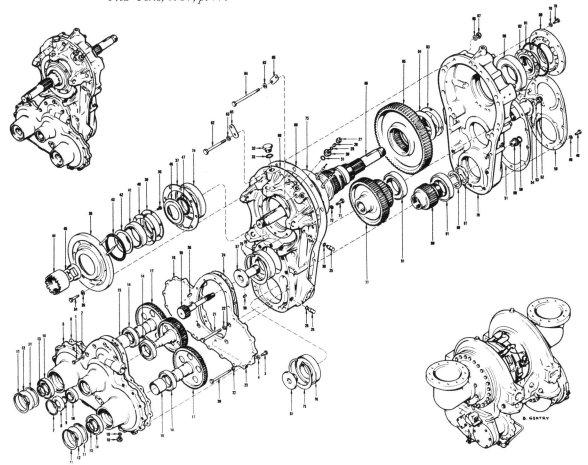

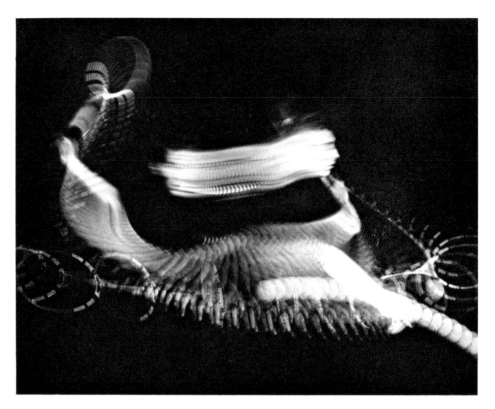

Fig. 104. Harold E. Edgerton.
Swirls and Eddies of a Tennis Stroke. *1939. Stroboscopic photograph.*

The photograph by Harold E. Edgerton, *Swirls and Eddies of a Tennis Stroke* (Fig. 104), was made with the use of a stroboscopic light source. The image produced on the film is a record of movement. The form of the tennis player is obscured, almost eliminated, and in its place the pattern of man and tennis racquet communicates information, but not the kind of information usually found in a snapshot.

Bill Brandt's photograph of a nude reclining on the pebbly surface of a beach was made with an old wooden camera with a wide-angle lens. The form of the figure is altered from the common photographic standard, because the optical properties of the lens used are unlike those of the lenses found in the average camera (Fig. 105).

Both the above examples are photographic representations. The fact that they do not correspond to the image generally expected from a camera suggests that photographic representation has been accepted as a criterion for accuracy because it is the type of image most commonly seen as a representation of three-dimensional forms on a two-dimensional surface, and not because it has special attributes missing in other forms of image making. The observer cannot assume that pointing a camera at a scene and snapping the shutter will result in a picture that can be used to judge the accuracy of any other image of the same scene. The photographer is restricted by the same limitations that are placed upon any other maker of two-dimensional images. He can represent only a portion of the total amount of information that can be recorded about the subject of his choice. The selection of the significant detail and the means used to represent it are arbitrary decisions of the image maker.

The history of art abounds in examples of two-dimensional representations of the three-dimensional world that bear no relation to photographic representation. There is no evidence to suggest that these examples are solely the result of an inadequacy on the part of the practitioners in this field at so-called "primitive" or "decadent" periods of time, for many of them are to be found in cultures that were vital and highly complex. It is probable that these other representational systems satisfied most of the artists who used them and that the images produced were acceptable to their patrons.

FIG. 105. BILL BRANDT. Nude on a Pebbled Beach. *1953.*

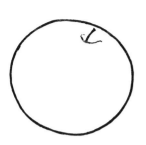

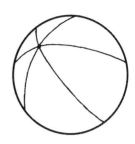

THE REPRESENTATION OF FORM AND SPACE

A form, as it is seen and known in nature, reflects light and stands out against a contrasting background. It may be touched; its shape, its texture, and its weight may be felt. We may walk about it. The exact process of knowing is a complicated and, as yet, incompletely explained part of perception, but it is known that the response to the shapes of objects is in the first levels of perceptual development in human beings.

A shape may be represented by a drawn outline with certain identifiable characteristics which seem to fit the awareness we have of the object in the three-dimensional world. The curved contours of an apple may be represented by a circle. The curved form of the apple and the curved form of the circle have a certain similarity. Other forms in nature are similarly curved, and the need to add identifying details to the drawing develops as we need to differentiate between apple, sun, head, ball, and so on. In each instance additional lines may be used, or the existing image may be altered to correspond to identifying characteristics (Diag. 44). This simple use of the outlined edge of forms for representation is the basis for a huge amount of the visual art that has been produced to the present time. Examples include the figures on a Greek vase of the fifth century B.C. (Fig. 106), a Japanese wood-block print of the eighteenth century (Fig. 107), and a head by Henri Matisse of the twentieth century (Fig. 108).

FIG. 106. *Two women putting away clothes, detail of a red-figured kylix attributed to the painter* DOURIS. *c. 470 B.C. Painted pottery. The Metropolitan Museum of Art, New York (Rogers Fund, 1923).*

FIG. 107. KATSUKAWA SHUNSHŌ. Woman in Red. *18th cent. Wood-block print, 27⁷/₈×6 ¹/₂ ". The Metropolitan Museum of Art, New York (Bequest of Mrs. H.O. Havemeyer, 1929; The H.O. Havemeyer Collection).*

FIG. 108. HENRI MATISSE. Upturned Head (Head of a Recumbent Figure). *c. 1906. Transfer lithograph, printed in black, 11¹/₈×10³/₄". The Museum of Modern Art, New York (Gift of Abby Aldrich Rockefeller).*

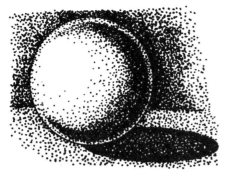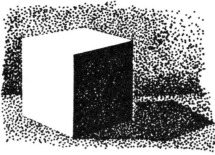

Diag. 45

Variations of this method of form representation include those which add an indication of the play of light on the surface of the object. Illumination from a single source of light will fall upon a three-dimensional object in a consistent pattern. Usually those surfaces nearest the light will receive the most illumination, and those surfaces which are turned from the light source will receive proportionately less illumination. The shape of the object has an effect on the pattern of light and dark areas produced in this way. Representing the light on the forms by graduated areas of dark and light color on the two-dimensional surface of the painting or drawing, the artist can combine this device with the use of contour edges to add to the illusion of form (Diag. 45).

In nature a form occupies space. The form remains constant, even though the space it occupies may change. That is, a sphere looks and feels the same whether it occupies one place on a table or another. However, space is not just that volume occupied by a form; it can also be the distance between forms (see Diags. 8, 9 in Chapter IV). Certain forms can be perceived to be in front of others. They can be seen to be close together or far apart. One form may be above another or below it.

Artists who have wished to represent the spatial relationships between forms in nature on the surface of a canvas have used one or more of the following six methods:

1. Overlapping planes
2. Variation in size
3. Position on the picture plane
4. Linear perspective
5. Aerial perspective
6. Color change

OVERLAPPING PLANES. Figure 109 is a typical example of the use of overlap to indicate the arrangement of forms in depth. In this thirteenth-century panel by a Tuscan painter the form of the child overlaps a portion of the form of the Madonna. This simple device indicates to the viewer that the child is placed in front of the mother. Overlapping may become much more complicated than the illustrated example (Diag. 46). Several planes may overlap in sequence, or some planes may appear to be transparent, so that the illusion of looking through a forward plane to one behind enhances the feeling of three-dimensional space (Pl. 37).

FIG. 109. Madonna and Child.
Tuscan, second half of 13th cent.
Panel, 60¹/₂ × 36".
The Metropolitan Museum of Art,
New York (Gift of
George Blumenthal, 1941).

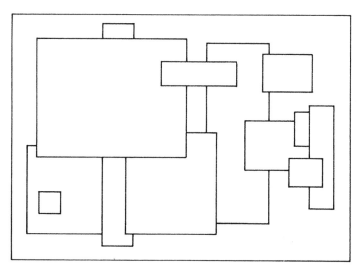

DIAG. 46

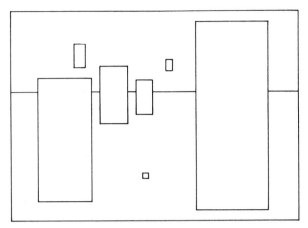 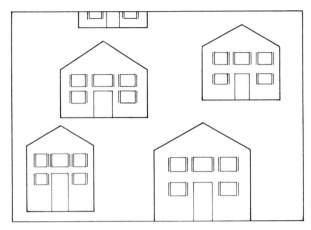

DIAG. 47   DIAG. 48

VARIATION IN SIZE.   Variation in the sizes of forms may be employed to indicate the relative importance of persons represented in a composition. This practice is often found in early Egyptian paintings and reliefs. Size change may also be used to suggest distance.

The observer who looks at a work containing objects of varying size may assume one of two alternatives: first he may say that the objects represented are, in fact, of different sizes in nature; or he may say that they are of the same size, but that the size differential in the representation corresponds to a difference in distance between the objects and the position of the observer (Diag. 47). This spatial interpretation of the size difference applies not only to objects assumed to be identical in size but also to objects having accepted proportional sizes; that is, a man is smaller than a house, and therefore the representation of a house drawn smaller than a man will suggest a much greater space differential than a similar comparison made between two houses. (See Pl. 38.)

POSITION ON THE PICTURE PLANE.   In certain paintings the system of spatial representation is based upon the position of forms relative to the bottom margins of the picture plane. This method is frequently found in the work of medieval Western artists and the artists of China and Japan. Those objects which are near the bottom are closer to the observer, indicating that spatial distance changes with corresponding positions as measured from the bottom of the work (Diag. 48). Sometimes this system is combined with changes in size, but it is not unusual to find works in which position and size are not correlated in spatial representation.

Duccio, an Italian fourteenth-century painter, painted a panel representing the Transfiguration of Christ (Fig. 110), in which six figures are represented on a rocky mound. The figures are grouped in two rows of three. There can be no doubt that the artist intended the upper row of figures to appear to be behind those in the lower group, and, in fact, they do seem to be. No overlapping is used here to achieve this effect, and the size of the figures does nothing to contribute to the representation of depth, for the lower group is somewhat smaller than those above. It is the position of the forms relative to the lower edge of the painting which serves to suggest their relative distances from the observer.

Fig. 110. Duccio. The Transfiguration of Christ, *from the back predella of the* Maestà. *1308–11. Panel, 18¹/₈ × 17³/₈″. National Gallery, London.*

LINEAR PERSPECTIVE.

> Take a piece of glass the size of a half sheet of royal folio paper, and fix it
> well ... between your eye and the object that you wish to portray. Then move
> away until your eye is two-thirds of a braccio [arm length] away from the piece
> of glass, and fasten your head ... in such a way as to prevent any movement
> of it whatsoever. Then close or cover up one eye, and with a brush or a piece
> or red chalk finely ground mark out on the glass what is visible beyond it;
> afterwards copy it by tracing on paper from the glass....[1]

This quotation from *The Notebooks of Leonardo da Vinci*, the great fifteenth-
century artist, is his description of "the way to represent a scene correctly." A
painter following this procedure would produce a drawing constructed in *linear
perspective*. A careful examination of Leonardo's description of the process suggests
some inconsistencies between the actual activity of looking at the world and the
requirements placed upon an artist who wishes to see a perspective image. Most
human beings do not go through life observing the world in the static manner
described by Leonardo. They do not hold their heads immobile, nor do they keep
one eye shut as they look about them. However, for the artist and the public in
fifteenth-century Europe linear perspective seemed to provide, as it still does for
many people today, a means of drawing an image that they considered the most
accurate representation of the real world on a flat surface. No existing drawing by
Leonardo illustrates his method of accurate drawing through the use of an instrument. The woodcut by Dürer (Fig. 111) shows a similar device.

---

[1] *The Notebooks of Leonardo da Vinci*, ed. and trans. Edward MacCurdy, Reynal & Hitchcock,
New York, 1939, pp. 877, 878.

The Visual Dialogue

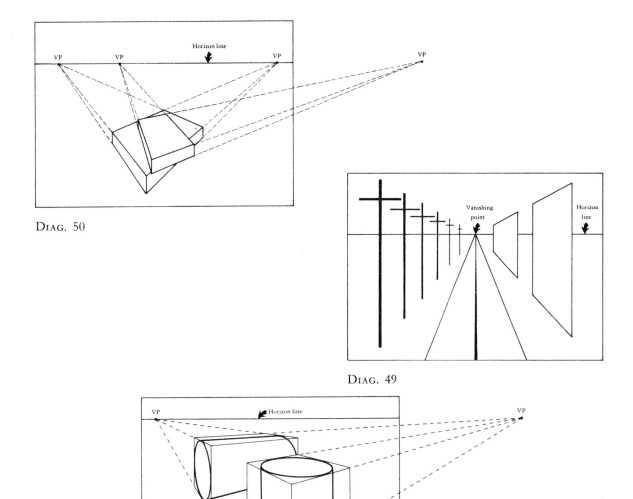

DIAG. 50

DIAG. 49

DIAG. 51

An analysis of a picture drawn by the linear-perspective method would reveal certain essential characteristics basic to all linear-perspective constructions. They are :

1. All parallel lines that exist in nature appear to converge at a point in the drawing. This is called the "vanishing point" (Diag. 49).

2. A different vanishing point exists for each set of parallels, but all points used to construct objects parallel with the ground exist on the same horizontal line. This line is called the "horizon line" (Diag. 50).

3. Round forms are drawn as though they are inscribed in the rectangles which have sides tangent to the curves (Diag. 51, Fig. 112).

Fig. 112. Leonardo da Vinci. *Perspective study for* The Adoration of The Magi. *1478–81. Pen and brush. Uffizi Galleries, Florence.*

There are certain exceptions to these rules, such as the use of supplemental vanishing points in drawing planes not parallel to the ground plane and the use of a vanishing point to converge the vertical parallels in objects seen from extreme up or down viewpoints; but they should not concern the reader, for they do not alter the basic concept of this description.

Before the development of the perspective system, artists used other devices for representing depth in two-dimensional art. For example, Roman mural painters as far back as the first century B.C. had a method of representing receding planes in architectural scenes. The edges of those planes, which would actually parallel the ground in the real object, were drawn at an angle to the horizontal axis of the painting (Fig. 113). These edges, and the lines parallel to them in the actual object, were sometimes drawn parallel to each other and sometimes at divergent angles. Rarely were they grouped into a systematic convergent arrangement.

The photographic image is remarkably similar to the linear perspective image in its rendering of depth. Actually the camera fulfills the demands made by Leonardo for the production of an accurate image. As a one-eyed instrument that does not move during the time it is "looking" at the scene before it, the still camera does not require the restrictive harness that a human being would require while he produced the picture. The sheet of glass on which the scene is drawn is replaced by the flat surface of the photographic film behind the camera lens. The image produced by the camera would seem to be the ultimate form of three-dimensional representation, and yet in the nineteenth century a number of artists found a need to represent some aspects of "reality" which were not communicated by either the photograph or its hand-made equivalent system, linear perspective.

FIG. 113. *Architectural view from the cubiculum of a villa at Boscoreale, Italy. 1st cent.* B.C. *Wall painting. The Metropolitan Museum of Art, New York.*

The Visual Language : The Representation of the Third Dimension

AERIAL PERSPECTIVE.   Another method of representing space, which often was combined with linear perspective after the sixteenth century, was *aerial perspective*. In this technique of spatial representation the artist approximates the observable atmospheric phenomenon by which distant forms lose the sharp definition of their edges and appear lighter and less distinct than objects close to the observer. In aerial perspective the artist paints distant forms in lighter and less brilliant colors than those in the foreground. He also softens the contours of these forms so that they appear to blend into the areas adjacent to them. In the painting by Velázquez, *The Surrender at Breda* (Pl. 39), note the strong contrast of the dark and light areas in the front plane and compare this portion of the painting with the background forms.

COLOR CHANGE.   The color of a form may differ from the color of another form in several ways. It may be lighter or darker. It may be more or less brilliant. And finally, but perhaps most obviously, one color may differ from another in its location on the spectrum. The identity of the colors located along the spectrum is designated by the common words associated with color—red, orange, yellow, green, blue, violet.

As noted above, aerial perspective uses changes in the dark and light quality and changes in the brilliance of color to indicate distance. Some painters have augmented the illusion of aerial perspective by giving distant forms in their paintings a bluish tint, but, in the main, aerial perspective does not employ spectrum color change as a device for indicating spatial relationships.

The colors on the spectrum are often referred to as belonging to a "warm" or "cool" group. This division places those colors which are close to the red end of the spectrum in the "warm" family; those adjacent to the blue end are called "cool." Under certain conditions warm colors give the illusion that they are closer to the viewer than are cool colors, and some artists have exploited this quality to enhance the distance of space in their paintings. By painting foreground forms in relatively warmer colors and background forms in relatively cooler colors, the artist can enhance the sense of space. Note must be made of the reference to *relatively* warm and cool colors, for it is possible to have one red that is cooler than another; that is, a red with a bit of blue in it will appear to be cooler than one without a blue cast. If spectrum color change is used consistently, the warmer red will appear to be in front of the cooler red.

Other spatial indications are possible through a consistent use of the variations in color. All these effects are achieved through the *consistent* use of some characteristic quality of color—its value, its brilliance, or its spectrum difference. In each instance the artist uses change in color as an equivalent for change in spatial distance, and in each distance the success of the method he employs is directly related to the consistency with which he uses it. Possible color changes that might be used for the indication of space could include:

1. Variations in brilliance, the most brilliant colors in the foreground and progressively less brilliant colors receding to the back (Pl. 40).

2. Variations on a single spectrum color against a background painted in a single color. Colors which vary in contrast to the background would come forward in proportion to their contrast. If the background was painted red, forms painted in green, which is the color greatest in contrast to red, would separate from the

PL. 31. JOHN MARIN. *From the Bridge, New York City.* 1933. Water color, 21⅞ x 26¾".
The Wadsworth Atheneum, Hartford.

PL. 32. EL GRECO. *The Vision of St. John the Divine.* 1608–14. Canvas, 88½ x 76″.
The Metropolitan Museum of Art, New York (Rogers Fund, 1956).

PL. 33. EDOUARD MANET. *Boating*. 1874. Canvas, 38¼ x 51¼". The Metropolitan Museum of Art, New York.

PL. 34. CHAIM SOUTINE. *Portrait of Moise Kisling.* Date unknown. (c. 1930).
Canvas, 39 x 27¼″. Philadelphia Museum of Art.

red most obviously and therefore would appear to be farthest away from it. Red-violet forms in this system would be closer to the red and therefore not so close to the foreground (Pl. 41).

CONTEMPORARY SPATIAL REPRESENTATION

The camera is not moved when it is used to produce a still photograph. The artist who produces the linear-perspective drawing draws as though his perception of the world were based upon a single, one-eyed view, in which neither the eye nor the head moves during the period of perception. He acts like a camera.

In the late nineteenth century, a period which burgeoned with new industry and technology, the idea of change and movement was in the air everywhere. Transportation was developing. Steam locomotion on land and on the sea added to the sense of dynamic change in the world. For scientists such as Darwin and Maxwell, the world and the people who inhabited it were parts of a nonstatic changing condition. Some of the artists who lived in this period responded to the same forces that affected the scientists. They saw about them a world of change, a world which could no longer be considered a static series of forms, spaces, and actions. Linear perspective was a product of a world which saw itself as a series of unchanging, separate views, a world which could accept as the most accurate representation of itself the one perceived from the immobile viewpoint of the bound observer described by Leonardo.

Let the reader lift his eyes from this page. As he looks about the room in which he finds himself, does he see that room from one unmoving position? The normal process of perception requires that an observer move his eyes, his head, and quite often his whole body as he perceives the space about him. That space and the forms within it are not seen all at one time, from a single viewpoint. They are seen a part at a time, each movement of the observer, his eyes, or his body giving him a different view. And yet if a still photograph of that room were to be made, it could be shown only from the stationary position of the camera at the time the photograph was taken (Fig. 114). The picture taken by the camera and the perception of the mind–eye

Fig. 114. *Photograph of a hallway, with the camera lens on an axis parallel with the floor.*

169

complex may be similar (though not identical) during each separate fixation of the eye as it looks at the room, but the perception of the room is based upon many fixes, and the perception of a landscape or of a table is accomplished in the same way.

How, then, can an artist, working with a medium that requires him to represent his perceptions on a single flat surface, communicate the perception of the room as he has seen it? It may be done by separating the picture area into several separate sections and placing a different picture, seen from a single viewpoint, in each section (Fig. 115). Or it may be done by attempting to combine a number of separate views within the format of a single picture, representing each portion of the room as it was seen from the position required to view it most comfortably. This latter technique was the method devised by Paul Cézanne, a French painter of the nineteenth century, and continued by a group of artists who were identified as the cubists, in the twentieth century.

Paul Cézanne was born in 1839 in the south of France. His development as a painter took place in an era of great and significant changes. The political, economic, and social life of Europe was in ferment. The political revolutions of the late

FIG. 115. *Photomontage of separate photographs of the same hallway (Fig. 114),*
taken with the camera lens directed at portions of the walls, floor, and ceiling.

Fig. 116. *Photograph of a still life, with the camera lens directed at the center of the table.*

eighteenth century, combined with the industrial revolution which began at about the same time, were matched by comparable great developments in technology and science. Cézanne, retiring and hard-working in personality, excited little interest through his personal appearance or his manner of living, but his painting was as revolutionary as the other forces that were stirring in Europe at the time (Pl. 42).

The traditional forms of painting and drawing which were the basis for the arts in the nineteenth century were extensions of the modes established during the Renaissance. Linear perspective was the unquestioned standard for the representation of form and space in the artist's vocabulary. Even the controversial painters who were contemporaries of Cézanne, impressionists such as Claude Monet and Camille Pissarro, used a traditional linear-perspective construction in their representation of forms. The controversy stirred by their works concerned their use of color and the methods of paint application they employed, but basically they followed in the Renaissance tradition when they drew forms in space (for example, Pls. 10, 11). The construction of the illusion of space was based upon the single horizon line and the fixed point of view. (See the following section of this chapter for a discussion of impressionist color.)

The photograph of a table and the objects on it in Figure 116 is the equivalent, in its basic structural essentials, of a linear-perspective drawing. The single lens of the camera took in the entire scene without changing position, just as Leonardo suggested that the artist look at the scene before him. The four photographs in the following sequence (Figs. 117–120) were all taken from the same position, but

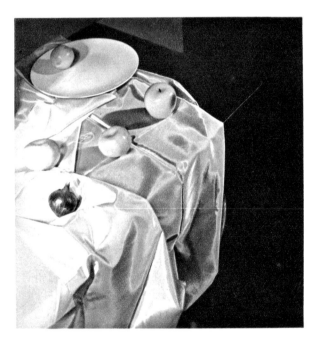

FIGS. 117–120. *Photographs of the same still life (Fig. 116),*
with the camera lens directed at different portions of the table.

The Visual Dialogue

the camera was directed to separate portions of the table, much as a viewer would direct his eyes when looking at portions of the table. By combining portions of the photographs (Fig. 121) and so constructing a composite montage, we can arrive at a representation of the table which differs considerably from a perspective representation.

Which picture gives a more accurate representation of the table? This question cannot be answered, for, as has been noted before, the difference in the pictures is not due to their accuracy but to the kind of information they present. The perspective representation seems to emphasize the forms of the objects, enabling the viewer to "read" the detail in a single, cohesive, isolated moment of time. The composite representation gives the viewer a sense of the dynamics of the experience of vision. It was this kind of representation which became an important aspect of Cézanne's work. In his still-life painting (Pl. 42) note the similarities to the composite photograph. The back edge of the table breaks and rises, as does the front edge. The bottle is drawn with a number of shifts to the left as it rises from the table, giving it a tipped appearance. Similarly, the dish on which the rolls are placed is drawn from one viewpoint for the left contour and from another, higher point for the right. Cézanne's attempts to a paint a new kind of formal and spatial representation were part of a searching study that he carried out during the course of his entire painting career. His initial inquiry into nonperspective spatial representation has had a major influence on painters from the beginning of the twentieth century to the present time.

FIG. 121. *Photomontage of the same still life (Fig. 116), made up of the separate portions shown in Fig. 117–120.*

FIG. 122. GEORGES BRAQUE. Violin and Pitcher. *1910.*
Canvas, 46^1/8 × 28^5/8″. Kunstmuseum, Basel
(Gift of Raoul La Roche).

FIG. 123. JUAN GRIS. Guitar and Flowers. *1912.*
Canvas, 44^1/8 × 27^5/8″. The Museum of Modern Art, New York
(Bequest of Anna Erickson Levene, 1947).

In Paris, during the first decade of this century, Pablo Picasso, Georges Braque, and Juan Gris cooperated to extend the concept of the representation of a nonstatic seeing experience. The result of their studies is called "analytical cubism." In their painting of this period one can follow the development of a progressively greater complexity of construction, multiple viewpoint combined with multiple viewpoint until the overlapping edges of the separate views became so numerous that the objects defy identification (Figs. 122–124).

Movement and change fascinated many people about the turn of the century. In the United States, as early as the 1880's, Eadweard Muybridge experimented with

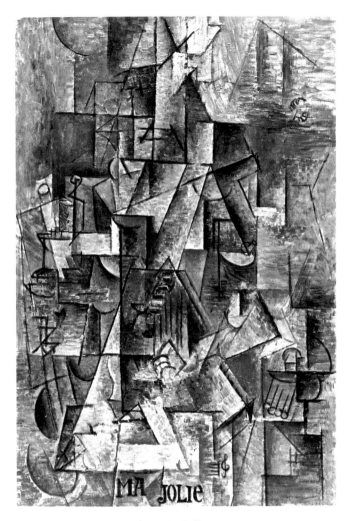

FIG. 124. PABLO PICASSO. Ma Jolie
(Woman with a Guitar or Zither). *1911–12. Canvas, $39^3/_8 \times 25^3/_4''$.*
The Museum of Modern Art, New York
(Acquired through the Lillie P. Bliss Bequest).

stop-action photographs of human and animal subjects in motion (Fig. 125). A similar interest in the representation of movement gave rise to the system of futurism, specifically proposed by a group of Italian artists in a "manifesto" published in 1909 and well exemplified by the work of Giacomo Balla (Fig. 33), one of the founding members of the group. These artists conveyed the sense of motion by depicting a sequence of poses caught in stopped action, one after the other, in the course of a movement, or by forms derived from the overlapping of such poses, as in the well-known *Nude Descending a Staircase,* by Marcel Duchamp (Fig. 126).

FIG. 125. EADWEARD MUYBRIDGE. Walking, Hands Engaged in Knitting.
Photographed July 28, 1885; time interval 178 seconds. From Animal Locomotion,
Philadelphia, 1887, pl. 39. The George Eastman House Collection, Rochester, N.Y.

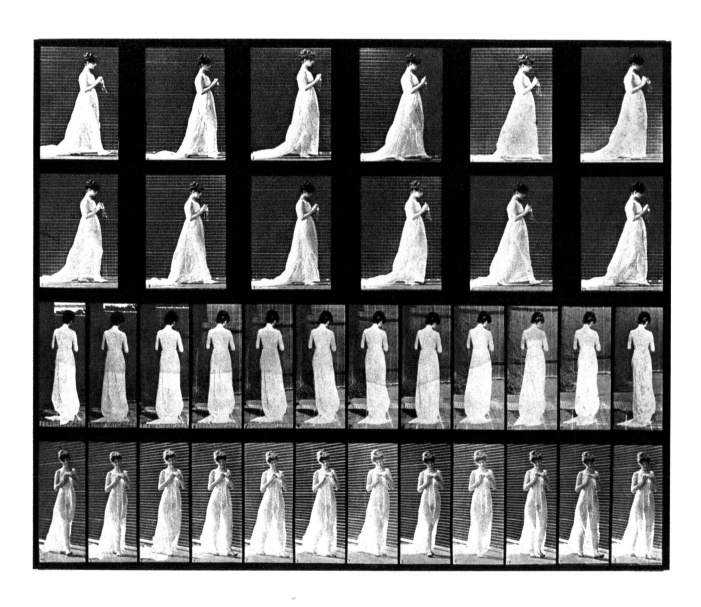

FIG. 126. MARCEL DUCHAMP. Nude Descending a Staircase, No. 2. *1912.*
Canvas, 58 × 35″. Philadelphia Museum of Art (The Louise and Walter Arensberg Collection).

THE REPRESENTATION OF COLOR AND LIGHT

An awareness of the physical world is not limited to forms and spaces. Descriptions of objects are just as likely to refer to their color as to their shape or texture. "The coat is tan." One way of making a visual equivalent for that statement is to draw the form of a coat and paint the enclosed area within the form a single shade of the indicated ground color. This method of color representation is to be seen in Plate 43, a Japanese print of the eighteenth century. But is the coat always seen as a single tan color? When shading is employed to represent form, the color of the coat is made lighter in the illuminated areas and darker in the shaded areas. The tan of the coat would be called its "local color," but that specific color would be only one of many different tans the painter would have to use to create the illusion of a tan coat seen under natural conditions of light. This system of color representation, local color that is shaded, was used throughout the Renaissance and is still in use today (Pl. 44).

The use of shaded local color for the representation of color in nature was not completely satisfying to some artists of the seventeenth and eighteenth centuries. The shaded areas they saw in nature did not always seem to be the color produced by adding black to a local color. Nor were the highlighted areas always the color produced by combining white with the local color. It is not unusual to find blue and green tones in the shadows of red clothing or on the heads of the subjects in paintings by Rubens (Pl. 29) and Fragonard. Fragonard's painting *La Bonne Mère* (Pl. 45) clearly shows the use of blue in the shadowed areas of foliage at the upper left. The artist's use of warm colors in the foreground sunny areas and cool colors in the shadows is to be seen throughout the painting.

In the nineteenth century, spurred on by the experiments in light and color by such scientists as Rood, Maxwell, and Chevreul, a number of painters began to experiment with new methods of color representation and paint application. These artists recognized that the apparent color of an object is affected to a considerable degree by the color of the light that shines upon it. The morning light is quite blue, as compared with the reddish light of the sunset. (Let doubters take photographs of the same scene, in color, before 8 A.M. and after the sun has begun to set in the evening and compare them.) The color of the light not only affects the forms in the light but also alters the apparent colors in shadow, usually introducing hues that are the opposite of the color of the light source, for example, bluish shadows and yellowish sunlight. Some painters, including Camille Pissarro, Claude Monet, and Alfred Sisley, realized that it was impossible to represent the brilliance of the colors of natural forms seen under sunlight by using the traditional methods of painting inherited from the Renaissance (Pls. 11, 46, 47). The paints available to these artists were just not bright enough to reproduce the color experience they had when they looked at a field at noon or the façade of a Gothic cathedral shimmering in the evening light.

Led by Monet, a group of artists, who were later given the name of "impressionists," introduced a revolutionary method of paint application and color usage. They found that areas of the canvas painted in small strokes of color would appear, from a distance, to be more brilliant than similar areas painted in flat or in gradually modulated tones. They also found that an area of green appeared more intense and even greener when it had within it small numbers of red or orange spots. Blues could be made more brilliant by a similar introduction of orange. In effect what they did was to create a form of optical vibration, which occurs when contrasting hues of similar value are juxtaposed. The vibrating small spots of color gave the surface of the canvas a shimmering quality, which seemed to make the light and colors represented in the painting more like the original subject.

The impressionist painter was excited and challenged by the light and color in nature. He saw form and space as secondary aspects of the light that delineated them. Objects, for the impressionist, were not things to be touched but things to be seen. The method of representing this visual world made it almost impossible to represent forms with the detail and concern for texture that were traditional before the work of Monet and his colleagues. Application of paint in small broken strokes prevented the creation of sharp contours and surface variation, which are typical of the paintings of an artist who wishes to represent objects in a sculptural manner. Compare the detail from a painting by Monet with one by his contemporary Jean Léon Gérôme (Pls. 47–50). Monet's use of paint makes it impossible to represent form with the concern for detail we see in the work of Gérôme, but Gérôme's use of paint precludes the possibility of representing light and color with the brilliance of Monet's surfaces. Once again we are faced with the conclusion that it is impossible to represent all aspects of real experience on the same canvas.

NONREPRESENTATIONAL PAINTING

A discussion of the representation of the "real" world on the flat surface of the artist's canvas would be incomplete without noting that many contemporary painters have turned from representational painting into other types of two-dimensional art. The creation of an illusionary world based upon the "real" world no longer interests them. There is no single reason for this change in attitude. In part the movement away from representation must be related to the tremendous growth of the use of the camera. Certainly the change in painting coincides with the development of photography as a means of representing the real world on a two-dimensional surface. Since the beginning of the nineteenth century, the use of the photograph has become the dominant form of pictorial representation. When it was combined with the engraving technology which permitted the reproduction of photographs in magazines and newspapers, the product of the camera became the most influential image maker of the twentieth century. Competition with a camera seems a fruitless activity for many of the present-day artists.

Another factor which appears to have influenced the movement away from representation is an increased concern with the personal, inner world of the individual. Many artists have turned their vision inward, exploring and expressing their subjective reactions to the world about them, and in some cases even creating a world of their own through the medium of paint and canvas. Chapter VIII examines the expressive content of the visual arts, and though the point is made that the expression of the artist's personal response to experience has been a part of the visual arts for many years, the period since the beginning of the twentieth century has seen a growing concern with the subjective statement.

A third influence on the artist which has reduced the importance of representation in contemporary painting is an increasing interest in the work of art as an object, a beautiful or exciting combination of forms and colors that satisfies an esthetic

FIG. 127. *Cruciform page from the Lindisfarne Gospels. c. 700. Illumination. British Museum, London (Ms. Cotton Nero D. IV).*

need, without depending on the image-making or representation potential of the work. In the past, decorative painting has been used to enhance the surfaces of buildings, and it is to be found, too, in manuscript illuminations. Frequently decoration was combined with representation, as in Figure 127, which is a page from the Lindisfarne Gospels, painted about 700. The complex tracery is joined here with forms that suggest the heads of birds. The total effect is one of highly enriched surfaces at once mysterious and precious, for the arabesques seem to hide the images even as they lend a sense of importance and value to the page.

A detail (Fig. 128) of the painting by Jackson Pollock (Pl. 51) has much of the same quality as the tracery in the Lindisfarne Gospels. It is a much larger work than the book page, and obviously the arabesque is more freely drawn, but it, too, suggests a mysterious web, delicate and rich. The viewer is enmeshed in skeins of color, which offer a potential response as ornamented surface and/or secretive screens that seem to obscure some hidden image.

Each of the representational systems described in this chapter is, in effect, a consistent combination of the plastic elements used by the painter. Form, color, texture, and the drawn line are arranged on the picture plane to create equivalents for three-dimensional form, space, light, and color. Though it is true that many contemporary artists no longer concern themselves with the problems of representation, there are many who still continue to do so, and the representational painting of today, though often quite different from the earlier traditional modes, remains an important part of the visual arts.

SCULPTURE : Representation and Esthetic Organization

CHAPTER VII

When the painter concerns himself with representation of the physical world, he is faced with the necessity of indicating the third dimension on a two-dimensional surface ; he must construct a system of form, color, texture, and line to suggest mass, space, surface, texture, and light. His is an art of illusion. This kind of illusion does not concern the sculptor. Because he works in three dimensions, the sculptor can, if he wishes, produce an exact replica of the forms and spaces in natural objects. Yet this imitative potential rarely satisfies him, for though natural forms share their three-dimensionality with sculpture, the differences between a statue and its subject require a sculptor to develop representational equivalents that often seem far removed from the physical appearance of animals and human beings.

What differences do exist between a human being and an exact duplication of the forms of that human being in a sculptural form? The most obvious difference would be found in the potential of the human body for movement and the static immobility of the sculpture. Even at rest a living form moves. Each breath animates the forms of the body—eyelids flicker, nerves pulse—and, of course, larger movements are possible—changes in the position of legs, arms, torso, and head. The human form devoid of movement seems to lose some of its essential character.

A second difference between sculpture and living forms, the difference in material, is almost as obvious as the first. Sculpture may be formed of a great variety of metals, woods, stones, and plastics, and there are obvious differences in color and surface texture between these materials and skin, hair, and cloth.

Finally it is important to note that living forms do not exist in isolation. The sense of reality conveyed by the appearance of the human body depends in part upon the fact that the body is seen in the context of some surrounding environment. Life seems to flow around the living. Light changes ; the air moves and brings with it the sounds associated with human experience. The figure exists in a landscape or within the interior space of a room filled with the evidence of the presence of real people. The sculptor usually produces a figure that is isolated from an environment. With the exception of certain forms of bas-relief, to be discussed later in this chapter, which have characteristics similar to painting, sculpture tends to isolate single or multiple representational images from the environment that would normally surround the figure.

Though the sculptor can copy the *forms* of a human being exactly, the differences between the statue and its subject remain significantly obvious. The sculptor, like the painter, can produce only an equivalent for his subject. When he seeks to represent a subject in the world about him, the sculptor must devise a combination of forms and surfaces in space which will suggest, symbolize, or become a surrogate for that subject.

Of considerable interest and importance in the study of sculpture are the great variety of three-dimensional images which have been used throughout history as equivalents for human and animal figures. Even if the study is restricted to the human figure, the range of representational images is remarkable. Compare a Cycladic statuette carved on an Aegean island about 4,500 years ago (Fig. 129); a figure of Hermes by the Greek Praxiteles, about 390–330 B.C. (Fig. 130); a thirteenth-century Virgin and Child from Spain (Fig. 131); a twelfth-century figure from India (Fig. 132); a Maori figure from New Zealand (Fig. 133); one from

Fig. 130. Praxiteles. Hermes. *c. 390–330 B.C. Marble, height c. 7'. Museum, Olympia, Greece.*

Fig. 129. *Cycladic statuette of a woman. c. 2500 B.C. Marble, height 14¹/₄". The Metropolitan Museum of Art, New York (Fletcher Fund, 1934).*

PL. 35. GEORGES BRAQUE. *Violin and Pipe with the Word "Polka."* 1920–21. Oil and sand on canvas, 17 x 36½". Philadelphia Museum of Art (The Louise and Walter Arensberg Collection).

PL. 36. GABOR PETERDI. *The Pregnant Earth*. 1959. Color intaglio, 16⅞ x 23¹³⁄₁₆″. Yale University Art Gallery, New Haven.

PL. 37. IRENE RICE PEREIRA. *Oblique Progression*. 1948. Canvas, 50 x 40″.
Whitney Museum of American Art, New York.

PL. 38. BEN SHAHN. *Miners' Wives*. 1948. Canvas, 48 x 36″. Philadelphia Museum of Art.

Fig. 131. Virgin and Child. *French,*
13th cent. Oak, height 31¹/₂″.
The Wadsworth Atheneum, Hartford.

Fig. 132. *Figure from India. 12th cent.*
Stone, 22 × 13³/₄″.
The Metropolitan Museum, New York
(Gift of Robert Lehman, 1947).

FIG. 133. *Maori figure from New Zealand. 19th cent.(?) Wood, height 43¹/₈". The Museum of Primitive Art, New York.*

FIG. 134. *Seated figure, probably Haida, from British Columbia. 19th cent.(?) Bone, height 6". The Museum of Primitive Art, New York.*

the Northwest Coast Indians of British Columbia (Fig. 134); and finally two more recent examples by Alberto Giacometti and Henry Moore (Figs. 135, 58). All these examples represent the human figure for some society or individual. The figure by Praxiteles seems to correspond most closely to the forms of the human figure as it appears in nature, and yet, as suggested above, it too must be considered an abstraction from real life.

Actually, a child's doll, in which a single piece of wood represents a torso, to which is added a crosspiece suggesting arms, a knob for a head, and two additional lengths of wood for legs, is easily recognized as a symbol for the human body. The body is so much a part of each person's experience that even the crudest simulation of parts combined into a figurelike group will be recognized as a figural image.

The particular combination of forms that satisfies a sculptor when he wishes to represent a real subject may be strongly influenced by the traditions of his culture. This is demonstrated by the examples above from Greece, India, Spain, New Zealand, and British Columbia. Working within these stylistic canons, an

The Visual Dialogue

FIG. 135. ALBERTO GIACOMETTI.
Walking Man. *Undated, c. 1947–49.*
Bronze, height 27".
Collection Joseph H. Hirshhorn, New York.

artist may be able to indicate differences of sex, movement, and expression. These
potentials are certainly utilized in the sculpture of the Greeks. Often, however, the
style is more restrictive, and in the figures typical of a cultural group the artist
seems to have disregarded some or all of the individual differences that exist between
human beings.

In the work of Giacometti and Moore we have two contemporary artists
who do not conform to any single stylistic pattern imposed upon them by an
external group or culture. Each artist has developed a symbolic image of the human
form that satisfies his own expressive and esthetic needs.

Because the image of the figure is so readily grasped, even when a figural piece
is markedly different from the forms of the real subject, the contemporary sculptor
is free to depart from imitative surfaces and forms in his work. He may combine
representation with a highly subjective comment about individuals or societies, or
he may emphasize the purely organizational aspect of his composition and seek to
produce an esthetic object that satisfies or delights its beholders.

FIG. 136. AGESANDER, ATHENODORUS, *and* POLYDORUS. The Laocoön Group. *Roman copy of a Greek original of c. 50 B.C. Marble, height 7' 11¹/₄". Vatican Museums, Rome.*

MATERIALS AND ESTHETIC ORGANIZATION OF SCULPTURE

Sculpture is an ordered arrangement of actual masses that exist in a real space.

The plastic elements of sculpture, as has been said earlier, are form, space, line, material, and texture, and the sculptor, like the painter, seeks to organize these elements into a unified composition.

The organization of sculpture begins with the material. Stone, wood, metal, clay, and other substances are formed through a number of processes into the final shapes and spaces, which are, in total, the finished work.

There are examples of sculpture which seem to be unrelated to the material as a basic compositional element in their organization. Greek sculpture of the first century B.C. differs little, whether it was carved in marble or cast in bronze. Compare the *Laocoön Group* (Fig. 136) with the *Boxer* (Fig. 137), both dating from the first century B.C. There is no major stylistic difference between these two statues, though the former is a marble piece and the latter bronze. A similar lack of concern for the qualities of material as an influence on composition is to be found in the Renaissance. A comparison of three statues by Donatello—the so-called *Zuccone, David,* and *St. Mary Magdalene*—suggests the similarity in this artist's approach to sculpture in marble, bronze, and wood (Figs. 138–140).

The Visual Dialogue

FIG. 137. BOXER. *c. 50* B.C.
Bronze, height 50".
Museo Nazionale delle Terme, Rome.

FIG. 138. DONATELLO. Habakkuk
(called "Zuccone"). 1423–25. Marble,
height 77". Museo dell'Opera
del Duomo, Florence.

FIG. 139. DONATELLO. David.
c. 1430–32. Bronze, height 62¹/₄".
Museo Nazionale, Florence.

FIG. 140. DONATELLO.
St. Mary Magdalene. *1454–55.*
Wood, height 74".
Baptistery, Florence.

FIG. 141. *Bakota funerary figure, from Gabon, Africa. 19th cent.(?) Wood, copper, and brass, height 21¹/₂". The Museum of Primitive Art, New York*

FIG. 142. *Maya-Toltec head of the god Tlaloc, from Yucatán, Mexico. Pre-Columbian, 10th–11th cent. Stone, height 13³/₄". The Museum of Primitive Art, New York.*

FIG. 143. *Bamenda mask, from British Cameroons. Late 19th–early 20th cent. Wood, height 26¹/₂". Rietberg Museum, Zurich (Von der Heydt Collection).*

194

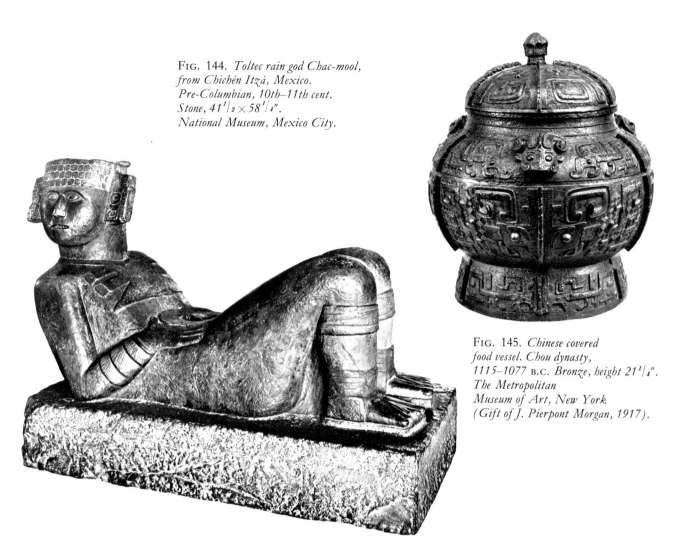

Fig. 144. *Toltec rain god Chac-mool,
from Chichén Itzá, Mexico.
Pre-Columbian, 10th–11th cent.
Stone, $41^1/_2 \times 58^1/_4''$.
National Museum, Mexico City.*

Fig. 145. *Chinese covered
food vessel. Chou dynasty,
1115–1077 B.C. Bronze, height $21^1/_4''$.
The Metropolitan
Museum of Art, New York
(Gift of J. Pierpont Morgan, 1917).*

About the beginning of the twentieth century sculptors trained in the traditions that stemmed from the Renaissance became aware of the existence of a body of sculpture that did not conform the esthetic canons of European art. Wooden and bronze pieces from Africa (Fig. 141), stone carvings of the pre-Columbian cultures of South and Central America (Fig. 142), the sculpture of the Far East and India (Fig. 132), the American Northwest (Fig. 134), and the islands of Polynesia (Fig. 133) gave the twentieth-century artist an expanded vision of the nature of sculpture. The simple and direct way in which many materials were used in these non-European arts suggested that there was a vitality and expressive quality to be found in each material available to the sculptor. The wooden masks of the Bamenda of the British Cameroons derived their forms in large part from the woodworking methods (Fig. 143). The hardness of stone and a limited ability to cut it gave the figures of the Mayans from Chichén Itzá (Fig. 144) a monumental simplicity. The inscribed designs on the bronzes of the Chou period in China gave new insights into the possibilities of this long-used material (Fig. 145).

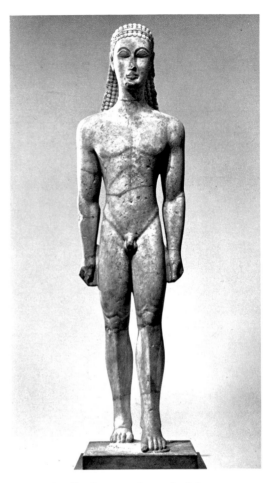

FIG. 146. *Egyptian statue, from Luxor. 19th dynasty,*
14th–13th cent. B.C. Stone, height 7′ 5³/₄″.
The Metropolitan Museum of Art, New York
(Contribution from Edward S. Harkness
and the Rogers Fund, 1921).

FIG. 147. *Greek statue of a youth of the*
"Apollo" type. 615–600 B.C. Marble, height 73¹/₂″.
The Metropolitan Museum of Art, New York
(Fletcher Fund, 1932).

Artists and critics were stimulated by this tradition-shattering art to see positive values also in periods of Western sculpture which had long been neglected because the work of these eras did not fit the criteria derived from the Renaissance. Egyptian sculpture, Cycladic statuettes, the sculpture of pre-fifth-century B.C. Greece, and the work of the Etruscans and of Romanesque and early Gothic sculptors took on an importance in the twentieth century which they had not had in the preceding centuries (Figs. 146–149).

Today much of the esthetic concern in sculpture is directly related to the materials employed by the sculptor and the way in which he works them, and an appreciation of sculpture can be enhanced by an understanding of the processes involved in its manufacture.

Essentially the sculptor can work in two separate and distinct techniques. He may build up his work from small parts, such as bits of clay or wax pressed together to produce a *modeled* figure ; or he may cut away or carve into a block of stone or wood larger than the finished work, eliminating the extraneous parts of the block and leaving the statue as a result of this process of reduction. The first method is called "additive sculpture" and the second "subtractive sculpture."

The Visual Dialogue

FIG. 148. *Etruscan fighting warrior.*
7th–6th cent. B.C. *Bronze, height $6^{11}/_{16}$".*
The Metropolitan Museum of Art,
New York (purchased
by subscription, 1896).

FIG. 149. *St. James the Greater, St. James the Lesser,*
St. Bartholomew, St. Paul, and St. John. 13th cent.
Stone. Cathedral of Chartres, south portal.

Fig. 150. Auguste Rodin.
The Little Man with a Broken Nose. *1882.*
Bronze with some gilt, height 5".
California Palace of the Legion of Honor,
San Francisco (Spreckels Collection).

ADDITIVE SCULPTURE.   The term "additive sculpture" is almost synonymous with the word "modeling." Both terms refer to the use of a pliable material, such as wax or clay, which can be formed into three-dimensional masses. This procedure permits the artist to make quick, spontaneous sketches, as well as prolonged studies. Because the material is soft and easy to manipulate, the artist can use a great variety of tools, as well as his fingers, to shape it.

Auguste Rodin's *Little Man with a Broken Nose* (Fig. 150) is an example of this sculptural technique. The completed form of the work was cast in bronze, but the original was clay. Clay models are fragile and perishable, so that it is usual for works constructed in the additive technique to be cast in another, more durable material. Sometimes the clay is baked at high temperature in a kiln, like pottery. The resultant product is called "terra cotta," and it is considered a satisfactory finished material for certain limited uses.

The person interested in the appreciation of sculpture need not get involved with the intricacies of the complex technology required to transform an original clay model to a finished metal statue. However, he should realize that the sculptor who works in this method, in order to integrate his idea with the material he has used, must think as he works in terms of the final casting and not of the clay. He must look at the gray clay forms and see bronze. He must consider the bronze surfaces, the patina they will take, the manner in which the light will be absorbed or reflected from the metal. He may ask himself, "Will the forms I have used look suitable in metal? Will they suggest the ductility, the strength of the material?" These questions are typical of those which would influence the appearance of the finished work. The answers given by contemporary artists have produced a great variety of sculptural forms and surfaces. Some works have been polished until their surfaces took on the quality of a mirrorlike skin, reflecting the light in flashes or star-bright brilliance. Other surfaces have been made to suggest the fluid quality of metal hardened into rough, lavalike incrustations. Still others are engraved and worked after the casting process to contrast the inner color of the metal with the color of the outer surfaces.

Sculpture cast in metal has all these possibilities, but for the contemporary sculptor it has one important disadvantage. It is relatively expensive. In the past, when patrons would commission works, it was not too difficult for the artist to find the financial support to have his pieces cast or to cast them himself. Much of the work of the contemporary sculptor is done before a buyer is found. He frequently must take on the economic burden of the casting procedure. As a result of this obvious problem, many sculptors were frustrated in their desire to create permanent metal sculpture. One solution to this problem was the introduction of the techniques and procedures of the industrial metalworker into the studio. By forming his sculpture of small pieces of metal and welding them into larger, more complex structures, the artist was able to work directly in steel, brass, or even precious metals and produce a work with all the permanence of a cast piece.

The problem of costs was not the only reason for the introduction of *direct metal sculpture*. Many artists were drawn to this process because it had esthetic and expressive values to which they responded. One of the first men to work in this medium was Julio González, who came from a family of ironworkers in Barcelona, Spain. Trained as a painter, González turned to wrought-iron sculpture late in his life, in the late 1920's and the 1930's. *Torso* is an example of the use of flat sheets of iron hammered into curved forms (Fig. 151). These sections were then welded together. The completed construction combines the image of a female torso with the surface, edges, and beaten forms of the ironworker's craft.

FIG. 151. JULIO GONZÁLEZ. TORSO. *c. 1936*
Hammered and welded iron, height 24³/₈″.
The Museum of Modern Art, New York
(Gift of Mr. and Mrs. Samuel A. Marx).

FIG. 152. SEYMOUR LIPTON.
Sanctuary. *1953.*
Nickel silver over steel,
height 29 ¹/₄".
The Museum of Modern Art,
New York (Blanchette
Rockefeller Fund).

González was followed by others, and today one can name artists such as
Seymour Lipton, Ibram Lassaw, Richard Lippold, and Richard Stankiewicz, among
many who work directly in metal.

Lipton beats metal sheets in the manner of the González *Torso.* His construction
Sanctuary (Fig. 152) is made of welded steel covered with a layer of nickel silver.
Ibram Lassaw covers a wire skeleton with layers of bronze, copper, and silver to
produce a linear composition in which melted metal seems to have solidified into a
weblike complex (Fig. 153). A similarly open construction, in which the forms are
reduced to thin lines of light, is the work of Richard Lippold, who welds wire and
rods into complex geometric structures (Fig. 61). Some sculptors, including
Richard Stankiewicz, use the metal refuse found in junk yards as the components
of their work. Sections of pipe and cast-off gears and wheels are welded together.
Marionette (Fig. 154) becomes a grotesque doll while still retaining the identity of
the pipes and assorted hardware that were combined to form it.

The Visual Dialogue

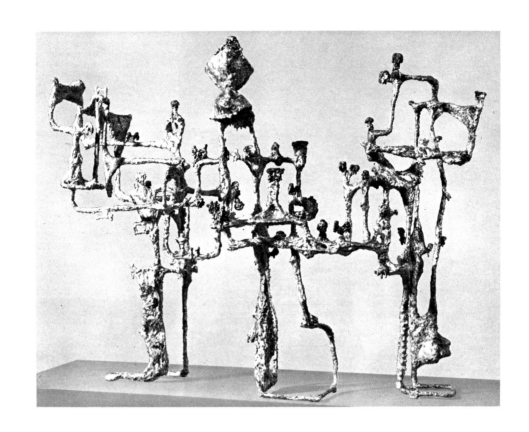

FIG. 153. IBRAM LASSAW. Procession. *1955–56.*
Wire, copper, various bronzes, and silver, length 40".
Whitney Museum of American Art, New York.

FIG. 154. RICHARD STANKIEWICZ.
Marionette. *1960. Steel, height 55".*
Collection Mr. and Mrs. Robert Mayer, New York.

FIG. 155. JOHN ANDERSON. Big Sam's Bodyguard. *1962.*
Ash wood, 82^1/$_2$×81^1/$_2$". Whitney Museum of American Art, New York.

FIG. 156. GABRIEL KOHN. Bird Keys. *1962.*
Wood, 39×40". Marlborough-Gerson Gallery, New York.

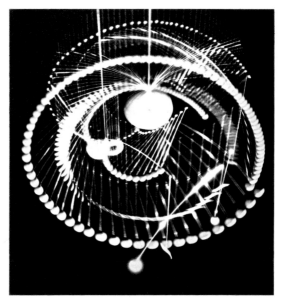

FIG. 157. ALEXANDER CALDER. Lobster Trap and
Fish Tail. *1939. Steel wire and sheet aluminum,*
c. 8¹/₂×9¹/₂". The Museum of Modern Art,
New York (Gift of the Advisory Committee).

FIG. 158. *Stroboscopic photograph.*
ALEXANDER CALDER. Hanging Mobile *(in motion).*
Aluminum and steel wire, width c. 28".
Collection Mrs. Meric Callery, Paris.

The word "assemblage" has been used to describe the category of art works,
including such constructions as that of Stankiewicz, created by combining separate
and distinct ready-made parts found and manipulated by the artist. These parts
may be used as they are found or they may be altered slightly by shaping, cutting,
or changing their color. The work of John Anderson called *Big Sam's Bodyguard* is
constructed of sections of wood, still retaining much of their treelike appearance,
which are combined with other sections carved into related forms by the sculptor
(Fig. 155). Gabriel Kohn, who also produces work which might loosely be described
as assemblages, laminates flat sections of machine-cut lumber into carefully crafted
forms and joins them into spatial constructions (Fig. 156).

Mobile sculpture is a variation of direct metal sculpture, in which portions of the
piece are united by articulated joints. This structural device enables the parts to
move, changing their positions relative to the other parts in the composition.
Through the use of motors or the action of the wind, mobile elements can be made
to flutter, wave, undulate, or spin in small and great arcs. Alexander Calder pio-
neered this form of sculpture and remains one of the foremost exponents of kinetic
art, that is, works constructed to move. For Calder the joints of his constructions
are as important as the forms, for the joints control the kind of movement that will
occur when the connected elements are activated (Figs. 157, 158). As can be seen
from the stroboscopic photograph of a Calder mobile, the movement produces a
pattern in space, and this pattern is directly related to the way in which the parts
are connected.

Fig. 159. Jean Tinguely.
Homage to New York: A Self-constructing
and Self-destroying Work of Art. *1960.*
Assemblage of piano, machine parts, bicycle parts,
weather balloon, fireworks, etc.

Early in his experiments with an art of movement Calder used electric motors to provide the motion in his sculpture. He abandoned their use because he felt that the movements produced by motors were too predictable and preferred the unexpected and random motion provided by air currents. In the late 1950's and the 1960's a number of sculptors have become interested in the possibilities of motorized constructions. Their work, along with mobiles like those of Calder, have been brought together under the general category of "kinetic art."

The esthetic and expressive potential in kinetic art ranges from the assemblages of Jean Tinguely, rather crudely joined machines made from the material available in junk yards, to the exquisitely crafted constructions of Pol Bury. Tinguely's machines move like insane or drunken robots, shaking, creaking, sometimes singing with the voice of a pretuned radio, sometimes erupting in a frenetic dance of self-destruction (Fig. 159). To the casual observer Bury's geometric compositions appear interesting but static. Unexpectedly, parts begin to quiver, vibrate, or slowly shift position in a manner which causes the viewer to doubt that he did, in fact, see any movement at all (Fig. 160).

Subtractive Sculpture.   As the word "modeling" is synonymous with additive sculpture, the word "carving" is often substituted for subtractive sculpture. The sculptor starts with a block of wood or stone and gradually reduces it to the forms he wishes to retain. This process requires no small physical effort on the part of the carver. Cutting into wood, or into the even harder stone, is a laborious and time-consuming process, and it is for this reason that carved pieces often lack the quality of spontaneity to be found in many examples of modeled or direct metal

PL. 39. VELÁZQUEZ. *The Surrender at Breda*. 1635. Canvas. c. 10 x 12′. Prado, Madrid.

PL. 40. PIERRE BONNARD. *The Breakfast Room.* 1930–31. Canvas, 63¼ x 44⅛″.
The Museum of Modern Art, New York.

Pl. 41. Hans Hofmann. *The Golden Wall*. 1961. Canvas, 60 x 72½". The Art Institute of Chicago.

PL. 42. PAUL CÉZANNE. *The Basket of Apples.* 1890–94. Canvas, 25¾ x 32″. The Art Institute of Chicago (Helen Birch Bartlett Memorial Collection).

Fig. 160. Pol Bury. Thirty-one Rods,
Each with a Ball. *1964.*
Motorized construction of wood, cork,
and nylon wire, height c. 40″;
wooden box 29³/₄ × 6¹/₂″.
The Museum of Modern Art, New York
(Elizabeth Bliss Parkinson Fund).

sculpture. An artist who must devote extended periods of time to the completion of a work does not begin to carve on a whim or a capricious fancy. Modeling is an ideal method for the production of the quick sketch, and many sculptors precede their work in stone or wood with studies in clay, but carving tends to be a serious business, and the attitude of the carver usually finds its way into his finished work.

Materials suitable for carving may differ in many ways. Their hardness may vary; their initial size may vary. They may have a neutral physical structure that does not affect the cutting action of the sculptor's tools, or they may have a structure, such as the pronounced grain of certain woods, that may draw the chisel along certain definite paths.

A sculptor may produce his original model in a flexible material like clay or wax or perhaps in plaster. It is then possible to transfer this original, through a complex measuring process called "pointing," to the block from which it is to be carved. The final process of removing the excess stone may be carried out by craftsmen employed by the sculptor, or he may do it himself. This rather mechanical approach to carving is not so popular today as it once was, for many contemporary sculptors feel that each new block has within it a hidden form, and that the sculptor's function is to reveal and release this form by removing those portions of the block which seem to obscure the essential image. As he works, there is a continuous interaction between the original concept of the carver and the material. Each cut may reveal a new clue to the structure and the formal characteristics of the stone or wood. Though the sculptor initially chooses his raw block because he feels that it has a potential which corresponds to his original conception, he can adjust his composition to the structure revealed to him in the material as the work proceeds.

FIG. 161. RAOUL HAGUE. Sawkill Walnut.
1955. Walnut, height 42".
Whitney Museum of American Art (Gift of
the Friends of the Whitney Museum).

Raoul Hague is an American sculptor who is known for his massive wood carvings. *Sawkill Walnut* is a typical piece by this sculptor, and it exemplifies his involvement with the material he uses (Fig. 161). Many of Hague's carvings are named after the wood he shaped to form them, indicating the importance he gives to the material. In *Sawkill Walnut* the forms seem to be a result of the growth process itself. Note how the grain becomes an integral part of the composition, flowing with the forms, reinforcing their directional movement, and at the same time enriching the surface. Even the wedged cracks in the wood seem to become a part of the composition, adding a textural variation to a flattened plane.

The hardness of stone and the textural possibilities inherent in the carving process are suggested by the *Head of Christ* by another American sculptor, William Zorach (Fig. 162). The material here is black porphyry, a very hard rock. It has been polished to a smooth, satiny finish on the surfaces that represent skin, but

The Visual Dialogue

Fig. 162. William Zorach.
Head of Christ. *1940.*
Black porphyry, height 14³/₄".
The Museum of Modern Art
(Abby Aldrich Rockefeller Fund).

the marks of the sculptor's tools are retained on the forms of the hair and beard. Over all there is a sense of the hard stone, which gave way reluctantly to the hammer and the steel edge of the chisel.

In both the wooden and stone examples above, the surface texture of the material plays an important part. Each material offers a carver the possibilities of a number of surface treatments. By choosing his cutting tools and methods of polishing, a sculptor can exploit the external faces of his material as he uses its internal structure. Development of the surface can emphasize color as well as the tactile quality of stone or wood, and here, too, is another integral material factor at the disposal of the carver.

As noted earlier in this chapter, the sculptor faces the same problem as the painter when he wishes to organize his work. He must create an esthetic unity which includes within it enough variation to create contrasts and complexities that will challenge and surprise the viewer who seeks to understand the order in a piece of sculpture. Once again it is necessary to note that the esthetic organization of sculpture cannot truly be isolated from its expressive or representational aspects. Ideally, esthetic organization, expression, and representation are all interrelated, but like the painter, the sculptor can use *repetition, continuity,* and *contrast* as esthetic devices to assist in the organization of his work. Important in the composition of sculpture is the recognition of the fact that a statue is a three-dimensional object. Except in the case of relief sculpture, the organization of sculpture is not restricted to one surface or face. The sculptor must organize his work so that the back is related to the front, and both front and back are related to the sides. In fact, when discussing a great many pieces of sculpture, it becomes difficult to describe them as though they had four distinct surfaces, for the artist has formed them into groups of elements which appear to have a continuing relationship through a 360-degree arc. A form or plane or linear movement may begin at one point, and a viewer may have to move around the piece of sculpture before he can trace the entire shape or path of that element.

The sculptor's material can have a strong unifying effect on a composition. The material can provide a unity of color and surface texture. However, once the sculptor begins to shape that material, he must organize his forms, carved or modeled surfaces, and linear movements so that they are integrated. Repetition of shape and surface and continuity of edges and planes are frequently used to this end. The sculptor may repeat the size or shape of forms and spaces. He may repeat surface treatment, that is, rough or smooth textures. Without repeating the shape of forms exactly, he may give them a similar character. They may be angular and cubelike or softly rounded and sensuous.

In his use of the inscribed line, the hard linear edge of forms, and the linear edge of the silhouette of his work the sculptor can produce a unity based on a continuous movement.

In *Man with Mandolin,* Jacques Lipchitz used repeated rectangular and triangular forms to unify the work. When seen from the front (Fig. 163), the repeated vertical edges of some of the forms produce the primary emphasis in the composition. This vertical movement is contrasted against a number of diagonals created by form edges. Note how the diagonal on the left ties together a series of small

FIG. 164. *Side view of Fig. 163.*

elements as it moves along on the left side of the lower contral group and then continues upward along the right side of the upper forms of the head. Cylindrical forms also are used on this face of the sculpture, as a subordinate and contrasting part of the composition, but the curves move away from the viewer, so that their characteristic arcs do not interrupt the vertical and diagonal emphasis. The face of the large plane on the right is placed at an angle so that it directs the viewer around toward the right side. On this side (Fig. 164) the sculptor has carved forms which echo those on the front face of the piece. Diagonals and verticals dominate the composition again, but the curved forms are somewhat more insistent. A study of the rear view and the left side of this carving would reward the viewer with the discovery of further unifying relationships similar to those noted here. The problem for Lipchitz was to tie each view of his composition to the view that was exposed before. The composition of the side had to appear inevitable, once the front of the piece had been seen. Yet the skillful sculptor has to arrange his forms so that, though they seem to be an inevitable extension of the views already seen, they are, at the same time, unexpected, surprising variations of the other faces of the structure.

FIG. 165. MICHELANGELO. Deposition from the Cross (Pietà).
Left unfinished, 1555. Marble, height 7' 5". Cathedral, Florence.

FIG. 166. *Side view of Fig. 165.*

A composition based upon strong planar movements is to be found in the *Deposition,* or Florence *Pietà*, by Michelangelo (Fig. 165). Here the figure of Christ twists so that the left arm, the head, and the knee form the forward edge of a plane that moves back from this line and around toward the left. It is intersected by another plane created by the female figure at the left, which continues this movement back behind the central axis of the group. To the right the forms of the other female figure interlock with those in the foreground and move back, this time in a secondary direction toward the right. Another planar movement runs upward from the juncture of the knee and the hand in a slow curve to form an arc with the hooded head of the figure behind Christ, which leans forward over the dead body.

Linear movements are carried along the edges of the forms and through the axis of the fallen figure and those which support it. A slow arc is repeated over and over again: in the body of Christ, in the position of his left arm, in the right arm of the female figure to the left, in the hood of the rear figure, and in the arch of the body of the female figure at the right. The whole group could easily be enclosed by a form shaped like a tall cone with slightly curving sides (Fig. 166).

In some contemporary examples of sculpture, particularly those made in welded metal, the organization of space is emphasized over the organization of forms. Ibram Lassaw's *Procession* (Fig. 153) is a composition based on the repetition of roughly vertical and horizontal movements. The irregular, elongated forms of the sculpture bulge out into lumpy masses and surfaces, but they retain their essential linear character. Rectangular spaces of many sizes and shapes are trapped between the thin solid elements. These spaces are arranged so that they can appear like a flat screen, but they also move back away from the observer to form a three-dimensional maze, which appears to change when seen from different viewpoints. Because they are so thin, the forms become movements in space, which connect the three major clusters of the construction and provide for secondary movements within the large groupings.

As noted earlier, most sculpture can be fully understood only when the observer can move around the entire piece so that the relationships and movements uniting all the parts can be seen. There are exceptions to this rule. Some compositions in three dimensions are based upon a series of contrasting forms set vertically one above the other. *Torso of a Young Man* (Fig. 167), by Constantin Brancusi, is a brass figure set on a base of wood and marble designed by the artist to create a symmetrical organization of the whole along a major vertical axis. The forms of the figure and the base contrast against one another, as do the textures of the mate-

Fig. 167. Constantin Brancusi.
Torso of a Young Man. *Brass, height 18",
on original base of marble and wood.
Collection Joseph H. Hirshhorn, New York.*

216

FIG. 168. The Transfiguration of Christ,
from the Gospel Book of Otto III. c. 1000.
Illumination. Bayerische Staatsbibliothek,
Munich (Ms. lat. 4453, fol. 113r).

FIG. 169. The Transfiguration of Christ,
detail of reliefs on the Easter Column,
Church of St. Michael, Hildesheim, Germany.
Early 11th cent. Cast bronze.

rials used in the individual sections. It is the juxtaposition of one form, one texture, against another that produces the full esthetic effect of this piece. An extremely important factor in the organization of this work are the surfaces produced on the forms. They offer to the viewer the sensuous pleasure of touching the warm, living form of wood; the granular, yet smooth surface of marble; and the cold, machine-like perfection of polished metal. It is an esthetic satisfaction which can be sensed even though the piece is seen and not touched.

George Sugarman's work (Pl. 19) is also an exercise in sculptural organization based upon contrasts. Sugarman constructs a sequential group of forms into a composition which seems literally to be teetering in a precarious, unbalanced state. Each form is shaped to play against the forms above and below it, and the color accentuates the contrasts tying the work together in a series of related tensions.

RELIEF SCULPTURE.   Relief sculpture is produced by creating three-dimensional forms which rise from, or are cut into, a flat, two-dimensional surface. Relief combines many of the characteristics of painting and sculpture and, in general, seems to parallel painting in methods of representation and organization. A comparison between a miniature painting of the Transfiguration of Christ from the Gospel Book of Otto III and a relief version of the same subject on a column in the Church of St. Michael, Hildesheim, both dating from about the year 1000, reveals the similarities between these two art forms (Figs. 168, 169). In both examples the figures are placed against a neutral background. Both have a strongly

FIG. 170. LORENZO GHIBERTI. The Story of Jacob and Esau. *c. 1435.*
Gilt bronze, 31" square. Baptistery, Florence, door.

linear quality, with a flattened, stylized representation of the figure. The primary
difference is the method used to create the linear forms. In the painting these forms
are drawn on the flat surface of the manuscript page. Areas are separated from the
background by outlines and color changes. In the relief the linear elements are the
result of shadows cast by the slightly raised portions of the bronze surface. Instead
of using a drawn line, the sculptor has "drawn" with shadows and high lights. The
entire figure is separated from the background on the column, because it projects
from it, and again it is the variation of light and shadow produced by this change
in thickness that substitutes for the painted separation in the manuscript.

A similar comparison can be made between a relief by Lorenzo Ghiberti from
the Italian Renaissance, *The Story of Jacob and Esau* on the door of the Baptistery of
Florence, executed about 1435, and a painting of about fifteen years later in Padua
by Andrea Mantegna, *The Judgment of St. James* (Figs. 170, 171). This relief and the
painting show more concern with the illusion of depth and three-dimensional form

FIG. 171. ANDREA MANTEGNA. The Judgment of St. James. *1449–55.*
Fresco. Church of the Eremitani, Padua, Ovetari Chapel.

than the two earlier examples. Both demonstrate the use of linear perspective as a
means of representing deep space. The three-dimensional forms of architecture and
figures are represented by Mantegna by painted, shaded forms. This shading
suggests a single light source, which models the solids in the picture to produce a
strong definition of edges and masses. Ghiberti's relief is constructed so that some
portions of the composition extend out from the background farther than others,
producing stronger light-and-shadow effects on the masses in the foreground.
In fact, some of the foreground figures are almost formed in the round. It is important to note, however, that the representation of the space behind the figures owes
far more to the perspective illusion than to the actual difference between planes.

A more recent use of relief is to be found in examples of cubist art from the
early years of the twentieth century. Again, the similarity between painting and
relief is obvious. Picasso's 1914 collage drawing, *Pipe, Glass, Bottle of Rum,*
makes use of the cubist devices of overlapping planes, simplified forms derived from

FIG. 172. PABLO PICASSO. Pipe, Glass, Bottle of Rum. *1914. Pencil, gouache, and pasted paper on cardboard, 15¹/₄ × 20³/₄". The Museum of Modern Art, New York (Gift of Mr. and Mrs. Daniel Saidenberg).*

FIG. 173. JACQUES LIPCHITZ. Still Life with Musical Instruments. *1918. Stone relief, 23⁵/₈ × 29¹/₂".*
Collection Mr. and Mrs. Joseph Pulitzer, Jr., St. Louis, Mo.

FIG. 174. ROBERTO CRIPPA. Composition. *1959. Bark mounted on plywood coated with paint, sawdust, and plastic glue, 78⁷/₈" square.*
The Museum of Modern Art, New York (Gift of Alexandre Iolas).

objects seen from several points of view, and an emphasis on the division of the flat picture plane rather than on an illusion of deep space (Fig. 172). A stone relief by Jacques Lipchitz, *Still Life with Musical Instruments*, dated 1918, exhibits similar qualities (Fig. 173). Hard edges and changing planes provide the linear and tonal elements in the relief, as they did in the earlier examples of this art form. The same emphasis on the picture plane is seen here, as are the compositional use of repeated shape and the continuity of edges.

The separation between relief sculpture and painting has become increasingly vague since the beginning of the 1950's. Painters such as Roberto Crippa are constructing collages with thick pieces of three-dimensional material glued to board. Crippa's *Composition* (Fig. 174) is made from sections of bark mounted on plywood coated with paint, sawdust, and plastic glue. Lee Bontecou, a sculptor, works with welded wire and painted canvas. *Relief* is a typical example of her constructions, a bulging hollow form that rises like a tent from the vertical surface of the wall on which it is hung (Fig. 175).

FIG. 175. LEE BONTECOU. Relief. *1959. Steel, cloth, and wire, 58¹/₈ × 58¹/₈ × 17³/₄".*
The Museum of Modern Art, New York (Gift of Mr. and Mrs. Arnold H. Maremont).

It could be properly said that many contemporary artists seem to work in a combination of painting and sculpture, bringing the potentials of both arts into their work. Bontecou is working as a painter when she organizes the linear elements of her constructions and tints the raw forms that are attached to the wires. Crippa concerns himself with three-dimensional masses and surfaces, and, in so doing, thinks in terms common to sculptors. Both these artists, and others who are working in a style that unites painting and sculpture, share with the artists working in more traditional modes the problems of esthetic organization and the expression of their responses to the world about them. For each the form and substance of his art derives from the necessity that motivates the artist to work. Differences in style, method, and materials result from differences of intention, personality, and sensibility.

THE EXPRESSIVE IMAGE

CHAPTER VIII

THE APPEARANCE of a piece of sculpture or a painting can offer great satisfaction to a viewer who is sensitive to the organizational structures in the visual arts, but frequently the idea, the evocation, the *expressive image* projected by the actual physical presence of the art object, offers the greatest esthetic reward.

An expressive image in painting and sculpture may be one of three things: (1) the representation of an emotional or atmospheric quality in the *subject* of the work; (2) the symbolic equivalent for the *artist's response* to a subject or an experience; or (3) that aspect of a painting or piece of sculpture which elicits an *emotional or psychological response from a viewer*.

At the outset it should be noted that part 3 of the definition may apply to the other two parts. That is, a viewer may have a subjective response to the faithful representation of a beautiful landscape, such as that by Jacob van Ruysdael (Pl. 52). He may also respond to an artist's expressive representation of a landscape, such as the painting by Van Gogh (Pl. 53). However, a viewer's response to the expressive image need not be tied to a representational form of art. In certain paintings and sculptural constructions the image that communicates strongly to an observer may not represent a specific physical object. The paintings of Mark Rothko are evocative combinations of form and color which may suggest or create an environment or atmosphere that a sensitive viewer can feel as an expressive image (Pl. 54), and in the sculpture *One and Others,* by Louise Bourgeois, the wooden forms are not figural, but their cramped placement on the space of their base has an implication of crowding which can produce the uncomfortable feeling of a claustrophobic society pressed together in a suffocating world (Fig. 176).

FIG. 176. LOUISE BOURGEOIS.
One and Others. *1955.*
Wood, height 18¹/₄".
*Whitney Museum of
American Art, New York.*

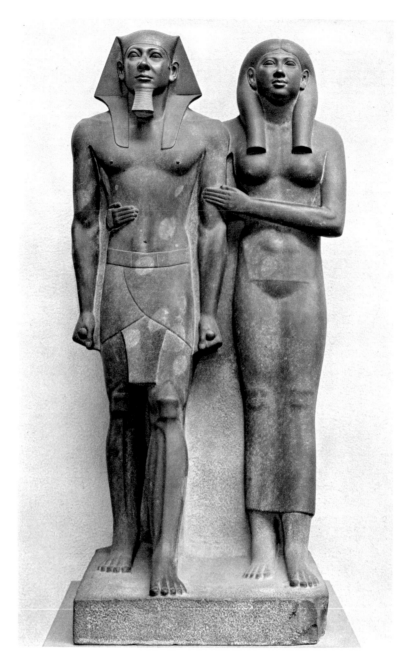

FIG. 177. King Mycerinus (Menkure) and His Queen. *4th dynasty, 2525* B.C. *Painted slate, height 56". Museum of Fine Arts, Boston.*

THE EXPRESSIVE IMAGE
IN REPRESENTATIONAL ART

Figures 177–179 are pieces of sculpture produced in ancient Egypt over a period of 2,500 years. For this great span of time the stylistic conventions of representation remained remarkably consistent in Egyptian art. With the exception of a short period during the reign of the pharaoh Ikhnaton, 1375–1358 B.C., when Egyptian art showed the personal preference of the pharaoh for a freer, more naturalistic style, the sculpture produced by Egyptian artists exhibits a stiff fron-

The Visual Dialogue

PL. 43. TOSHUSAI SHARAKU. *Iwai Hanshiro IV as Chihaya.*
1794–95. Wood-block print, 12¾ x 5¹⁵⁄₁₆″. Museum of
Fine Arts, Boston.

PL. 44. GIOVANNI BELLINI. *Madonna and Child.* 1509. Panel, 41¾ x 33⅜". Detroit Institute of Arts.

PL. 45. JEAN HONORÉ FRAGONARD. *La Bonne Mère.* c. 1775. Canvas, 25¼ x 20¾".
Museum of Fine Arts, Boston (Gift of Robert Treat Paine II).

PL. 46. ALFRED SISLEY. *Flood at Port-Marly.* 1872–76. Canvas, 23⅝ x 31⅞″. Louvre, Paris.

FIG. 178. Ramses II. *19th dynasty, c. 1250* B.C.
Stone. Temple of Amon, Luxor.

FIG. 179. Taharqa,
from Gebel Barkal, Nubia.
25th dynasty, 7th cent. B.C.
Stone, height 149".
Khartoum Museum.

tality. In statues of standing figures the head, shoulders, and hips are placed in parallel lines, the left leg is placed before the right, hands are most often at the sides (although there are some exceptions), and the eyes stare directly forward. The finished statue still retains the sense of the block of stone from which it was carved.

The description above could apply to the two-figure group, *Mycerinus and His Queen,* which dates from about 2525 B.C. (Fig. 177). It could also apply to the great figures from the court of Ramses II in Luxor (Fig. 178), which were produced about 1250 B.C. Carved five or six hundred years later, in the twenty-fifth dynasty, the statue of the pharaoh Taharqa, from Gebel Barkal (Fig. 179), retains the early conventions of representation.

When one considers the qualities that may be associated with a human figure, the body movements, and the indication of personal feelings or emotion, it is

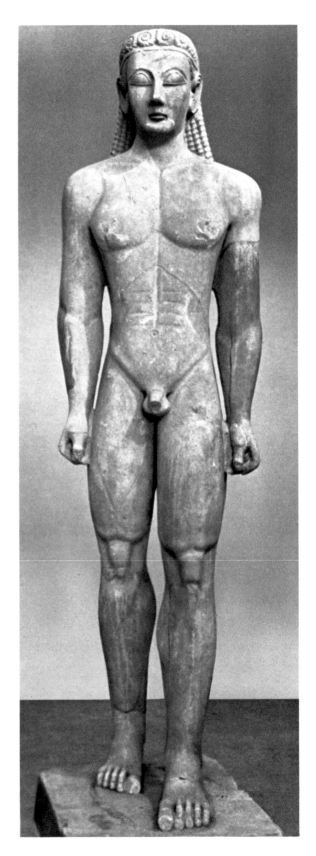

FIG. 180. Apollo, *from Sounion (right).*
c. 600 B.C. *Marble, height 11'.*
National Museum, Athens.
Detail of Fig. 136 (above).

The Visual Dialogue

obvious that the conventional treatment of this subject in much of Egyptian sculpture indicates a disregard for the aspects that other artists, at another time, in another place, might have considered important.

Explanations for the consistent style of ancient Egyptian art often refer to the static society and to the emphasis on the eternal life after death that was a major factor in the religion of Egypt. This cultural climate would tend to reduce the possibility of stylistic changes in the art. Once adequate visual symbols had been developed for religious and social purposes, those symbols would remain satisfactory as long as the culture continued without major changes.

Across the Mediterranean from Egypt, the Greeks developed an art form starting with many of the static conventions of Egyptian sculpture, but within a period of five hundred years it developed into an art concerned with movement and the expression of emotion. Compare the *Apollo* from Sounion (Fig. 180), dated about 600 B.C., with the central figure in the *Laocoön Group* (Fig. 136), which was completed in the first century B.C. The archaic *Apollo* has much in common with the Egyptian figures illustrated here. It is a frontally oriented work, stiff and immobile. It shares these stylistic qualities with most of the figure pieces produced in Greece at this time. The central figure of the *Laocoön Group* is in sharp contrast to that of *Apollo*. It breaks from the frontal plane and twists the upper portion of the torso away from the direction of the legs. The head is bent back in an attempt to indicate action. This same concern for movement seems to account for the manner in which the feet touch the ground plane, not flat and solidly placed, but bent at the toes as though frozen in movement. The face is contorted in a grimace of pain; even the muscles of the figure are shown in the strain of an emotional experience. Surely for the sculptor who produced this work the concept of man and the world he lived in was quite different from that of the artist who was working five hundred years before.

The changes which occurred in Greek art during the period between the sixth and first centuries B.C. reflected parallel cultural changes. Greece went from an aristocratic society, with wealth and the power concentrated in the possession of landowners who had deep roots in the past, men who desired the continuation of the ideals and the values of their fathers, to a materialistic society whose wealth was derived from trade. Greece of the second and first centuries B.C. was a country in which the old aristocracy gave way to a new one. Instead of maintaining the *status quo,* this new group broke down many of the old attitudes and values. Men were concerned with the present, with the transitory rather than the traditional. The art of this period presents a new concept of man and the world he makes for himself.

Though it is possible to point out a significant difference between Greek art of the first century B.C. and that of the sixth century, it is important to note also that these two styles have much in common. Both of them represent the physical form of the human being in quite similar ways, and they share this quality with the art of Egypt. Each of these styles retains the essential proportions of the human body. The head, the torso, and the limbs are similar in size and position to those of a real person. When the artist of late Greek sculpture wished to express emotion or give character to his images, he did it by making his forms in stone or bronze correspond to similar forms he had seen on the faces and the bodies of human beings under stress.

Fig. 181. The Temptation
of Christ, *scene on a capital.*
12th cent. Stone.
Cathedral, Autun, France.

However, this form of equivalency is not the only way in which emotion can
be communicated. In Figure 181, a capital from the twelfth-century Cathedral at
Autun, France, is a representation of the New Testament story of the Temptation
of Christ. The representational conventions in this work are quite different from
those illustrated in the previous examples. The posture of the figure of Christ is
rigid and stylized, as is the representation of the robe about the figure. The
anonymous artist of this capital wished to indicate something other than physical
appearance in the figure representing the Devil. He did not use the conventional
proportions that appear in the Christ figure; instead, the proportions were changed
to intensify the communication of a frightful expression. He distorted the conventional method of representing the figure to express the significance of the Devil.
The figure of the Devil in the Autun capital differs from the example of the central
figure in the *Laocoön Group*, in that it deviates from the conventions of pure
representation for greater expression. The forms corresponding to the mouth, the
eyes, and the nose are similar to those used in the head of Christ, but they have been
enlarged and shaped in a manner that abandons the convention, and so are more
expressive. *Whenever a cultural period develops standard modes or styles of representation,
artists are usually expected to work within those styles. When they depart from them to any
significant degree, this departure can be used to indicate an expression of emotion within the
subject or within the artist who produced the work.*
Another use of the departure from a representational convention is to be found
in the late paintings of El Greco. A study of his *Purification of the Temple*, now in the
Frick Collection, painted between 1595 and 1600, will reveal that the treatment of
a number of the representational features in the painting do not conform to the
conventions common at the turn of the seventeenth century (Pl. 55). When this
painting is compared with an earlier work on the same subject by the same artist,

in Minneapolis, some significant contrasts in the approach to representation are evident (Pl. 56). In the earlier painting the representation of form and space in the subject matter corresponds, in the main, to that of late Italian Renaissance painting. Proportions of the figures in the painting are similar to those usually associated with the human body; shading from light to dark has been used to indicate three-dimensional form, with the source of light appearing to come from the upper right; linear perspective has been used to indicate spatial relationships; and the pattern of light-and-dark shadows and high lights seems directly related to the desire of the artist to represent human and architectural forms in a detailed and consistent manner.

Though the mode of representation in the Frick painting conforms, in general, to that of the earlier work, the figures in the late painting are noticeably attenuated. The forms are defined by shading, but the source of light is not clearly indicated. The light-and-shadow pattern on the central figure of Christ is painted as though the source were at the right, yet there are unexplained shadows on the right side of the kneeling figure at the lower right. Other inconsistencies of lighting can be noted in the figure group at the upper right and the central group at the left. The illusion of three-dimensional space in the Frick painting is one of compressed volume. Figures seem forced together. Even the bit of landscape through the central arch has lost the deep spatial effect that is present in the early painting.

The effect of the Minneapolis painting is that of a tableau, a staged scene, in which the emotional expression depends upon the poses of the actors within the picture frame; but in the later painting the light-and-dark pattern of flickering forms, the agitation of the contours defining the forms, and the attenuation of the forms themselves accentuate the drama and reinforce the communication of emotion.

The artist of the twentieth century has no single set of conventions for the representation of form and space. Unlike the artists of ancient Greece, the medieval sculptors of the French Romanesque cathedrals, or El Greco in the late sixteenth century, the artist of the present has no single style to use as the standard form of representation. Enriched by the availability of examples and reproductions from the entire history of art in the West, aware of the great variety of representational approaches used throughout the world, the twentieth-century artist can choose from among them all the style best suited to his own expressive requirements. If he cannot find one that seems adequate, he is free to invent a new one, his only restrictions being those of his imagination, his skill, and his previous experience.

The two drawings (Figs. 17, 18) by Picasso discussed in Chapter II demonstrate one artist's ability to choose and utilize two distinctly different approaches to the problem of representation. The contrast is obvious; the choice of representational conventions, from the almost Renaissance approach of the nude figure to the cubist approach of the *Guernica* study, was apparently made to suit the artist's need. Obvious, also, is the contrasting use of the drawing line in each work—the smooth, flowing movement of the line in the figure and the seemingly crude, scribbled, apparently uncontrolled use of the pencil in the head. As in the two examples of El Greco, the elements of the Picasso drawings have been controlled for expressive purposes.

As long as the artist conformed to the conventions of his time in the construction and the production of works of art, his exploration of the expressive possibilities in the plastic elements had to be extremely limited. Under these conditions the painter or the sculptor conceived of his subject matter and executed his work within the patterns set by his traditions, but given the freedom of the present day, an artist may choose his visual language. Without concern for a particular form of representation, he may consider the expressive use of each element and the possible combinations of elements. What kind of line will best express anger? What combination of hues will communicate a feeling of gaiety? What kind of space is required in a mural to convey a condemnation of aggression? These and other questions have been answered by contemporary artists, who have found their own solutions to the creation of expressive visual symbols.

The possibility of a choice of expressive visual images exists today, but the artist does not always make a conscious selection of that style which is most relevant to his intentions. Often the choice is made without a logical predetermination of how a feeling or an idea can best be expressed. The artist may be affected by works of art he has seen before, without knowing that they are acting as an influence. The selection of a visual language is rarely an arbitrary decision. A critic, or even the artist himself, may be able, after the work is completed, to analyze the reasons for the choices that inevitably produced the unique qualities of a particular art object, but in the process of creating that work a complex series of conscious and intuitive actions and interactions produces the visual language that satisfies the needs of the sculptor or painter.

In 1911 a Russian painter and theorist, Wassily Kandinsky, published a book in which he attempted to define his new concepts of art. In *On the Spiritual in Art* Kandinsky developed his belief in an art based on an inner conviction. He felt that art should be derived from actual experience but also that it should develop out of the personal, subjective reality of the individual artist, without any attempt to represent, pictorially, the appearance of the outer world. To do this he suggested the use of a "language of form and color." He ascribed expressive values to particular colors and forms and asserted that it was essential for the artist to paint with a primary concern for these values, because they represented the artist's subjective, that is, his "spiritual" response to experience.

> In reality, no picture can be considered "well painted" if it possesses only correct tone values [illusionistic use of color] .... One should call a picture well painted if it possesses the fullness of life. A "perfect drawing" is the one where nothing can be changed without destroying the essential inner life, quite irrespective of whether this drawing contradicts our conception of anatomy, botany, or other sciences. The question is not whether the coincidental outer form is violated, but only, if its quality depends on the artist's need of certain forms irrespective of reality's pattern. Likewise, colours should be used not because they are true to nature but only because the colour harmony is required by the paintings individually. The artist is not only justified in using any form necessary for his purpose, but it is his duty to do so.[1]

In *Point and Line to Plane,* published in 1926, Kandinsky continued his development of the idea of a visual language. He attempted to establish particular meanings for colors and forms and their combinations(Pl. 57).

---

[1] Wassily Kandinsky, *On the Spiritual in Art*, The Solomon R. Guggenheim Foundation, New York, 1946, p. 92.

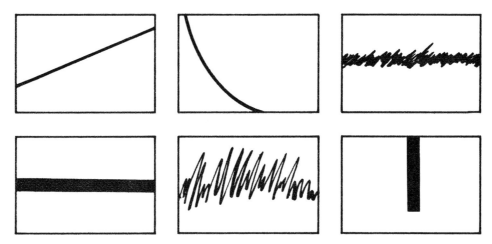

DIAG. 52

Kandinsky realized that his analysis of the expressive qualities of the elements of art could only brush the surface of the problem. He and other artists who have attempted to relate pure color, form, line, and texture to the expression of visual meaning have not come to any general agreement concerning the specific meanings of particular elements or the meanings of their possible combinations. To assume that a single kind of line or a single color will express love, or hate, or happiness is simplifying the problem unrealistically, but it is possible to suggest certain general, and perhaps obvious, kinds of meaning that may be achieved by a selective use of line, form, and color.

For example, short, staccato lines will suggest more agitation than lines that have a flowing continuity. The line itself may be rough or smooth. It may be oriented on the diagonal or curve, placed with a vertical emphasis or a horizontal emphasis. (See Diag. 52.)

Color can be selected to contrast sharply in value or hue, or color combinations can be harmonious and quietly unified, suggesting obvious expressive possibilities.

Even when the forms in a composition are restricted to identical squares and those squares are arranged in horizontal and vertical lines, variation in color can produce significant differences in the expressive content of the designs. The two examples shown here illustrate color changes in value. Diagram 53 shows variations of value in contrast, and the quality produced is one of agitation, excitement, conflict. Diagram 54 is composed of squares of closely related values, and the effect is quite different. Words such as "still," "quiet," "mysterious" might very well apply to this effect.

DIAG. 53

DIAG. 54

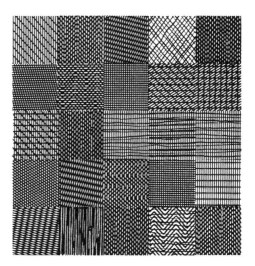

Fig. 182. Wilhelm Lehmbruck.
Kneeling Woman. *1911.*
Cast stone, height 69¹/₂".
The Museum of Modern Art, New York
(Mrs. John D. Rockefeller, Jr., Fund).

The forms selected may be massive and sculptural, or they may be small and complex. The spatial systems used may be simple and logical or inconsistent and confusing. Even the manner of applying paint to the surface of a canvas can contribute to the expressive content of a painting. Paint applied with a frenzied violence can have a real value as a part of this kind of expression. Deliberation and control in the application of paint can suggest calm and repose. Each artist, whatever the medium he uses, can find in it qualities capable of producing a great variety of non-physical meanings.

All that has been said here about the expressive potential in the plastic elements of the painter is equally true for the sculptor's art.

Compare the *Kneeling Woman* by Wilhelm Lehmbruck with Gaston Lachaise's *Standing Woman* (Figs. 182, 183). Neither of these works pretends to be an accurate replica of the forms of a female figure. The work of Lachaise is composed of bulging, massive, spherical forms, which seem to burst with strength and vitality. The bronze

FIG. 183. GASTON LACHAISE.
Standing Woman. *1932.*
Bronze, height 7' 4".
The Museum of Modern Art, New York
(Mrs. Simon Guggenheim Fund).

glows as though under stress, appearing to be drawn taut under the effort of restraining the burgeoning energy within. This figure becomes a symbol of woman as the source of life, fertility, strength, and power.

Lehmbruck elongates the forms of his figure from those which would be considered an accurately proportioned representation of a young woman. This attenuation and the restrained modeling of the forms produce a quiet image. The stone surface has a slightly flowing quality and a surface that is warm and free from active high lights. This figure is all that Lachaise's is not, and it, too, becomes more than the portrait of an individual. The *Kneeling Woman* suggests grace, introspection, a sense of withdrawal from life.

To be sure, the stance of each figure is an important part of the image it projects, one aggressive and active, the other passive and reposed, but equally obvious is the arbitrary treatment of the forms and surfaces used by each sculptor, and this organization of elements speaks as clearly as does the representational statement.

FIG. 184. FRÉDÉRIC AUGUSTE BARTHOLDI. Statue of Liberty (Liberty
Enlightening the World). *1874–85. Copper and iron, height of figure 151'.*

An additional expressive factor should be mentioned as important to the
sculptor, and that is *scale*. In sculpture the size of a piece can have a very real effect on
the observer. The reaction to a painting also often includes a response to size. One
does 'not feel the same about a tiny illumination in a manuscript as about a mural
that covers a great wall. But in sculpture, perhaps because the three-dimensional
work exists as an actual mass in space, scale seems to have an even greater importance than it does in the two-dimensional media. A sculptural work that towers over
the observer has an importance deriving from its size. The *Statue of Liberty* in the
harbor of New York City is not a figure of great esthetic value; it takes its significance from the values it symbolizes, but its importance comes also from its scale
(Fig. 184). Reduced to the size of a man it would lose its impressive appearance and
become far less than it now is. In contrast, a small piece of sculpture with the
qualities of a jeweler's art may be esthetically satisfying, but the same work enlarged
many times might appear preposterous.

EXPRESSION OF THE "INNER WORLD"

The common man of the fifteenth century who wished to know himself had only to look at his fellow men or look in the mirror. He understood men in terms of their overt actions. The man of the twentieth century, even the untrained observer, has been made to realize that "understanding" is not that simple. It has become usual to explain our actions by referring to the unconscious and subconscious aspects of our behavior. Psychology and psychiatry have taught us to consider whole areas of unseen, and in some cases unknowable, experience as a real and important part of our lives.

With the introduction of the idea of the unconscious into the realm of human experience, artists found a new source of subject matter. This source was themselves. They attempted to examine and represent those areas of experience and personality which were kept behind the gates of their conscious lives. These artists have been grouped, generally, into the category of surrealism. Their first attempts to touch their inner experience followed the paths of current psychological techniques. Paint or ink was blotted without an attempt to determine the final appearance of the forms. Bits of torn paper were allowed to drop onto a surface, producing chance combinations or groups. The artists hoped that these blots and bits of torn paper would suggest images that were locked in the recesses of their minds (Fig. 185).

Fig. 185. Jean (Hans) Arp. Automatic Drawing. *1916.*
Brush and ink, 16 ³/₄ × 21 ¹/₄″. The Museum of Modern Art, New York.

One of the early surrealists, Max Ernst, wrote:

> The investigations into the mechanism of inspiration which have been ardently pursued by the Surrealists, lead them to the discovery of certain techniques, poetic in essence, and devised to remove the work of art from the sway of the so-called conscious faculties. These techniques, which cast a spell over reason, over taste and the conscious will, have made possible a vigorous application of Surrealist principles to drawing, to painting and even, to an extent, to photography. These processes, some of which, especially collage, were employed before the advent of Surrealism, are now modified and systematized by Surrealism, making it possible for certain men to represent on paper or on canvas the dumbfounding photograph of their thoughts and of their desires.[2]

As surrealism was developed, it changed its methods. Such artists as Ernst, René Magritte, and Salvador Dali attempted to represent the world of their dreams through a technique of painting that approached the precision and clarity of a photograph. This approach was, technically, at the extreme pole from the spontaneous, uncontrolled images that resulted from the chance methods of the first surrealist experimentalists. Nevertheless, these artists insisted that the images in their paintings were spontaneous and directly related to the unconscious experience of their inner world (Figs. 186, 187).

Salvador Dali describes his method of painting as follows:

> After some time spent wholly in indulging in this kind of fancy summoned up out of childhood reminiscences, I finally decided to undertake a picture in which I would limit myself exclusively to reproducing each of these images as scrupulously as it was possible for me to do according to the order and the intensity of their impact, and following as a criterion and norm of their arrangement only the most automatic feelings that their sentimental proximity and linking would dictate. And it goes without saying there would be no intervention of my personal taste. I would follow only my pleasure, my most uncontrollably biological desire. This work was one of the most authentic and fundamental to which surrealism could rightly lay claim.
>
> I would awake at sunrise, and without washing or dressing sit down before the easel which stood right beside my bed. Thus the first image I saw on awakening was the painting I had begun, as it was the last I saw in the evening when I retired. And I tried to go to sleep while looking at it fixedly, as though by endeavoring to link it to my sleep I could succeed in not separating myself from it. Sometimes I would awake in the middle of the night and turn on the light to see my painting again for a moment. At times again between slumbers I would observe it in the solitary gay light of the waxing moon. Thus I spent the whole day seated before my easel, my eyes staring fixedly, trying to "see," like a medium (very much so indeed) the images that would spring up in my imagination. Often I saw these images exactly situated in the painting. Then, at the point commanded by them I would paint, paint with the hot taste in my mouth that panting hunting dogs must have at the moment they fasten their teeth into the game killed that very instant by a well aimed shot.[3]

---

[2] Alfred H. Barr, Jr., *Fantastic Art, Dada, Surrealism*, The Museum of Modern Art, New York, 1936, p. 37.

[3] Reprinted from *The Secret Life of Salvador Dali*, p. 221. Copyright © 1942, 1960 by Salvador Dali. Used with the permission of the publishers, The Dial Press, Inc., New York.

FIG. 186. MAX ERNST.
Alice in 1941. *1941.*
Canvas, 15 ³/₄ × 12 ¹/₂".
The Museum of Modern Art, New York
(Collection James Thrall Soby).

FIG. 187. RENÉ MAGRITTE.
The Liberator. *1947.*
Canvas, 39" × 31".
Los Angeles County Museum
of Art (Gift of William N. Copley).

FIG. 188. PAUL KLEE. Botanical Garden. *1921. Pen and ink, 9 ⁷/₈ × 15 ³/₈". Paul Klee-Stiftung, Berne.*

The Visual Dialogue

Dali's paintings and the works of others following this general approach have certain typical stylistic qualities. They usually provide the viewer with a meticulously drawn, ambiguous scene in which the realism suggested by the technique is in conflict with a representation of forms or events outside his experience. In some cases fantastic worlds are created, filled with frightening monsters or strange architectural structures. In other instances the artist will present a superficially conventional scene with some small detail that cannot be logically explained or that suggests a series of connected images extending beyond the limits of the canvas (Pls. 59, 60).

THE EXPRESSIVE IMAGE IN NONREPRESENTATIONAL ART

Somewhat apart from the movement of surrealism but developing along more or less parallel lines, the paintings and drawings of the Swiss artist Paul Klee bridge the gap between representational and nonrepresentational images in the visual arts. When Klee died in 1940, he left behind him an extraordinary body of work, in which was traced the artist's extended involvement with the problems of pure visual expression. Klee was a colleague of Wassily Kandinsky when they both taught at the Bauhaus, an experimental institute for instruction in the arts, which was established first in Weimar and then moved to Dessau, Germany. It was Klee who said in 1919 that art did not exist to reproduce the visible but to render visible what lay beyond the visual world. His work is a combination of a highly intellectual concern for plastic organization and an intuitive search for expressive images. Klee's researches (and one may truly refer to his paintings in this way) resulted in some paintings that appear to be formal exercises, others that are imaginary landscapes and cityscapes, and still others that contain enigmatic calligraphy and childlike figurative symbols. Paul Klee's paintings were always highly personal, and yet they opened doors for many artists who followed him in searching for visual, non-literary images (Fig. 188, Pl. 58).

Many present-day artists have forsaken a rational, conscious attitude toward art and instead depend upon spontaneous, intuitive responses to the emotional stimuli they feel. Their visual symbols develop in the very process of painting. Their methods and attitudes have much in common with those of the early surrealists who experimented with automatic writing and accidental collages, and they have a familial connection with the work of Klee.

William Baziotes is a painter who belongs to this group (Pl. 62). He discusses his work in the following way:

> There is no particular system I follow when I begin a painting. Each painting has its own way of evolving. One may start with a few color areas on the canvas; another with a myriad of lines; and perhaps another with a profusion of colors. Each beginning suggests something. Once I sense the suggestion, I begin to paint intuitively. The suggestion then becomes a phantom that must be caught and made real. As I work, or when the painting is finished, the subject reveals itself.[4]

Artists such as Baziotes combine the use of a language of pure form and color in the tradition of Kandinsky and the automatic intuitive development of expressive

---

[4] *Fifteen Americans,* ed., Dorothy Miller, The Museum of Modern Art, New York, 1952, p. 12.

images in the manner of the surrealists. They do not represent emotion; they try
to produce a visual equivalent for the emotional experience itself.

The phantom to which Baziotes refers in his statement may take the form of a
nonrepresentational, chimerical image, which becomes a threatening or beneficent
presence that a viewer may sense in the work of art. The painting *Beard of Uncertain
Return* (Fig. 189), by Jean Dubuffet, may be understood to represent the head of a
bearded man, and yet it is more than that. The highly textured surface of the single
large form dominates the center of the canvas. Here is a portrait of *something,* a
nightmarish presence that is far more than an area of textured canvas. The central
form becomes an image, rather than a part of an esthetic organization. It seems to
have a life of its own, rather than a function as a color or textural area in a compositional scheme.

PL. 47. CLAUDE MONET. *Sunflowers*. 1881. Canvas, 39¾ x 32″. The Metropolitan Museum of Art, New York (The H. O. Havemeyer Collection, Bequest of Mrs. H. O. Havemeyer, 1929).

PL. 48. Detail of Monet's *Sunflowers* (Pl. 47).

PL. 49. JEAN LÉON GÉRÔME. *Gray Eminence (L'Eminence Grise)*. 1874. Canvas, 38¾ x 25¾". Museum of Fine Arts, Boston (Bequest of Susan Cornelia Warren).

PL. 50. Detail of Gérôme's *Gray Eminence* (Pl. 49).

A similar nonrepresentational image appears in the bronze by Jacques Lipchitz called *Figure* (Fig. 190). This massive series of forms has elements of a figurative image in it, but its expressive content seems to derive from its scale (over 7 feet high), the simplicity of its forms, and a robotlike arrangement of the circular elements in the upper portion of the composition.

Kurt Schwitters, a German artist who died in 1948, produced collages which combine image and composition in a style quite different from that of Dubuffet. Schwitters organized bits of printed matter, commonplace scraps of paper, and cloth into meticulously arranged compositions (Pl. 25). The materials used in these collages often carry with them some of the meaning associated with their original use. A part of a calendar, a ticket stub, the handwritten corner of a note—these become more than textural and color shapes combined to form a pleasant design. They are the residue of the lives of unknown men and women, formed into a mosaic that provides the viewer with a shadowy image of past events.

FIG. 190. JACQUES LIPCHITZ. Figure. *1926–30. Bronze, height 7' 1¹/₄".*
The Museum of Modern Art, New York (Van Gogh Purchase Fund).

Frequently the image in nonrepresentational painting is an evocative atmosphere rather than a disquieting specter. The paintings of Josef Albers can be described as compositions based upon overlapping squares of color, but when a group of them is seen together, each subtle combination of colors seems to suggest a quite different experience or attitude. In fact Albers's titles for these paintings often have reference to highly personal experience (Pl. 63).

In some instances contemporary painters have increased the scale of their works so that they cover wall-size areas. These large canvases seem to create a personal world of form and color that functions as a man-made environment. They offer a viewer a world set apart from nature, charged with the emotion that initially stimulated the artist who produced it.

The late paintings of Jackson Pollock are examples of large oils which become expressive environments. *Number 1* (Pl. 51) measures 68 by 104 inches. It was painted in a technique that Pollock developed. The canvas was laid out on the flat surface of a floor. Pollock stood over it, using brushes, punctured cans, and sticks, which dripped paint to produce the tangled web of colored lines that covers the surface of the painting. The result is a complex screen that surrounds a viewer with a shimmering barrier through which there seem to be visible lights and forms of unknown origins.

The artist describes his involvement in this painting process as follows :

> When I am *in* my painting, I'm not aware of what I am doing. It is only after a sort of "get acquainted" period that I see what I have been about. I have no fears about making changes, destroying the image etc., because the painting has a life of its own. I try to let it come through. It is only when I lose contact with the painting that the result is a mess. Otherwise there is pure harmony, an easy give and take, and the painting comes out well.[5]

To review, the expressive image may be a representation of the attitude of a subject in a work of art ; it may be the expression of the artist's attitude toward a subject; or finally, in a nonrepresentational work, it may be an evocative symbol or atmosphere created by color, form, and the other plastic elements, which precipitates an emotional response in the viewer. The expressive image is in part shaped by the subjective response of the viewer, and because this is so, there cannot be a universal response to any particular expressive statement. So much of the response to an image depends on the variable qualities that make up each individual artist who produces an image and each individual viewer who looks at the result of the artist's work that some images are inevitably ambiguous and "meaningless" to some persons. It is enough to say that, for each viewer, some works of art will express some of the feelings and subjective attitudes that are an important part of the sense of life we all feel. The response to these expressive images is a part of the esthetic response that can be stimulated by the art object.

---

[5] Jackson Pollock, "My Painting," *Possibilities,* Winter 1947–48, in Eric Protter, *Painters on Painting,* Grosset & Dunlap, Inc. New York, 1963, p. 249.

ARCHITECTURE: Esthetic and Expressive Organization

CHAPTER IX

ARCHITECTURE, LIKE SCULPTURE, is a three-dimensional art form. As such, it has certain similarities with sculpture. Both are composed of forms arranged in space; both use texture, shape, material, volume, light, and color as constituent parts of their organization. But architecture is not sculpture, and the differences between them have a direct effect on the appreciation of each.

Architecture throughout history has concerned itself with sculptural problems, but it has never eliminated the concern for the interior volumes contained by the exterior shell. In our own time this concern often takes precedence over the esthetic relationships of the external elements in the design of a building, and the appreciation of architecture must include an awareness and concern for the nature and quality of interior space. This does not mean that it is impossible to be impressed by the exterior of a building. The size, the shape, the materials, and the over-all design of the outside of a building are often esthetically satisfying, even thrilling, but this is only a part of a building. As it is possible to respond to one small part of a painting, so, too, it is possible to respond to a portion of an architectural work. More complete understanding can come only with an interaction between the viewer and all of the building, inside and outside.

This kind of total appreciation presents problems more difficult in architecture than in any other form of the visual arts. As in the case of seeing sculpture, there is the problem of the partial view, the necessity of seeing only a portion of the work at any one time. In architecture the problem is amplified. All of a piece of sculpture may be seen from the outside, whereas the viewer must stand within the design of an architect to know it fully. The size of the architectural design is often a factor in complicating the process that leads to its appreciation. To understand a building that covers hundreds of square feet and is constructed on more than one level means that the observer must relate spaces and forms isolated by the barriers of walls and stairways. It requires the ability to see esthetic relationships between visual experiences separated by minutes and possibly by hours.

The esthetic organization of architecture is often based upon the principles of unity and variety common to both painting and sculpture. The Pazzi Chapel in Florence, by the Italian architect Brunelleschi, lends itself to this kind of examination (Fig. 191). The dominant element of the front of the chapel is a screenlike façade, which introduces the characteristic design elements used repeatedly through-

FIGS. 191, 192. FILIPPO BRUNELLESCHI. *Pazzi Chapel, Florence. 1429–43.*
(191) Façade (unfinished). (192) Interior.

out the building. Six columns with Corinthian capitals are set in two groups of
three. The same rhythm is repeated on the flat upper portions of the façade, but here
the columns are replaced by twin pilasters of smaller scale. Areas between the pilasters are filled with rectangular panels. An arch connects the two sections of the
screen, which flank the entrance, focusing attention on the front doors just beyond
the porch. A combination of horizontal and vertical elements, curved arch forms,
and Corinthian detail are the unifying stylistic devices used by Brunelleschi within
and without the building.

Repeated pilasters adorn the outer walls of the chapel, echoing the division of
space established on the front screen. This same rhythmic scheme is found inside
the building on both of the long walls (Fig. 192). Tall, narrow windows topped with
arches are placed between the pilasters, and they, too, are found repeated as decorative moldings within.

The interior space is covered by a large ribbed dome, which rises from supporting arched elements, echoing the curves in the porch. Each flat wall surface is
tied to the general decorative scheme in a consistent repetitive use of vertical,
horizontal, and curved motifs. Even the domed space of the main body of the chapel
finds its introduction in a smaller dome over the entrance of the porch and its
echo over the alcove that houses the altar.

FIG. 192

The plan of this building shows an essentially symmetrical composition, but it does not suggest the variety of spaces produced within this basically simple scheme (Fig. 193). The sheltered, shadowy space of the porch leads the viewer into an inner volume that rises upward into the interior dome, which is illuminated by a group of circular windows between the ribs.

A more detailed analysis would find many more repetitive elements that tie the parts of this structure into a single unified composition. Here, then, is an example in which the architect used one of the classic methods of esthetic organization, repetition, as a means of producing an elegant series of planes and spaces.

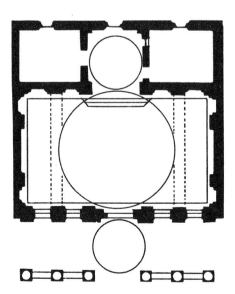

FIG. 193. FILIPPO BRUNELLESCHI.
Plan of the Pazzi Chapel.

253

FIG. 194. FRANK LLOYD WRIGHT. *The Solomon R. Guggenheim Museum, New York. 1959.*

FIGS. 195–198. FRANK LLOYD WRIGHT.
*The Solomon R. Guggenheim Museum,
New York, interior details. 1959.*
(195) Ramp and reflecting pool.
(196) View into the dome.
(197) Auditorium. (198) Stairwell.

FIG. 195

Fig. 196

Repetition is also used as the primary compositional device in the Solomon R. Guggenheim Museum. In this building the architect, Frank Lloyd Wright, used the curve as the basic design motif (Fig. 194).

The museum exhibition area is a great open, spiral ramp, which descends six stories from a ribbed, translucent dome to the ground level. This spiral is housed in the southern portion of the museum. From the outside, the inner structure is mirrored in the inverted truncated-cone form of this main section of the building. To the north a smaller cylindrical mass houses the administrative offices and library. The two curved sections are tied together with a massive horizontal band, which contrasts against the curves while also functioning to relate the building to the ground plane and to provide the dramatic emphasis for the entrance. A secondary repeat of the horizontal occurs above the lower band, in a form of cornice, which creates a sharp angular contrast above the rounded corner of the building at the northwest.

A visitor enters the museum under the horizontal mass. The low ceiling height of the shadowed entrance dramatizes the great volume of space and light that expands out and up from the entry. Nowhere is one permitted to forget the unity of this extraordinary composition. Throughout the building curved forms are repeated: on the exterior, in the design of windows, screens, walls, and planting areas, and, of course, in the two masses comprising the main features of the façade; in the interior, in the shape of the lavatories, the elevators, and even the pattern of the terrazzo flooring, which echoes the motif. An intimate auditorium in the basement has a stage, seating area, and ceiling which continue the circular repeats (Fig. 197).

Contrasts to the dominant shape are to be found in the spiral itself. Instead of permitting the rising curve to continue unbroken from floor to dome, Wright interrupted the corkscrewlike movement with a section on each story that bulges out in a reversal of the main arc (Fig. 195). Another important contrast is to be found in the design of the main stairwell, which abuts the ramp. In this area it is the

FIG. 197

triangle that unites all elements of the design (Fig. 198). Like the repeated curves in the gallery, the triangular repeats are to be found everywhere, including the exterior shape of the stairwell pylon, which intersects the coil of the spiral on the east side of the building. Stairwell and main gallery are joined compositionally by the introduction of the triangular shape in recessed lighting fixtures, which dot the ceiling of the ramp, and finally in the ribs of the dome which crowns the building (Fig. 196).

Like the painter or sculptor, both Brunelleschi and Wright sought to order their compositions by using repetition, continuity, and contrast; but, unlike their counterparts in the other two visual arts, the architects had to consider more than the esthetic organization of their designs when faced with the problem of creating these two structures. Before Brunelleschi's building was a complex composition of curves and horizontal and vertical elements, it had to be considered as a *chapel*—a structure that would stand erect, a shelter in which a group of people expected to worship their God. Before Wright's design could exist in space, it had to be constructed with strength enough to function as a ramp that would carry the weight of hundreds of people and to support the dome over it. It also had to resolve the problems of lighting and displaying a collection of paintings and sculpture.

An architect applies the principles of composition employed by other artists, but he must conceive of these principles within an esthetic scheme which includes practical, functional limitations that do not apply to the other two visual arts.

Vitruvius, who wrote his *Ten Books on Architecture* in the first century B.C., stated that the fundamental principles of architectural design were convenience, beauty, and strength. In our own time, the word "function" has often been substituted for "convenience," and to this requirement has been added the idea that beauty and strength (that is, esthetic order and the structural use of materials) are inseparably united. In some instances architects and critics of their art have insisted that all three are part of one unity. "Form follows function" is a phrase often used

Fig. 198

in architectural criticism. Louis Sullivan, an American architect who worked at the end of the nineteenth century, was one of the leaders in the development of this idea. In an essay discussing the problems inherent in the design of tall office buildings, Sullivan stated his beliefs as follows:

> It is my belief that it is of the very essence of every problem that it contains and suggests its own solution. This I believe to be natural law. Let us examine, then, carefully the elements, let us search out this contained suggestion, this essence of the problem.
>
> The practical conditions are, broadly speaking, these:
>
> Wanted—1st, a story below-ground, containing boilers, engines of various sorts, etc—in short, the plant for power, heating, lighting, etc. 2nd, a ground floor, so called, devoted to stores, banks, or other establishments requiring large area, ample spacing, ample light, and great freedom of access. 3rd, a second story readily accessible by stairways—this space usually in large subdivisions, with corresponding liberality in structural spacing and expanse of glass and breadth of external openings. 4th, above this an indefinite number of offices piled tier upon tier, one tier just like another tier, one office just like all other offices—an office being similar to a cell in a honey-comb, merely a compartment, nothing more. 5th, and last, at the top of this pile is placed a space or story that, as related to the life and usefulness of the structure, is purely physiological in its nature—namely the attic. In this the circulatory system completes itself and makes its grand turn, ascending and descending. The space is filled with tanks, pipes, valves, sheaves, and mechanical etcetera that supplement and complement the force-originating plant hidden below-ground in the cellar. Finally, or at the beginning rather, there must be on the ground floor a main aperture or entrance common to all the occupants or patrons of the building.[1]

---

[1] Louis H. Sullivan, "The Tall Office Building Artistically Considered," *Kindergarten Chats and Other Writings,* George Wittenborn, Inc., Publishers, New York, 1947, p. 203.

How different are the functions of a building of commerce rising out of the streets of Chicago or New York in the twentieth century from the functions of a building dedicated to an ancient god, sited on a plateau overlooking the Mediterranean over two thousand years ago! Geography, history, economics, politics, religion—all these can have their effect on the function of any single building in the architectural continuum. But essentially there are three major functional areas that concern the architect: *the operational function, the environmental function,* and *the expressive,* or *symbolic, function.* Often one of these areas dominates the other two in the development of a particular stylistic period. Ideally they would all make important contributions to the resolution of any one architectural design.

THE OPERATIONAL FUNCTION

Who is to use the building? How many people will occupy it? What will they be doing when they are within it? These are questions which would apply to the operational function of a building. In the extensive study of architecture entitled *Forms and Functions of Twentieth Century Architecture,* edited by T. F. Hamlin, the table of contents lists forty-two building types. Under the headings "Buildings for Residence," "Buildings for Popular Gatherings," "Buildings for Education," "Government Buildings," "Commerce and Industry," "Buildings for Transportation," and "Buildings for Social Welfare and Recreation" the contributors discuss the problems relating to the design of each of these categories. Our society has grown so complex, its needs served by so many specialized groups and highly sophisticated organizations, that it is no longer possible to restrict the forms of architecture to a few limited types.

A partial list of the limitations facing an architect who must design a space suitable for the operational requirements of the occupants includes traffic patterns; room sizes and shapes; location of various areas of activity; wall, floor, and ceiling finishes; acoustics; plumbing; lighting; and ventilation. The simple problem of how the occupants are to reach the upper levels of the building may take on a major significance in the development of a design. Finally, it must be noted that one of the most pressing practical concerns of the architect is cost. With rare exceptions, the architectural designer is always faced with the problems of budgets and the concern of his client to control the construction and operating costs of the building. One must always remember that the architect's designs are never complete on the drawing board. They reach completion only after the drawings are transformed by the efforts of masons, carpenters, plumbers, and electricians, each of whom requires instruction and supervision, and, of course, recompense for his labor.

THE ENVIRONMENTAL FUNCTION

Given the forty-two building types mentioned above, the architect must consider his building not just as an efficient machine designed to facilitate the activity of its tenants but also as an environment in which human beings will spend a portion of their day. This obvious statement is not so self-evident as it may seem. The human being has often been considered a cog in some huge mechanism. Often his physical needs have been satisfied, but little concern has been given to his emotional or esthetic needs. Today, however, there is a growing awareness of the connection between environment and human efficiency in the production of goods by the efforts of men and women. Office buildings and huge assembly plants, as well as other structures designed for commercial, industrial, and public purposes, house great populations for a substantial portion of their lives. The atmosphere in which these people work cannot fail to affect them, and, of course, whatever may be said for the buildings that shelter our public and economic complex is equally, or even more importantly, pertinent to the design of our residential architecture.

Light, color, the size of rooms, the kinds of materials used—all can have a significant effect on the physical and psychological response to the architectural environment. The architect begins with the individual human being—his size, his need for identity as an individual, his response to sound and movement in his restricted sphere of activity. Within the restrictions imposed upon him by the operational functions of the building, the architect can try to create the environment that best suits the needs of his building. Are the occupants required to be alert? Are they required to be impressed by the social, or perhaps the political, significance of the structure?

Richard Neutra is a contemporary architect who has concerned himself with the problems of architectural design as the creation of environment. He notes that we are most conscious of possible effects of an architectural environment upon us when they are presented to us in the extreme. As an example he cites the design of certain "fun houses" in amusement parks, in which the rooms are built askew and the angles and planes of the walls are constructed in bizarre relationships. The occupant of such a room is placed in a different environment from that which he has normally experienced, and often he becomes puzzled or even frustrated by it. His sense of the pull of gravity no longer relates to the visual experience he is having. Size and space relationships are confused.

> The whole is a striking example of how deep down the disturbance will reach if we break the co-ordination of visual experience and gravity sense in the inner ear and the many muscle-senses, which help our usual balancing act. This stereognostic co-ordination is slowly acquired from infancy and, through a network of nerve connections, governs glandular secretion, blood circulation, the rhythmic intestinal movements. Reassured feelings are related to this established harmonization of sensory clues, termed stereognosis, and other emotions arise promptly from a disharmony among them.[2]

Neutra feels that this extreme example is part of the whole complex interaction between the individual and his environment. In Neutra's concept the architect can produce an environment designed for the ideal physiological and psychological requirements of the inhabitants of the buildings. He explains his point of view in his book *Survival Through Design*.

> In human dwelling places, complex *inner* stimuli derive from the design of the rooms and the articles in them with which we surround ourselves. The chair, together with the desk, determines our posture; so does the couch on which we read with a light source, either well or inconveniently placed. Or, for example, that same couch may be planned and placed in poor relationship to a magnificent window and make us crane our neck in vain to

[2] Richard Neutra, *Survival Through Design*, Oxford University Press, New York, 1954, p. 155.

enjoy the view. The problems of posture relate a vast number of other sensory experiences to vision, which concerns and directs not only our eyes but our whole body.

It is clearly the design of a room and its furniture which call for certain habitual movements and placements of our body. The taking and holding of a posture, the going into any muscular action, in turn establish what is called a kinesthetic pattern, a pattern of successive and simultaneous inner stimuli. Important responses are then elicited by such stimuli, reflexes are touched off, conditioned by a routine usage of furniture, lighting fixtures, and a thousand little items which, in their placement and function, may be variously right or wrong. The responses mentioned are frequently not conscious ones, and in many cases not motor responses directed toward a remedial action. Often these responses are emotional but cumulative, so that lasting depressions or exhilarations may be their effect, and thus the effect of the room in which we spend our time.[3]

The creation of an architectural environment is directly dependent upon the esthetic aspect of the interior spatial design of a building. As in other art forms, the architect is concerned with the creation of an esthetic organization. He attempts to use form, texture, and color in a spatial order, but these plastic elements are related to and are, in part, created by the structure of the building, which is, of course, related to the operational function.

As noted earlier in this chapter, it is possible to examine an architectural design in a manner similar to that of studying the esthetic organization of painting or sculpture. However, it should be obvious from the discussion of the functional areas of operation and environment that an observer often cannot respond immediately to the characteristics of an architectural composition directly related to these factors.

To appreciate the operational function of a building it is necessary to know what operations take place in it and how the operational necessities have been satisfied. This information is frequently not available to the lay observer, and judgments on the efficiency of many buildings must inevitably be left to those who use them. However, many types of buildings are used by the public at large (stores, offices, apartment houses, schools, and residences), and it is possible for a large portion of the nonspecialist public to draw pertinent conclusions about the ingenuity and imagination employed to accommodate the needs of the occupants.

The environmental function of an architectural design is, once again, that aspect of a building which most affects the people who use it. An occupant would find it difficult to isolate those elements in an environment which produced a state of pleasure or well-being, but he would know when that state existed. The appreciation of environmental design must inevitably come from an intuitive response to the combination of architectural elements acting upon the observer. Differences of personality and physiology between occupants of a building will color the reactions to a planned environment so that no single consistent response is possible. Each person who seeks to understand a building will have an individual subjective response to it, as a place to live and work, that will affect his appreciation. The subjective response to architecture operates also when one responds to the third function of architectural design, the expressive or symbolic function.

---

3 Ibid., p. 151.

Figs. 199, 200. Henry Bacon. *Lincoln Memorial, Washington, D.C., exterior and interior.*

THE EXPRESSIVE, OR SYMBOLIC, FUNCTION

Architecture has limits.

When we touch the invisible walls of its limits then we know more about what is contained in them. A painter can paint square wheels on a cannon to express the futility of war. A sculptor can carve the same square wheels. But an architect must use round wheels. Though painting and sculpture play a beautiful role in the realm of architecture as architecture plays a beautiful role in the realms of painting and sculpture, one does not have the same discipline as the other.

One may say that architecture is the thoughtful making of spaces. It is, note, the filling of areas prescribed by the client. It is the creating of spaces that evoke a feeling of appropriate use.[4]

These are the words of Louis Kahn, an American architect who is concerned with the symbolic function of architecture. Like many other architects, Kahn recognizes the need to consider a building as a symbol for the activity housed within it. A school, a church, an office building, and a seat of government must mean different things to those who use them and to those who pass through them.

The symbolic function of architecture depends in part upon the response of the public to the forms erected by the builder, as the agent of the architect, who satisfies the need of his client. A portion of this response will most certainly be conditioned by buildings of the past, which have had a historical significance in some aspect of the culture of the contemporary society. One need only look at the hundreds of government buildings in this country and abroad which have been influenced by the appearance of Greek and Roman architecture to realize that the columned temple has been identified with public buildings. The Lincoln Memorial in Washington, D.C., is one of many examples of an architectural design modeled on Greek antecedents (Fig. 199). The monument was completed in 1912 and is in the

---

[4] Louis I. Kahn, "Structure and Form," Voice of America Forum Lectures, 1960, in Vincent Scully, Jr., *Louis I. Kahn*, George Braziller, Inc., New York, 1962, p. 118.

Fig. 200

form of an unpedimented Doric temple. Certainly one of the buildings of great significance to many Americans, this monument derives much of its expressive content from the classic style chosen by the designers. The colonnade surrounding the great statue of Lincoln in the interior announces to the visitor that he is about to enter a space of importance (Fig. 200). The scale of the building and the white marble surfaces of its walls and columns add to the grandeur and the emotional impact that most visitors feel before and within this monument. It does not debase this response to suggest that some significant portion of it is due to the stylistic connection between this building and other more ancient examples of monumental architecture.

If the Lincoln Memorial is compared with the Jefferson Westward Expansion Memorial, in St. Louis, Mo., which was designed by Eero Saarinen, the difference in conception is startlingly evident. The Lincoln monument is tied to the past, with all its associated meaning and content; the great catenary arch of the Jefferson Memorial has no stylistic precedent. Certainly the idea of an arch as the entrance or a gateway to an important space is operating here, but the stark simplicity of the form devised by Saarinen could have been conceived only in the twentieth century (Fig. 201). The grand scale, the gleaming surface of stainless steel, and the soaring form of the structure create an expression of the vision of Jefferson, the opening of the West, and the achievements of the early pioneers who traveled through St. Louis to reach the new frontiers beyond the Mississippi.

Expression in architecture is not confined to monuments. Each human activity can suggest the environment, the forms, and the spaces appropriate to the quality or character of the operational function that goes on within a building. The architect, if he is able, may select and combine those materials and structural systems which serve as both the container and the symbol of the activity for which the building is intended. A building may indicate wealth, power, modernity, tradition, ambition, or repose. It may suggest withdrawal from society or stand as an invitation to visit and share the hospitality of the owners. It may stand apart from the land, a man-made object suggesting the scientific technology that has resulted from the use of the human mind and the industry of the contemporary society (Fig. 65), or it may stay close to the earth, rising from the soil and rocks, a part of nature, tying man to all other forms of life, like the great rambling Arizona home and studio of Frank Lloyd Wright (Pl. 22).

FIG. 201. EERO SAARINEN. *Jefferson Westward Expansion Memorial,*
St. Louis, Mo. Nearing completion 1966.

FIGS. 202–205. *Eclectic buildings of "colonial" type.* (*202*) *Municipal offices.*
(*203*) *Residence.* (*204*) *Library.* (*205*) *Church.*

Expression in contemporary architecture cannot evade the traditions, the
common cultural heritage, of the society for which a building is intended. Architectural critics often condemn eclectic or imitative architecture because it does not
find its expressive forms in the present-day world; when a building is given a
superficial, imitative skin that camouflages an internal design with an anachronistic
shell, the inconsistency between the nature of the building and its appearance can
be bizarre and even ridiculous. To clothe a municipal office building, a residence, a

PL. 51. JACKSON POLLOCK. *Number 1*. 1948. Canvas, 5′ 8″ x 8′ 8″. The Museum of Modern Art, New York.

PL. 52. JACOB VAN RUYSDAEL. *Wheatfields.* c. 1660. Canvas, 51¼ x 39⅜". The Metropolitan Museum of Art, New York.

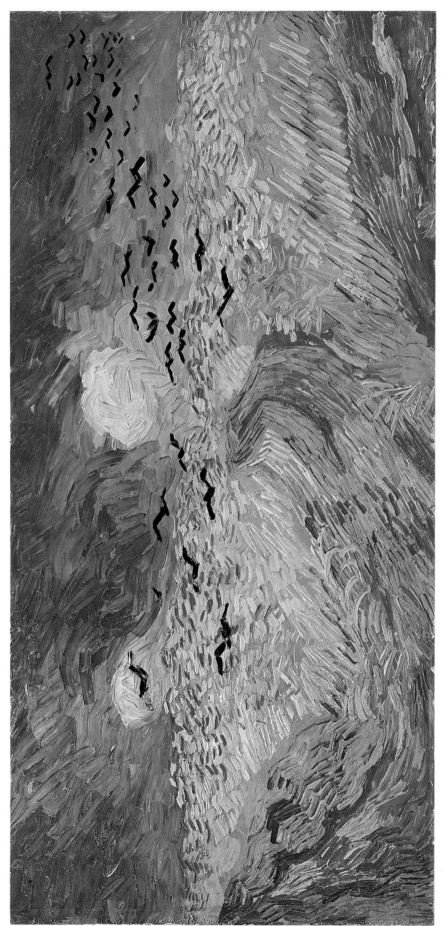

PL. 53. VINCENT VAN GOGH. *Crows over a Wheatfield*. 1890. Canvas, 20 x 40¾". Collection V. W. van Gogh, Stedelijk Museum, Amsterdam.

PL. 54. MARK ROTHKO. *Number 10*. 1950. Canvas, 90⅜ x 57⅛".
The Museum of Modern Art, New York (Gift of Philip C. Johnson).

library, and a church (Figs. 202–205) in the same architectural forms sacrifices expressive design to stylistic consistency. However, many of the personal and social activities common to men of the past still exist in a somewhat similar form today, and in these areas of our culture eclectic designs may serve in much the same way as their antecedents. The typical eighteenth- or early ninteenth-century house is still able to meet the needs of many twentieth-century families with but few alterations in design. For many people, particularly those who live in the northeastern part of this country, the so-called "colonial" house expresses security, the warmth of family life, and a continuity of earlier cultural values which, in total, provide a satisfying esthetic environment (Fig. 206). A man from New England may leave his home, a contemporary version of a 200-year-old design, and travel to his office in a steel-and-glass tower without feeling that there is an inconsistency between these two totally different environments. The fact that this dichotomy is possible may suggest a lack of cohesion in our culture, but the fact remains that many people can accept eclectic architecture as a part of contemporary life. In general, however, each cultural period has seen expression in architecture result from the forms and the materials common to the time. Each building speaks best when it speaks of its own time in its own idiom. Most attempts to look back to forms that were expressive in the past have produced a dilution of expression, a kind of sentimental nostalgia.

To review then, the expressive and esthetic organization of architecture shares with the other visual arts, and particularly with sculpture, the need for a unified focus. An architect may achieve some portion of this unity through the use of the organizational devices employed by the painter and the sculptor—repetition, continuity, and contrast, or opposition; but, unlike the other two visual arts, architecture most often has a functional basis for its unifying composition. It is the operational nature of a building which controls the selection of materials, the methods of construction, and, finally, the forms, spaces, and surfaces which are, in total, the building itself. In the ideal architectural design esthetic organization, expression, function, structure, and materials are all interrelated and interdependent. It is possible for an observer to respond to any one aspect of a building, but the full appreciation of architecture is dependent upon an awareness of all the factors that can influence design.

Fig. 206. *"Colonial" ranches. William A. Clark. Wilmont Homes, Pa. 1953.*

STRUCTURAL SYSTEMS OF ARCHITECTURE

CHAPTER X

INTIMATELY CONNECTED with the form, function, and expression of any structure are the methods of construction and the materials used to build it. In creating the space needed by his clients, the architect can never ignore the basic problems of how walls should be raised and what will support a roof. Practical, structural considerations are part of the total complex to be resolved in the architect's design. There are instances in which the structural problems of the builder do not seem to concern the designer or the person who looks at the completed work. A person who delights in the appearance of a large equestrian statue need not know that there is within the statue a complex skeletal structure. Just so, the person enclosed by the geometry of a classic Renaissance church (Fig. 207), the bombastic drama of a baroque building (Fig. 208), or the soaring arches of a contemporary ferroconcrete reception hall (Fig. 209) may have a rich and satisfying esthetic response without knowing how the building has risen. Nevertheless, there can be a connection between the knowledge of the way a structure has been erected and the satisfaction

FIG. 207. FILIPPO BRUNELLESCHI. *San Lorenzo, Florence. 1423.*

FIG. 208. GIACOMO BAROZZI DA VIGNOLA. *Church of the Gesù, Rome. Begun 1568.*

FIG. 209. GEORGE FRANCIS HELLMUTH,
JOSEPH WILLIAM LEINWEBER,
and MINORU YAMASAKI.
*Airport Reception Building,
St. Louis, Mo. 1953-55.*

FIG. 210. O. H. AMMANN *and* CASS GILBERT. *George Washington Bridge, New York. 1927–31.*

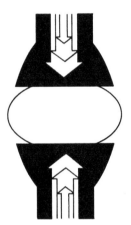

DIAG. 55. *(left) Forces of compression.*
DIAG. 56. *(below left) Forces of tension.*

a viewer can feel when confronted by the building. Understanding the manner in which the architect fights the forces of gravity that tend to keep the walls of his building from rising and the roof from remaining suspended above the earth can excite the mind and alert the senses. No one who has crossed one of the great suspension bridges can think of neglecting the part played by each thin strand of wire in the form, function, and esthetic impact of these structures (Fig. 210). The following section provides a short description of the major structural systems and a discussion of their significance in the design of architecture.

A material that is to be used structurally must resist certain forces which test its strength. It may be required to support weights that operate to crush it, exerting what is known as "the force of compression" (Diag. 55). Or perhaps it will be pulled and stretched like a rubber band, by the "stress of tension forces" (Diag. 56). Both of these forces, compression and tension, may be applied to a single element in a structural system, or, possibly, they may operate separately. In building it has always been man's problem to find materials that can resist these forces and structural systems in which his materials can serve to their best advantage. In his need to protect himself from the elements man has used his ingenuity to take materials from nature and form them to suit his social and physical needs. The range of materials includes the snow blocks of the northern Eskimo, the great stone blocks of the Egyptians, the animal skins and thin wooden frames of the American Plains Indian, and the living rock of India, from which monolithic temples were carved like sculpture. For the most part the early history of building is tied to the materials that were readily available to the peoples of a particular area, and characteristic architectural styles resulted from demands imposed by these materials. Only in the most primitive societies do we find people living within the hollow of a single tree or in the shelter of a cave or beneath a single rock. As soon as man has more sophisticated living quarters, he must cope with the problem of combining a number of separate pieces of a material into a larger unit. If he uses wood, each

piece must be attached to another piece. The pieces must be woven, tied, joined, nailed—somehow they must be united to form upright walls and, perhaps, a roof to protect the inhabitants from the weather.

Building in stone or brick requires the solution of similar problems. The examples in India of temples carved completely out of stone cliffs (Fig. 211), which become forms of giant hollow sculpture, constitute an incredible monument to man's perseverence and ingenuity, but they are rare exceptions; stone construction, perhaps to an even greater degree than construction in wood, requires the union of relatively small elements into larger structural units.

FIG. 211. *Kailasanatha Temple, Ellora, India. c.* A.D. *750.*

FIG. 212. *Hall of Amenhotep III, Temple of Karnak, Luxor. c. 1400* B.C.

FIG. 213. *Theseum (Hephaesteum), Athens. Begun 449* B.C.

THE POST AND LINTEL

One of the simplest and most universally used systems of construction is the post and lintel or wall and lintel. Examples of this method of construction are to be found in Egyptian temples dating back to 2700 B.C., in Greek temples of the sixth and fifth centuries B.C., and in buildings of the Roman Empire and the European Renaissance. The half-timbered medieval houses and the one-room cabins of the early Colonial settlers are found in this group, too. The Japanese, the Chinese, and the peoples of India and of the Yucatán peninsula learned to raise their buildings by this structural method. The system is nothing more complicated than the erection of two vertical elements, posts or walls, which are bridged by a horizontal element, the lintel. The repetition of these structural units in different ways has permitted the development of many architectural styles (Figs. 212–216).

FIG. 214. *Peristyle House of the Vettii, Pompeii. c.* A.D. *50.*

FIG. 215. *Eleazer Arnold House, Great Chamber, Lincoln. R.I. 1687.*

FIG. 216. *Construction methods, detail of the narrative scroll* Matsuzaki-tenjin engi. *1311. Ink and color on paper. National Museum, Tokyo.*

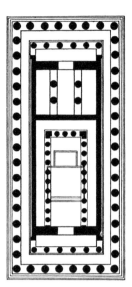

FIG. 217. ICTINUS. *The Parthenon, Athens. 447–438* B.C.

FIG. 218. *Plan of the Parthenon.*

A glance at the façade of a Greek temple will show the characteristic form of the post and lintel (Fig. 217). In the Parthenon, built during the fifth century B.C., a row of columns is placed at the perimeter of the building. Stone lintels bridge the spaces between the columns to create a horizontal band called the "entablature," a major design element in the typical Greek temple. A second row of columns on the east and west ends of this building is also used to support lintels. Stone walls within the line of columns act with smaller interior columns to support additional bridging elements to complete the structural system.

Though simple, post-and-lintel and wall-and-lintel construction can be used to create highly refined architectural designs, but the need for vertical supports to carry overhead loads limits the usable space in this system of building.

Reference to a floor plan of the Parthenon (Fig. 218) will show that much of the interior space is occupied by the columns or walls which support the roof. This abundance of supports is required because the stone lintels could not be very long in relation to their width and thickness. Stone, which is very strong in compression, is inefficient as a material for lintels, because it is not elastic and tends to give way under tension.

Diagram 57 indicates the way in which posts and a lintel work. Note that the weight W carried by the lintel is countered by an equal and opposite force exerted by the posts. This action of forces tends to bend the lintel in a bowlike manner (represented by the dotted lines). The upper portion of the lintel is forced into compression as the material yields to assume the bowed shape ; the lower portion is placed under tensile stress as the material tends to assume the bowed shape.

Wood is a more satisfactory material than stone in this method of construction, but it remained for the development of a material that was strong in both compression and tension before wide spaces could be bridged without the use of large numbers of vertical supports. This development occurred with the introduction of steel into construction, but it had to wait for the end of the nineteenth century before its use had a significant influence on architectural style.

The Visual Dialogue

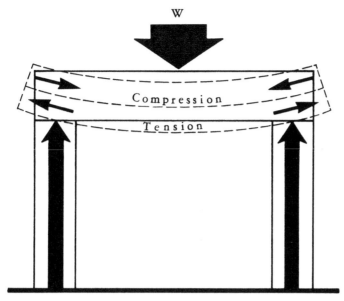

W

Compression

Tension

DIAG. 57

THE ARCH AND VAULT

Because stone is a permanent, fireproof, impressive material, it was used by builders wherever it was available. The earliest attempts at building with this material were probably no more than piles of rocks heaped one upon the other, with a small space left open within the pile. The open space was created by piling the stones about it so that the upper stones projected slightly beyond the lower ones, gradually converging from all sides until they joined at the top of the structure. This is corbeled construction (Fig. 219). Examples of this method of construction go back to the early history of architecture, but it was not until the development of

FIG. 219. *Treasury of Atreus (so-called),*
Mycenae, Greece. c. 15th cent. B.C. *Stone, height 44^1/$_2$'.*

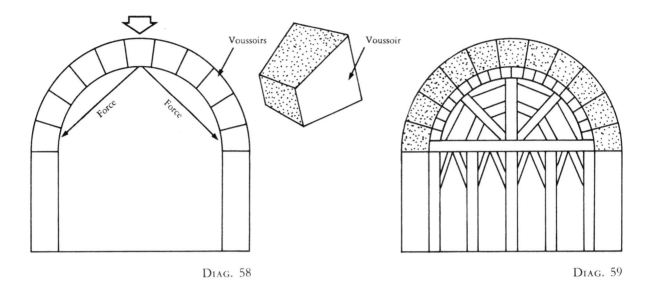

Voussoirs   Voussoir

Diag. 58   Diag. 59

the principle of the arch that stone construction reached its zenith. There are essential differences in the systems. Corbeled stone elements are laid parallel to the ground, layer on layer. Each course of stone projects out into the opening between the walls a bit farther than the course beneath. The weight of the upper courses pressing down on the stones beneath them permits a builder gradually to close the gap over an opening. The projections produce a characteristic saw-tooth form in the closure. In the arch the stone parts, called "voussoirs," are placed radially, with their axes directed toward a central focus. The wedge-shaped voussoirs direct the weight of the arch and the stone above it out at an angle, rather than down, the force attempting to spread the sides of the arch to flatten the form (Diag. 58).

The arch is a more sophisticated form of stone construction than corbeling, for it requires that the faces of the stone be dressed accurately, so that each voussoir is at the proper angle to its neighbor to form the semicircular structure. Incorrect cutting of these sides would cause the separate components of the arch to slip, producing a structural weakness that would result in its collapse. In addition to the requirement of skilled stonecutting, there is the necessity of building a temporary support for the single voussoirs until all of them are in place. An arch will not stand until each of its parts is in place, for it is dependent upon their interaction for its

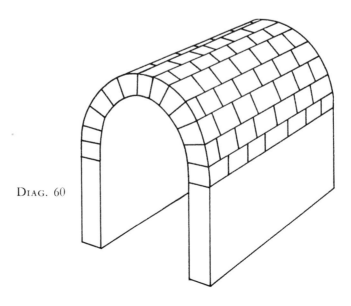

Diag. 60

strength. To hold them in position during the process of construction it is usual to build a semicircular wooden form called "centering." When the voussoirs have been fitted, the centering is removed and the arch stands unaided (Diag. 59).

The basic concept of the arch was used to provide buildings with continuous stone roofs. Setting one arch behind another produced a structure which resembled a tunnel (Diag. 60). This was the barrel vault. It provided early builders with stone roofs which could span impressively wide spaces and could, of course, be continued in length for extended distances (Fig. 220).

The forces working on the barrel vault act just as those on the arch do, but they exist over its entire length and require similar counterforces to counteract the tendency to collapse. As in the case of the arch, centering is required to support all parts of the vault until they are in position. This is a limiting factor in the construction of vaulted roofs, for centering is expensive and time-consuming. Another restriction imposed by the barrel vault is the limited amount of light admitted to a building covered in this manner. Builders were hesitant to pierce the sides of vaulted buildings for fear that the opening would endanger the strength of the vault. Any openings introduced were, of necessity, small. Only the arched ends of the structure were free for the entry of light. These problems of illumination and centering were partially resolved in the development of the groin vault.

FIG. 220. *Basilica of Constantine (or of Maxentius), Rome. Begun under Maxentius c.* A.D. *306–12, completed by Constantine.*

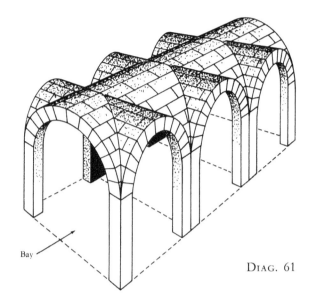

Fig. 221. *Baths of Caracalla, Rome,*
theoretical restoration of
a part of the interior.
A.D. *211–17.*

Bay

DIAG. 61

As early as the third century, builders in Rome experimented with variations on vault construction. They arrived at a vaulting system which eliminated many of the drawbacks inherent in the barrel vault. It was found that if two barrel vaults were built at right angles over a square area, they would intersect each other, producing openings at all four sides of the square. All the thrust of the two intersecting vaults would be concentrated at the corners between the openings. Even though it was necessary to provide an enormous amount of buttressing at these points, this new system freed the architects from the necessity for continuous, heavy walls. They could divide any building into squares, or bays, and cover each square with its own vault (Diag. 61, Fig. 221). Each vault was relatively free of the stresses from the other similar vaults in the building, so that upon the completion of each vault the wooden framework used in its construction could be removed and used elsewhere.

DIAG. 62

FIG. 222. *Arch of Janus, Rome. Early 4th cent.*

FIG. 223. *Structural drawing of the Arch of Janus, Rome.*
Banister Fletcher, A History of Architecture...,
Charles Scribneis Sons, New York, 1963, p. 223.

The design of Roman vaulting was highly refined. These early builders recognized that not all parts of the groin vault required the same strength. Most of the vault's work was carried by the arches at the outside faces and at the crossing. If these portions were built of heavy stone, the areas between them could be filled in with relatively light material. An additional advantage was that the major supports could be removed, once the heavy ribs, or arches, were in place. Since these elements remained freestanding, only the space between them, the web, required additional centering, and this could be supplied by material of much lighter weight (Diag. 62, Figs. 222, 223).

Stone vaulting remained at this stage of development until the end of the eleventh century. Until this time the design of a groin vault had been based upon the geometry of the circle. A round arch is a segment or arc of a circle, and the height of the arch cannot be more than half its width (Diag. 63).

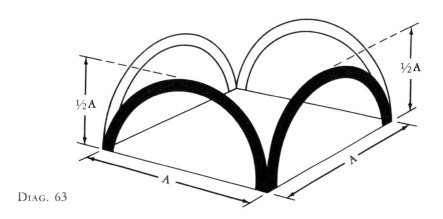

DIAG. 63

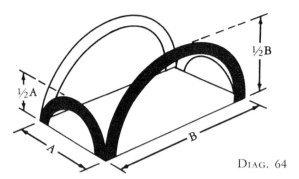

DIAG. 64

If a builder wished to construct a groin vault in which all the arches rose to the same height, he had to use arches of identical width and so produce square bays. On the other hand, if he wished to use a bay of rectangular plan, having unequal sides, he could not readily use round arches, for the vault would rise to different heights on the long and short sides of the bay (Diag. 64).[1]

This problem was solved by constructing arches in the form of two arcs rising upward to a pointed joint at their intersection. By changing the radius of the arc segments and the angle of their intersection, it was possible to vary the width of the arch while maintaining a single height (Diag. 65). Not only did the pointed arch permit the use of rectangular and irregularly shaped bays, but it also directed the thrust of the arch in a more nearly vertical direction, requiring less buttressing to counter the outward thrust of the normal arch forces (Diag. 66).

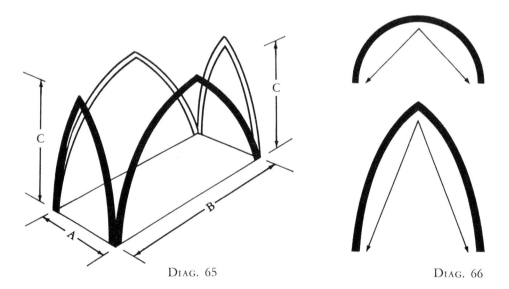

DIAG. 65   DIAG. 66

---

[1] Several methods of covering a rectangular bay with round arches were developed by Romanesque builders, but none of these was completely successful. During the Renaissance groin vaults were constructed with a combination of round and elliptical arches, employing a more sophisticated geometry than was used by the earlier builders.

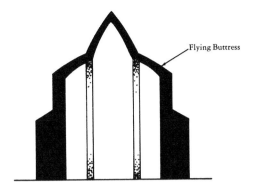

DIAG. 67

An additional refinement was added to the ribbed vault and the pointed arch. Instead of being carried on the exterior walls of the cathedrals, the thrust of the vaults was diverted by means of connecting arches to large vertical piles of masonry beyond the sides of the building. This device was called a "flying buttress" (Diag. 67). It reduced the forces playing on the walls of the buildings and allowed the builders to achieve heights beyond their early dreams. It also permitted the side walls to be opened up so that glass windows might be introduced.

The combination of these structural systems—the ribbed vault, the pointed arch, and the flying buttress—produced what is now called the "Gothic system" of construction (Fig. 224).

FIG. 224. *Cathedral of Notre-Dame, Paris. 13th cent.*

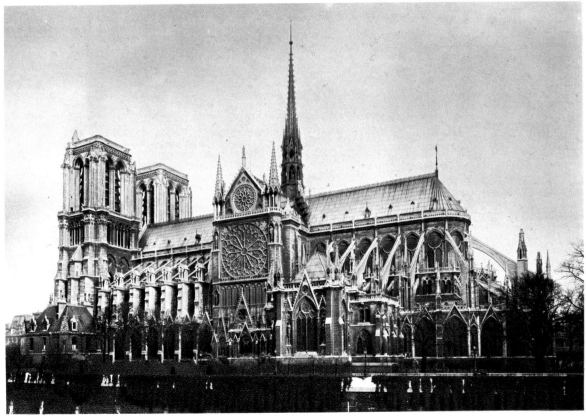

THE DOME

The dome was developed by the Romans after it had been invented in the Middle East. Essentially a hemispherical vault, the dome is subject to the same forces that work upon the arch and the vault, but the thrust of the dome is exerted around its rim for 360 degrees. It, too, must be buttressed so that its thrust is contained by heavy walls or by other, smaller, half domes pressing back in on it (Diag. 68).

Because the plan of a dome is a circle, the dome most easily covers a cylindrical building. The builder who wishes to use a dome as the roof of a building with a square plan is faced with the problem of covering the corners of his building and, somehow, joining the round edge of the circle to the straight edges of the walls (Diag. 69). One way of solving this problem is to fill in the corners with triangular wedges that sit under the edge of the dome. These wedges are called "squinches" (Diag. 70, Fig. 225). They help to make a transition from the rectangle to the circle by producing at the corners angles less acute than the usual 90 degrees and therefore easier to bridge.

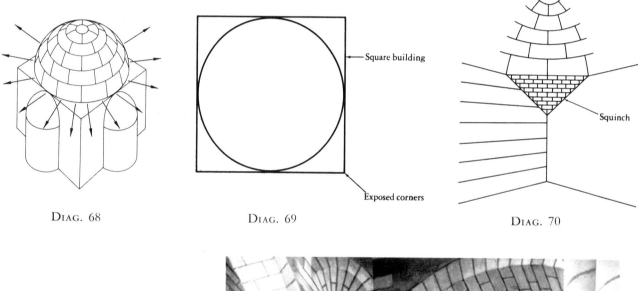

DIAG. 68   DIAG. 69   DIAG. 70

FIG. 225. *Squinch construction. Church of St. Hilaire, Poitiers, France. Consecrated 1049.*

PL. 55. EL GRECO. *The Purification of the Temple.* 1596–1600. Canvas, 16½ x 20⅝". The Frick Collection, New York (copyright).

PL. 56. EL GRECO. *Christ Driving the Money Changers from the Temple.* 1571–76. Canvas, 46 x 59".
The Minneapolis Institute of Arts (The William Hood Dunwoody Fund, 1924).

PL. 57. WASSILY KANDINSKY. *Composition (4)*. 1914. Canvas, 64 x 31½".
The Museum of Modern Art, New York (Mrs. Simon Guggenheim Fund).

PL. 58. PAUL KLEE. *Senecio*. 1922. Canvas, 16 x 15″. Kunstmuseum, Basel.

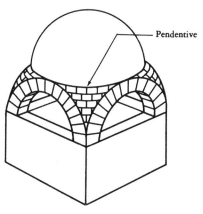

Pendentive

DIAG. 71

FIG. 226. *Dome on pendentives. Hagia Sophia, Istanbul. 6th cent.*

A more elegant solution was developed in the Near East. It consists of erecting four arches above the sides of the building, each arch springing from the two corners of the wall on which it sits. The space between two adjacent arches is filled with stone to produce a curved triangular form with a point at the corner of the building. The two rising edges of the triangle are formed by the sides of the arches, and the upper edge curves between the top of the adjoining arches to form one quarter of the base of the dome (Diag. 71). This structural device is called a "pendentive," and it became an important architectural element in Byzantine architecture (Fig. 226).

King Truss

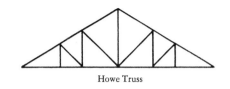

Howe Truss

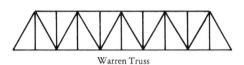

Warren Truss

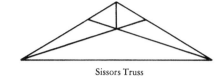

Sissors Truss

DIAG. 72. *Examples of trusses.*

THE TRUSS

A triangle is a geometric form which cannot be forced out of shape once the sides are joined. This stability permits a designer to join pieces of wood, iron, or steel into triangular structures called "trusses," which can be used to span large spaces. Individual members in the truss design may be under compressive or tensile forces, and frequently their cross section is altered to suit the demands of their function. Many different kinds of trusses have been designed by combining triangles of different angles and sizes (Diag. 72). The design of a truss frequently becomes the basis for interior or exterior architectural forms.

CONSTRUCTION IN THE NINETEENTH CENTURY

With the beginning of the nineteenth century a new chapter opened in the development of architecture. Out of the industrial revolution, which was born in England and spread throughout Europe and the United States, new building methods were slowly developed, based on the use of iron and then steel, which were made available, and the concept of standardized mass-production techniques. The changes that occurred did not happen overnight, but by the end of the century it was plain from the appearance of many of the public and private structures which had been built that the revolution in architectural design was as significant as the social and economic changes preceding it.

THE BALLOON FRAME

Building in wood had previously been based on the post-and-lintel system used in the earliest forms of construction. Heavy wood timbers were joined together with complicated joints and wooden pegs to produce a basic framework upon which the rest of the house depended for its strength (Fig. 215). The work was slow and tedious, requiring highly skilled joinery. Nails were used sparingly, for they were hand-wrought and therefore expensive.

With the improvement of sawmill machinery and the invention of machines which could manufacture quantities of inexpensive wire nails, a novel method of wood construction was made possible. About the middle of the nineteenth century a system was developed for nailing together pieces of wood only 2 inches wide, instead of the heavy timbers which had been used previously for the erection

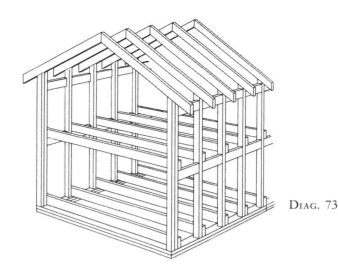

of wooden buildings. Substituting many thin, easily handled pieces of wood for a single massive timber and nailing them together, rather than cutting into the wood to form joints, produced a structure that was strong and easy to erect. This is the method most commonly used for the construction of wooden buildings and interior partitions today (Diag. 73, Fig. 227). Though its use is universal in our own time, it was considered daring, even dangerous, at the time of its introduction. Old-time builders refused to believe that anything so frail in appearance would have the strength necessary for substantial walls and roofs. They described it as "balloon construction," and this term of derision remained.

Although this method was used, in the main, to construct houses that were similar in exterior appearance to those built before its introduction, it is a significant example of the influence of technology on building.

FIG. 227. *Balloon construction.* W. F. SEVERIN. *Terra Linda, Marin County, Calif. 1954.*

Fig. 228. *Cast-iron construction.* Abraham Darby. *Severn Bridge, Coalbrookdale, England. 1779.*

CAST-IRON CONSTRUCTION

Prior to the industrial revolution ferrous metals were used only sparingly in buildings. Though iron was known to the Greeks and the Romans, they preferred to use nonrusting bronze, and bronze was used in only limited amounts for primarily decorative purposes. Renaissance architects were as reluctant to use iron as a structural material. With the development of iron technology, iron became the symbol of the nineteenth century. Used originally in railroad tracks, it was quickly introduced into the building trades. The use of cast iron actually predates the nineteenth century; for example, there is a cast-iron bridge in England that was erected in 1779 (Fig. 228).

FIG. 229. HENRI LABROUSTE. *Bibliothèque Nationale, Paris,
reading room in the Department of Prints. 1858–68.*

Cast iron was adopted for columns in building by those who realized that the great strength and the relative ease of its production made it an admirable building material. Many of the new buildings astounded the public, with their light-filled interiors, designed with vast areas of glass and daring open arches and trusses of a cobweblike strength that seemed to deny the force of gravity. One of the most daring examples of cast-iron construction was the Bibliothèque Nationale in Paris, designed by Henri Labrouste and built between 1858 and 1868. Throughout this building, and particularly in the reading room, the new potentials of cast iron were exploited (Fig. 229).

DIAG. 74. *Masonry construction of a multistoried building.*
Bottom story carries the weight of all upper stories.

FIG. 230. H. H. RICHARDSON. *Marshall Field Wholesale Store, Chicago. 1885–87.*

THE STEEL FRAME

Until the late nineteenth century a building stood erect because its walls formed part of the necessary structural system. The Gothic cathedral, whose vaults and flying buttresses produced a system in which the wall was not a primary structural element, is the major exception to this rule. In the post-and-lintel system and the vaulted constructions of the Romans and the Renaissance, the walls supported the roof or the floor of the next highest story. In multistoried buildings all the weight of the upper floors was finally carried by the lower walls. Windows were essentially holes cut through this operative construction, with the weight above the windows supported on lintels or arches (Diag. 74).

The Marshall Field Wholesale Store, built in Chicago in 1885–87, designed by H. H. Richardson, was one of the last important multistoried masonry buildings erected in this country (Fig. 230). The weight of the interior floors and the roof of the building was carried, for the most part, on cast-iron columns and wrought-iron beams, but the outer walls were self-supporting masonry construction, massive elements of granite and sandstone.

At the end of the nineteenth century the introduction of steel as a building material permitted the development of a structural system which freed the exterior walls from their load-bearing function. A skeleton steel-and-iron framework was erected prior to the construction of walls, floors, or interior partitions. This skeleton supported the walls. The strength and relatively light weight of the metal frame reduced the cost of multistoried office buildings and permitted an increase in the number of stories which could be erected on a single site (Diag. 75).

William Le Baron Jenney was one of the early innovators of the steel-frame building. His Home Insurance Company Building, constructed in Chicago between 1883 and 1885, was the first major example of a structure that did not depend upon its outer walls for support (Fig. 231).

The façade of Jenney's building appears much lighter in weight than the Marshall Field Store, but it still seems quite heavy when compared to buildings such as Lever House, in New York (Fig. 232), which is constructed on the same structural principles.

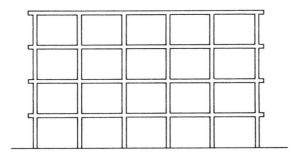

DIAG. 75. *Steel-frame construction of multistoried building. Steel frame is self-supporting and carries the weight of masonry and glass exterior walls, floors, and interior partitions.*

FIG. 231. WILLIAM LE BARON JENNEY.
Home Insurance Company Building, Chicago. 1883–85.

FIG. 232. SKIDMORE, OWINGS, *and* MERRILL.
Lever House, New York. 1952.

The esthetic need for a masonry wall remained an important factor in the design of steel-frame buildings for many years, even though the practical need no longer existed. At the end of the nineteenth century and into the twentieth the appearance of masonry on the exterior of a large building seemed to provide a sense of strength and stability that was expected in a major building, particularly a tall building. Only gradually did the function of the external wall find expression in the thin glass and metal skins that are so common today.

In contemporary architecture the wall has been given a new meaning. When necessary, it may still function structurally to support a roof or floors, but there are instances in which the wall is nonstructural, when it functions to protect the interior areas from the weather or perhaps when it becomes a means of achieving visual or audio privacy. Specific wall materials may be selected to satisfy any of these three separate functions; glass, plastic, thin sheets of metal, even cloth, may serve best in any one instance. Materials may, but need not, have multiple functions. This flexibility offers the architect alternatives that were not possible before and increases his opportunity to suit his design to a functional and expressive purpose.

The Visual Dialogue

Fig. 233. John Smeaton. *Eddystone Lighthouse, English Channel. Demolished 1882. Engraving by William Cooke.*

FERROCONCRETE CONSTRUCTION

Concrete is a mixture of small stones or gravel bound in a cement mortar. As it is mixed, this material has a heavy, fluid consistency. To be used in building, concrete is poured into molds which shape its final appearance. When the concrete has dried and the molds are removed, it keeps its shape and has structural properties similar to those of stone. This material was known and used during the time of the Roman Empire. Its use was forgotten until the end of the eighteenth century, when it was rediscovered and employed in the construction of lighthouses (Fig. 233).

Since concrete has qualities similar to those of stone, it is extremely strong in compression but equally weak as a tensile material. By the end of the nineteenth century a building method had been developed in which metal rods were imbedded in the concrete, combining the tensile strength of the rods with the compressive strength of the concrete. This combination is called "ferroconcrete," or "reinforced concrete" (Diag. 76). It is an extremely strong and versatile material.

Diag. 76. *Reinforced concrete beam (left) and slab (right).*

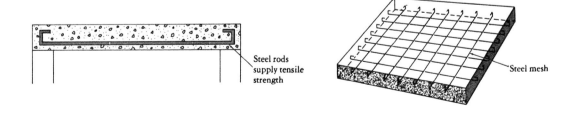

Steel rods supply tensile strength

Steel mesh

Architects and engineers have been quick to adopt ferroconcrete and have learned to make use of its ability to take on the shape of whatever forms were constructed to mold it (Fig. 234). This freedom of design has been expressed in recent years in dramatic, thin, concrete shells, which are being used in our most advanced structures. Vast spaces have been covered by domes and complex geometric surfaces with shells less than 1 inch in thickness. This latest development in building presages an entirely new landscape for both city and suburb in the not too distant future.

Among the most remarkable and esthetically satisfying examples of construction in ferroconcrete are the buildings of the Italian architect Pier Luigi Nervi. In 1957 Nervi designed an enclosed stadium for the Olympic games held in Rome in 1960. It is a concrete shell supported on Y-shaped columns (Figs. 235, 236), one of three major buildings designed by Nervi for the athletic events of the games. This building, like all Nervi's work, is an example of the esthetic potential inherent in the technological developments of recent years.

Nervi has said: "It is obvious that engineering and the mental make up produced by engineering do not suffice to create architecture. But it is just as obvious that without the realizing techniques of engineering any architectural conception is as non-existant as an unwritten poem in the mind of the poet."[2]

[2] Pier Luigi Nervi, "Nervi's View on Architecture, Education and Structure," *Architectural Record,* December, 1958, p. 118.

FIG. 234. *Concrete construction, with forms still in position and vertical steel reinforcement still showing in upper story. First Federal Savings & Loan Building, Atlanta, Georgia.*

FIGS. 235, 236. PIER LUIGI NERVI. *Palazzetto dello Sport, Rome, exterior and interior. 1957.*

THE GEODESIC STRUCTURE

Perhaps the most dramatic example of the development of architectural forms based upon structural innovations is to be found in the geodesic domes of R. Buckminster Fuller (Figs. 237–239). Fuller is a designer who for many years has experimented with new structural systems. His domes are based upon his own system of mathematics, which he calls "energetic-synergetic geometry." Essentially, these structures are based upon the combination of tetrahedrons, a figure constructed of four triangles. By joining tetrahedrons into more complex groups and extending them to form segments of spheres, Fuller and his associates have produced a large number of designs which combine extremely light weight with a seemingly infinite ability to cover huge volumes. These domes are constructed of small modular elements, which are joined together. The resulting web can then be covered with any of a number of materials to make the enclosed space weatherproof. Plastics, cloth, aluminum, and sheet steel have been used as skins for Fuller domes. Domes based on this structural system have been made of cardboard, waterproofed with plastic, and used by the United States Marines as temporary structures. A geodesic dome has been calculated which could span 2 miles and cover the area of midtown Manhattan.

FIG. 237. R. BUCKMINSTER FULLER. *Kaiser Dome, Hawaii. 1957.*

Fig. 238. R. Buckminster Fuller. *Union Tank Car Company Dome, Baton Rouge, La. 1958–59.*

FIG. 239. R. BUCKMINSTER FULLER. *Monsanto "Geospace" Dome, type used for emergency housing in Puerto Rico. 1961.*

Buckminster Fuller believes that structure and design are intimately wedded. He would extend this idea far beyond its application in architecture to include all aspects of human life.

> My experience is now world-around. During one third of a century of experimental work, I have been operating on the philosophic premise that all thoughts and all experiences can be translated much further than just into words and abstract thought patterns. I saw that they can be translated into patterns which may be realized in various *physical* projections—by which we can alter the physical environment itself and thereby induce other men to subconsciously alter their ecological patterning.[3]

---

[3] R. Buckminster Fuller, *Education Automation,* Southern Illinois University Press, Carbondale, Ill., 1962, p. 8.

THE VISUAL DIALOGUE

CHAPTER XI

I would venture to affirm that a man cannot attain excellence if he satisfy the ignorant and not those of his own craft, and if he be not "singular" or "distant," or whatever you like to call him.[1]

What I want to show in my work is the idea which hides itself behind so-called reality. I am seeking for the bridge which leads from the visible to the invisible.

. . . .

One of my problems is to find the ego, which has only one form, and is immortal—to find it in animals and men, in the heaven and in the hell which together form the world in which we live.[2]

THE FIRST of the two quotations above is attributed to Michelangelo, who was working in the time of the Renaissance. It is the expression of an artist who felt that he was important in his society, a society which had slowly made the transition from the medieval world, in which individuality was severely limited. The second quotation is the statement of the German expressionist painter Max Beckmann, painting in the twentieth century and completely immersed in his own personal search for those things and values which are meaningful to him. Though not in the same way, or to the same degree, both Michelangelo and Beckmann turned from those about them to look inward for the basis of their art, and it is this attitude which is representative of the great majority of contemporary artists.

For the artist today, and for many others, there is no single meaningful, all-encompassing concept of man, his society, his ethics, and morality. Instead, there is the recognition of a world fragmented into many separate, though often related, cells, divided by language, custom, religion, economic development, and geographical location. For any single individual in this conglomerate group the significance of the events which occur from day to day, the nature and meaning of past events, and the expectation of what is yet to happen can differ so widely that it is not strange to think of one artist in one studio in one small part of the world focusing on only a small part of this immense fabric, attempting to express his singular involvement with it.

---

[1] *Artists on Art,* eds. Robert Goldwater and Marco Troves, Pantheon Books, New York, 1945, p. 67.
[2] *Ibid.,* p. 447.

303

Fig. 240. Pablo Picasso. Girl before a Mirror, *detail of Pl. 8. March, 1932. Canvas. 63³/₄ × 51¹/₄". The Museum of Modern Art, New York (Gift of Mrs. Simon Guggenheim).*

PL. 59. SALVADOR DALI. *Apparition of a Face on the Seashore.* 1938. Canvas, 43½ x 57″. The Wadsworth Atheneum, Hartford.

PL. 60. PIERRE ROY. *Electrification of the Country*. c. 1929. Canvas, 29 x 20″.
The Wadsworth Atheneum, Hartford.

Today each artist must isolate that which is important to him, and then he must find the visual equivalent for it. The present-day artist is faced with a situation that never faced his predecessors. He lives in a world for which the visual image is commonplace. The most inexperienced art student is conversant with visual art forms more varied and more numerous than those known to the master artist of the previous century. Each year the history of art grows larger, and access to the art of the past becomes easier. Museums and galleries in our cities have made possible a first-hand knowledge of major art objects from the very beginning of history to the present, and what the museums have been able to do for their visitors, mass magazines have done for their readers. Color reproductions of works of art seem to find their way to the pages before the paint is dry on the artist's canvas. This esthetic bounty has increased the interest in the visual arts, but at the same time it has driven the contemporary artist to a search for new forms of visual communication. As the exposure of paintings and sculpture has grown, the need for new forms of communication has grown with it. The forms of a painting style which seem to express a sincere and direct sensitivity to human experience at one time in history may become the basis for a stylistic cliché at another. Picasso used the cubist treatment of a head in his paintings of the 1930's as a vital expressive device. By showing composite views of the head, it was possible for him to intensify the emotional content of his figure symbols. This device has become relatively common in contemporary painting and has even made its way into advertising art, drained of its emotional impact, now a clever stylistic treatment (Figs. 240, 241).

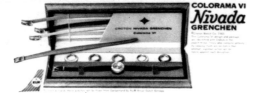

FIG. 241. *Advertisement for Croton Watch Co., Inc. February, 1962.*

Fig. 242. Francisco Goya. Tampoco (Nor These), *from* The Disasters of War. *c. 1820. Intaglio, 5³/₈ × 7¹/₂". The Metropolitan Museum of Art, New York (Schiff Fund, 1922).*

The artist searching for the plastic means to say the things that are important to him cannot use forms, symbols, and symbolic structures that have been drained of their meaning through overexposure and repeated use. He must find those combinations of the plastic vocabulary which will have the impact and the directness that he feels is deserved by the importance of what he has to say. He searches for a way to bypass the cliché, not to be ambiguous and incomprehensible, as many critics have charged, but for exactly the opposite reason—to be explicit, to be meaningful. He is an extension of the artistic tradition that preceded him, but he also tries to expand that tradition so that those aspects of it which are no longer effective for real communication are reinforced or superseded by more vital forms.

Many of the expressive forms of art have been conceived as a result of the artist's need to solve more practical problems. This is particularly true in architecture, where the structural and operational problems are such an important part of the design, but it is important to note that there are frequently many possible solutions to any given practical problem : a roof may be covered by a round vault, a pointed groin vault, or a flat plane. The choice of a structural method depends upon availability of materials, cost, and the skill of the available craftsmen, but it also depends upon the esthetic response of the designer. Certain forms and spaces satisfy him more than others, without having structural or operational necessity as a basis for their use.

In painting and sculpture the need and the desire to represent important objects and experiences in the real·world do not limit the style chosen to satisfy this need.

Certain painters and sculptors working at the present time feel that their function is to comment on the social and moral condition of their world, using visual images that can be understood by a mass audience. For the most part, artists

committed to this belief in the social function of art use the traditional forms of visual communication, the forms which have had the greatest exposure and so are most familiar to the public. In our own time these forms are generally similar to photographic images.

Often these socially conscious works have an immediate and expressive impact, but just as often the power of their expression declines as the social conditions change. There are exceptions which seem to possess values untouched by time. The etchings by the Spanish painter Francisco Goya were a damning commentary on the bestiality of war when they were drawn about 1820, as a result of the Napoleonic invasion of Spain (Fig. 242). Today, perhaps because the images of rape, murder, and torture still cry out, these etchings continue to move a large audience. On the other hand, when one looks at Figure 243, by the contemporary American Ben Shahn, there is little response to its message. Shahn produced this painting as one of a series devoted to the trial of Sacco and Vanzetti, which took place in 1921, and their execution, 1927. At the time, this series of paintings was considered a powerful indictment of what many considered a grave miscarriage of justice. Today, without the aid of a written historical account of the event, what does this painting describe or express to the viewer who is unfamiliar with the story?

It is not possible simultaneously to extend the form of language and to appeal to a mass audience. With new forms of communication come difficulties of understanding, the problem of a confusion of symbolic meanings. New language forms may give the artist an opportunity to intensify the content of his message, but at the same time they restrict his audience, and he must choose between an expressive vocabulary and a large public. In times of crisis the choice has often been for the latter. Today, however, with photography serving as an active and efficient visual art form for the communication of ideas to a mass public, the painter and the sculptor seem destined to concern themselves with the development of visual forms of expression which have limited audiences but, at the same time, extend the area of expression.

Why does the artist wish to paint, to carve stone, to organize steel and stone on his drawing boards ?

The most obvious answer is that it pleases him, it satisfies him. In manipulating the materials of his art there is a satisfaction akin to that of the games of children. The sensuous and kinesthetic pleasures expressed in the scribble of the infant as he discovers the lines made by his crayons and the almost animal delight of squeezing clay between the fingers are still to be found in the mature artist. Of course, there is more. There is the act of discovery. There is the satisfaction that the artist feels when he identifies in the work developing before him the concrete expression of a reality he had sensed, half-formed, in his mind. There is the satisfaction of establishing order, of being able to control the material and organize the forms and the color of a work to achieve the ends that inspired it. It is at this level that the artist needs to find that combination of the plastic vocabulary which will do for him what no other combination is capable of doing.

Finally, the work of art functions for the artist as a form of communication. When he is through with it, after the last brush stroke has been placed and the last mark of the chisel has been ground from the surface of the stone, the artist offers his statement to those who are capable of reading his message.

Art seems to have a real value for the artist, but why should anyone else be concerned with it? The answer, of course, is obvious: no one *should* be concerned, but many people *are*.

For some, the concern they feel comes from an awareness that certain products of the artist have given them pleasure, and they seek more. It is, perhaps, impossible to establish the basis for this feeling. It seems to have been present in man from his earliest days on earth. The ornamentation of simple tools and weapons testifies to its importance in almost every culture (Fig. 244).

At one time, when art alone fulfilled the function of visually recording and representing the physical world, accurate representation was the aspect of greatest concern to many viewers. Today this function, in the main, has been assumed by photography, but there are still many persons who find pleasure in seeing a painting that is essentially representational, in the manner of a photograph. For the most part, the satisfaction offered by such work, as distinguished from the photograph, is similar to that found in the work of the craftsman, the identification of skilled labor, the sense of participation in the technical problems that have been solved to produce the work. When such a work gives the viewer a sense of reality surpassing that of the photograph, the pleasure to be realized is like that of discovering some new bit of information, some new insight, a revelation about a world one already knows.

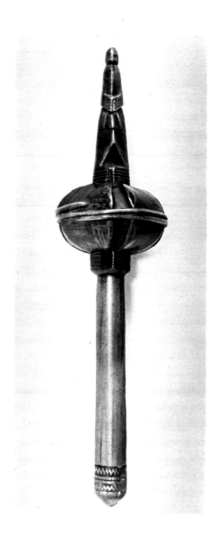

FIG. 244. *Folk spindle (rocca),
from Calabria, Italy. 19th–20th cent.
Carved and incised wood with
rattling seed pod, height 9³/₈".
Collection Mamie Harmon, New York.*

The paintings of the American Andrew Wyeth have found wide public and critical acclaim. They combine photographic representation with an extraordinary skill in the application of paint, and, in addition, they often project or evoke an intimate sense of a highly personal sensitivity to everyday experience beyond the perception of most people (Pl. 64).

The revelatory aspect of art and the satisfaction it can produce is not reserved to the forms that approximate photographic representation. An art form that is evocative, that seems to point to certain aspects of reality without rendering them clearly in a symbolic form that is readily understood, also has in it the potential for discovery. It permits an emphatic, subjective response. The reality it offers need not be pleasant in itself; the pleasure is derived from the experience of finding the meaning, whatever it may be. There is also the satisfaction to be found when the observer feels that he has been transported into a world apart from his own, a world which has order and reason to a degree that he cannot often find in the complexity of his own, or which offers him some respite from the realities of the immediate experience and permits him the luxury of a temporary existence in an environment created by the artist.

Finally, there are the direct sensory pleasures to be had from the response to color or the touch of a smooth piece of marble, or perhaps the exhilaration that is felt when one stands in the center of a great architectural space.

There are, then, many effects of art on those who do not produce the works : the satisfaction of the senses of the individual, the stimulation of his imagination, the isolation of his consciousness in a world of clarity or in one of reverie. All these offer the observer an opportunity for experience he might otherwise not have, experience which adds to the riches of life in a way that cannot be duplicated by other means.

The public cannot, however, place the total responsibility for its response upon the artist. It is not enough to say that the artist *must* produce an object which makes the public respond, for the appreciation of art results from an *active* participation on the part of an observer. The work of art and the person who stands before it take part in a *dialogue*, in which each contributes a portion of the whole experience.

This dialogue has its counterpart in the studio, for the creation of the work of art frequently results from a process in which the artist acts upon his work and is in turn acted upon by it. The artist begins the process. In painting, a red mark placed upon the canvas will be followed by other marks. The initial impulse that caused the marks to be made may have been due to a desire to represent an object, to express a feeling, to produce an object, or any combination of the three, but once the marks are there, outside the painter, they become part of a process which continues until the painting is complete. Each spot of color on a canvas has at least some minutely accidental qualities in it. No matter how precisely he works, an artist cannot control every possible variable in each stroke of his brush, and for painters who work in a broad and vigorous manner the factor of accident may be very large, indeed. The painter learns, as do artists in the other visual arts, to use the unexpected or unplanned effects that appear in the work in progress, to permit a *dialogue* to take place between the artist and the art object, the artist producing an image which then acts upon him.

A continuing interaction can take place as the work progresses, but though the appearance of some portions of the completed art object may be traceable to accidental or unconscious factors in its creation, it is the artist who has the final responsibility for the work of art. It is he, having seen the accidental areas, who decides to retain or eliminate them.

It is true that an artist who believes he is carrying on a dialogue with his work as it progresses to completion is, in reality, speaking to himself, but this does not alter the fact that a dialogue does *appear* to take place between two *active* participants. The production of a work of art is a dynamic activity, in which the artist acts and then responds to the result of his acts as he proceeds to the next step in the sequence that finally produces his finished work.

As noted, the interaction, or the dialogue, that takes place between artist and art object has a parallel in the relationship between the viewer and the art object. The work of art exists as a completed physical entity when it is presented to the viewer, but it becomes an object of esthetic value only when it causes a response in that viewer, and the nature of that response is dependent upon the active participation of the viewer in the esthetic experience. The work of art has a statement to make, but it is the observer who shapes that statement into a personal communication by committing himself to the experience. The work of art can speak to those who are passively involved, but is speaks most eloquently and satisfyingly when it becomes a part of a visual dialogue.

DRAWING: Materials and Techniques

APPENDIX I

Drawn lines may result from two different processes. The first of these produces a mark by depositing minute particles of colored matter on a surface from a stick of material that is drawn against it. The second process produces a mark as a fluid is allowed to flow from an instrument to an absorbent surface. Both methods may be used to execute a solid line, without variation from dark to light, or gradually shaded areas of great delicacy.

The *dry* drawing media include silverpoint, pencil, pastel or chalk, charcoal, and wax crayon.

Silverpoint, one of the oldest traditional drawing media, is not in general use today. In this medium a silver wire is drawn over a prepared surface that is abrasive enough to cause small particles of the metal to adhere to it. As the metal particles tarnish, a line of delicate gray is formed. Silverpoint does not lend itself to a shaded line. Each line is as dark as every other line. If the artist wishes to develop gradations of tone, they must be built up slowly and carefully by making a series of lines close together, so that from a short distance they appear to become a solid area. If a darker tone is desired, the lines are placed closer together or even intersecting at various angles. The latter technique is called "crosshatching."

Pencil produces a line not unlike that of silverpoint (Fig. 90). However, it is possible for the artist to purchase pencils in a wide choice of hardness and softness, so that he may draw lines ranging from light and hard to rich black and soft.

Pastel, or *chalk,* is manufactured by combining colored pigment with a binder into an easily crumbled stick. *Charcoal* is formed by burning, or rather charring, selected sticks of wood or vine. These media produce lines in the same physical manner as silverpoint and pencil, but, unlike those, they are easily used to execute shaded areas (Figs. 89, 91). The particles of chalk and charcoal are so easily dispersed over the surface of a sheet of paper that they have a tendency to smudge and must be fixed with a spray of thinned varnish before they can be considered permanent media.

Pastel chalks are produced in an almost limitless variety of colors and are sometimes used as a painting medium. As such, they exhibit a brilliance unmatched by any other method of applying color to a surface.

Colored pigments may also be bound by wax into stick form to produce *crayons*. Wax crayons are usually associated with children's drawings, but they have been used by artists (Figs. 24, 93) who like the brilliant color and the slippery touch of this medium. (For lithographic crayon, see Appendix II.)

Fluid drawing techniques, for the most part, depend for their final appearance on the instruments used to apply them. These instruments may vary from a random stick to an expensive brush carefully constructed of the finest sable hairs. Pen points of all kinds, including those made from metal, bamboo, or quills, are also used (Fig. 188). Each instrument may be manipulated to produce a wide variation of line and texture, depending on controlled handling by the artist. When used with a brush, fluid drawing media may be applied in large washes in either flat or graduated tones.

In both the dry and the fluid media the surface of the paper (or similar sheet of material) can markedly affect the quality of the drawing made on it. Often the artist selects that surface which satisfies his expressive needs. Papers vary in roughness and in absorbency. They can help to produce drawings of precision or drawings in which an atmosphere or mood is achieved through soft edges and subtle tones.

It is possible for the artist to combine various drawing media in a single work (Figs. 18, 92). He may select that combination of materials which suits his purpose. Each one will react differently to the movements of his hand and arm. It is important to note the significance of this manipulation in the finished appearance of the drawing, for drawing, more than any other art form, is the direct expression of the manipulation of the artist's materials by his fingers, hand, and arm. A draftsman who is experienced and sensitive to the materials he uses will consider them as an extension of his own fingers and use them to unite material, manipulation, and artistic intent in one inseparable unit.

THE PRINT PROCESSES

APPENDIX II

A print is an impression of a composition produced by an artist on a master surface. The artist cuts into this surface or draws on it and treats the drawing chemically so that the original design can be transferred from this surface to paper. Many impressions may be taken from one master surface.

Prints fall into four major groups: those produced by relief cutting, intaglio prints, planographic prints, and those produced through a form of stencil process.

The following sections discuss the most common printmaking techniques. Others have been used by artists in the past and by those working today, but a familiarity with the techniques described here should give the reader sufficient background to find his way in examining the graphic arts.

RELIEF PRINTS

The relief print is perhaps the best-known form of printmaking. In this process the artist draws his composition on a block of material that can easily be cut with a knife or gouge. Those areas which he desires to print are left untouched, and the areas to be left white are cut away from the block surface. When the cutting of the surface is completed, the resultant block is charged with a viscous ink by a roller, or brayer. As the brayer rolls over the block, it touches only those areas which were left uncut. The areas cut into the block remain free of ink. A piece of soft, semi-absorbent paper is placed on the charged block, and pressure is applied by a press or, more frequently, by rubbing the back of the paper with a smooth instrument. The ink is offset onto the paper and the print results.

When the cutting process is carried out on the flat side of a block of wood, the print is called a "woodcut," or "wood-block print." Many kinds of wood may be used for this type of print, and the characteristic grain of each type can be integrated into the design. Different cutting tools can be used to produce lines and edges of varied quality. (See Figs. 97, 107, 111.)

The same method of cutting can be employed on heavy linoleum instead of wood. Prints made with this material are known as "linoleum-block prints." They differ from wood blocks only in the grainless structure of their surface. Unhampered by the changes in hard and soft cutting typical of a wood block, the artist who works in linoleum may cut his block more easily, but the softness of the material does not allow him to cut complex designs, for delicate sections tend to give way under the action of the printing process.

WOOD ENGRAVING

The end grain of a block of wood may also be used to make a print. This surface is considerably harder than the flat side of the wood and has a less noticeable grain. Prints made from designs cut into the end of the wood are called "wood engravings." They are usually more precise in the treatment of forms and textures, with many small lines and patterns rather than the bold, direct treatment usually seen in the woodcut.

Relief prints are usually printed without tonal gradations in the ink. Graduated tones may be produced by a very skilled and careful application of ink to the block, but the relief-print process naturally lends itself to strong contrasts of black and white areas, and this natural tendency is usually exploited by the printmakers.

Relief prints in a number of different colors are not unusual. The artist who wishes to produce a multicolored print must cut a separate block for each color. These blocks are designed so that they can be *registered* ; that is, one prints over the other in the precise position required by the design.

INTAGLIO PRINTS

The intaglio print differs from the relief print in that the areas that print on the paper are those which are depressed, rather than those which remain on the surface of the block. In this process a plate of polished metal is inscribed with lines, forms, or textures. After the plate is completed, ink is wiped over its entire surface. The ink is allowed to settle into the depressed portions of the plate but is wiped from its raised surface. Then the plate and a piece of dampened absorbent paper are placed in a press. Pressure is applied, and the ink which was originally in the depressions, is offset onto the paper, resulting in the completed print.

Intaglio prints may be produced by two basic methods : the depressed lines may be etched into the surface of the plate with acid, or they may be cut into its surface with special cutting tools. The first method results in an etching or aquatint; the second, in an engraving, drypoint, or mezzotint.

ETCHING

In an etching the surface of a metal plate is covered with a thin coating of acid-resistant material. The artist scratches his composition into the coating, leaving the exposed metal unprotected beneath the scratched lines. The plate is then immersed in an acid bath. Those areas covered by the resist remain unaffected, but the acid bites through the scratches, eating away at the metal to produce a bitten line. The depth of the line, which corresponds to its blackness in the print, is controlled by the length of time the acid is allowed to work. Gradual changes from light to dark or large areas of tone may be introduced into this process by a careful wiping of the ink on the completed plate at the time the print is made. It is, however, difficult to produce these effects in the plate itself. If they are desired, it is necessary to crosshatch areas in a manner similar to that described for silverpoint drawing.

Example of this type of crosshatching may be seen in Figures 22 and 23 in Chapter III.

AQUATINT

Aquatint is an intaglio method for the introduction of areas of tone into the printing process. In an aquatint the plate is covered with a coating of rosin dust before the acid resist is applied. When etched, the rosin produces a pitted surface on the plate, which prints as a tone. The resist is painted on in successive coats to cover different areas at different times. Those areas which are to print a light tone are etched very slightly. The plate is then removed from the acid, washed, and dried. The lightly etched area is blocked out with resist so that the acid can no longer attack it. This process is repeated for the next darker area and continued for each succeeding area in order from the lightest tones to the darkest. Etched lines may be combined with the toned areas to provide a contrast to the flat forms produced by this technique.

ENGRAVING

An engraving is produced by cutting the lines of the design into a plate with cutting tools called "burins." Because of the physical effort involved in engraving, the lines produced appear to be rather mechanical in comparison to the freedom of line possible in etching. After the plate is completed, the inking and printing process is identical with that of etching. (See Fig. 94.)

DRYPOINT

A variation on engraving is drypoint, in which lines are scratched into the surface of the plate with a hard point. A ragged metal edge called a "burr" is raised on the sides of the scratches. These burrs are allowed to remain, and when the plate is inked, they retain some of the ink, producing a characteristic blurred, fuzzy line in the print.

MEZZOTINT

The engraving and the drypoint, like the etching, cannot easily produce toned areas. This can be accomplished, however, in the mezzotint, a directly cut intaglio print process. In this form of printmaking the entire surface of the metal plate is textured with a grain imparted to it by a toothed metal rocker. The rocker is manipulated across the surface of the plate, producing a great many indentations. Areas to be developed by the artist are smoothed with a scraper, which burnishes the rocker texture; the smoother the texture, the lighter the printed tone. The scraper may be used to produce areas of pure white or tones ranging from white through a wide choice of grays to black.

The potentials for expressive and esthetic variation in the intaglio processes are intimately related to the technical facility of the artist in producing his plates (Figs. 96, 242). All print techniques, but perhaps most noticeably these, require a technical mastery of the medium, including both the production of the plates and the inking process, for the application of ink is a significant variable.

PLANOGRAPHIC PRINTS

A planographic print is produced from a flat printing surface. The print process utilizing this method is called "lithography." Lithography is based on the natural repulsion of oil and water. In this print method the face of a slab of limestone is specially grained with an abrasive to produce a flat, slightly roughened surface, free of all dirt and stains. A drawing is then made on the prepared surface with a wax crayon or a special ink called "tusche." When completed, the drawing is treated chemically so that those areas, including even the most minute grains of the stone, which remained untouched by the oil and wax will accept water and repel oil, while those areas touched by the crayon or ink will accept oil and reject water. The stone is kept damp during the entire printing process. When a roller charged with an oily ink is rolled over its surface, the ink does not adhere to wet areas, but builds up on the parts touched in the drawing process. In this manner a microscopic layer of ink is deposited on the stone in the image of the original drawing. At this point, with the stone still damp, a piece of dampened paper is placed on top of it and they are both run through a press. The ink is offset onto the paper and the lithographic print results. The process is repeated for each print.

Some present-day lithographers use grained metal and paper plates rather than stone. Prints made from paper or metal vary slightly in appearance from those drawn on stone, but the drawing and printing process is essentially the same.

In lithography, an artist may vary his drawing technique in a great many ways, producing prints which approximate the detail and tonal gradations of a photograph or the boldness and direct appearance of a woodcut. Textures and surfaces unobtainable in any other process are made possible in lithography by scratching, scraping, and rubbing the crayon in the drawing. (See Fig. 108.)

As in the other print processes, if more than one color is desired, each color requires a separate impression.

STENCIL PRINTS

Prints may be produced through the rather simple process of cutting stencils (perforated or cut-out designs) from paper or some similar sheet of material. When paint or ink is applied over them, the areas beneath the uncut material of the stencil are protected and remain white. In this process the positive areas, which are to print, are cut away from the stencil and the negative areas are left in place. Only the simplest designs are possible with cut stencils, for it is difficult to print very detailed forms clearly. There are further complications in the problems of keeping a highly detailed stencil intact throughout the period of its use. All the parts of a stencil must be connected, or they will lose their relative positions in the composition.

SERIGRAPHY

Unless some method is used to connect the separate parts of a stencil into a single, usable sheet, the artist is severely limited in the designs he can produce. For this reason the technique of silk-screen stenciling, or serigraphy, has become a popular stencil medium. In this process the stencil is attached to the underside of a porous screen of silk, nylon, or metal mesh. The screen reinforces the stencil and keeps all the separate parts of the composition in position relative to each other.

Paint is forced through the screen onto a sheet of paper or cloth beneath it. As in the other stencil process, the paint is kept from certain areas of the paper and allowed to deposit on others, producing the print.

Since the introduction of serigraphy new methods have been developed for the preparation of stencils to permit highly complex and detailed work. The serigraph, though it has its origin in ancient China, is a comparatively new print medium but is gradually finding its place with the other printmaking techniques in contemporary graphic art.

TABLE 1. PRINTMAKING PROCESSES, MATERIALS, AND CHARACTERISTICS

Process	Type	Materials	Characteristics
Woodcut, or wood-block print	Relief	Wood block, side grain Cutting tools	Many different woods suitable. Strong black-and-white effects.
Linoleum-block print	Relief	Heavy-gauge linoleum Cutting tools	Similar to woodcut but less detailed in forms because of softness of material.
Wood engraving	Relief	Wood block, end grain Cutting tools	More difficult to cut than woodcut. Lines usually finer, more precise.
Etching	Intaglio	Metal plate Resist Acid	No constraint of free use of line. Dark and light lines result from depth of acid bite.
Aquatint	Intaglio	Rosin-covered plate Resist Acid	Permits graduated tones in large areas. Works from light to dark.
Engraving	Intaglio	Metal plate Burins	Difficult cutting produces more controlled designs than etching.
Drypoint	Intaglio	Metal plate Needles	Burr on scratches holds ink to create soft line.
Mezzotint	Intaglio	Metal plate Rockers Scrapers	Permits large areas of tone. Scrapers lighten tones by smoothing plate surface. Works from dark to light.
Lithography	Planographic	Stone Wax crayons Tusche Grained metal and paper plates	Based on mutual repulsion of oil and water. Wide range of techniques possible.
Serigraphy, or silk-screen print	Stencil	Stencils Silk, nylon, or metal mesh	Screen holds small stencil elements in position, permitting complex designs.

PAINTING: Materials and Techniques

APPENDIX III

The distinction between drawing and painting is often a hazy one, but for the purposes of this text painting may be defined as a process in which a viscous material, paint, is applied by some method to a surface, or support. It is usual for the painter to use a number of different colors in a single work, though there are examples of paintings limited to white or black or one of these faintly modified by one other color.

COLOR AS PAINT

Color in painting is paint. This truism is not so obvious at it seems, for some people, when they look at paintings, tend to think only in terms of the objects, colors, or forms painted and forget the inherent qualities of the material itself. The artist tends to think of color in terms of the material he must use to supply it. Paint is for him the most basic of all the physical components of his work.

All paint is composed of three basic parts: the pigment, the vehicle, and the medium.

Pigment is that part of paint which supplies the color. In its raw state it may be a form of earth, a metal ore, an organic material, or a synthetic compound formulated by a chemist. Its raw form is that of a dry, colored powder. Alone, this powder would be impossible to use. It requires a binder to hold its particles in suspension so that it can be spread on in a film which will eventually harden to keep them permanently bound together and adhered to a surface. This binder is the *vehicle*.

The vehicle, in turn, often requires something which permits it to vary in viscosity, thins it out. This substance is the *medium*.

The combinations of vehicles and media are numerous, but they are usually grouped in two families: aqueous and nonaqueous, those thinned with water and those requiring other thinners. Table 2 lists the most common painting media and their individual characteristics.

Recent years have seen the introduction of a number of plastic paints. They are popular because they offer colors of extreme brilliance and dry quickly and work easily. Among the most popular of the new paints are the polymer temperas having acrylic resins as a medium and water as a vehicle. Various trade names (Liquitex, Aqua-tec) are used occasionally instead of the generic term to identify the material used in individual works.

TABLE 2. PAINTING TECHNIQUES, MEDIA, AND CHARACTERISTICS

Technique	Vehicle	Medium	Characteristics
Transparent water color	Gum arabic	Water	Pigments slightly transparent.
Opaque water color	Casein or other opaque water-soluble glue binders	Water	Permits freedom in application. Because of opacity, repeated changes possible. Paint may be built up into thick layers.
Tempera	Egg yolk	Water	Fairly transparent, though less so than transparent water color. One of the oldest techniques.
Fresco	Lime plaster	Water or lime water	Combination of pigment and lime water applied on wall while lime plaster still damp. When plaster dries, pigment integrated with plaster. Used primarily for large murals.
Oil	Linseed oil Varnish (sometimes)	Turpentine	Probably the most versatile technique. May be applied opaque or transparent, thin or thick.
Encaustic	Beeswax	Turpentine or heat	Pigment combined with wax. Thinned for application by heat or turpentine.
Mosaic			Colored bits of stone or glass fitted together to form design and held in position by plaster or cement. Not generally considered a painting medium, but important in producing two-dimensional art.

An acrylic-resin paint with turpentine as a vehicle may be combined with oil paint; it is produced under the trade name of Magna Color. It has many of the qualities of oil paint but shares the characteristic of rapid drying with the polymer temperas.

SUPPORTS AND GROUNDS

Necessary as paint is to the creation of a painting, it cannot serve without the support to which it is applied. Supports vary for the different paint media. Their selection is based in part on their permanence and in part on their suitability for the application of each type of paint. In general, supports fall into three major groups : papers or cardboards, wood or composition panels, and fabrics. Metal sheets and glass are also sometimes used, but they are not common.

Paper and cardboard supports are usually reserved for aqueous media. The surfaces of these supports are manufactured in varying degrees of roughness and absorbency. The selection depends upon the predilections of each artist. (See Pl. 31.)

Wooden panels were once the most popular form of painting support (Pls. 2, 3, 16, 23, 29). Before the introduction of canvas, in the sixteenth century, almost all small paintings were painted on wood. Today wood panels are used less often, but a wood composition panel (Masonite) has become very popular. (See Pl. 63, below.)

Fabrics have been used as supports for many years. Many Oriental water-color paintings have been executed on fine silk. Both cotton and linen canvas have become standard as supports for oil paintings over the entire world. The majority of the paintings reproduced in this book are in oil on canvas.

With the exception of paper, it is usual for all supports to be prepared with a surface that helps to bind the paint film to its backing. This surface is the *ground*. It may be a coating of white lead pigment in an oil vehicle or a form of chalk called "gesso," which is commonly used as a ground for egg-tempera paintings (Pl. 64). Grounds, like papers, may be selected for their absorbency and for the textured appearance they can add to the surface of the painting. Often they are applied by a mechanical process to supports prepared by commercial suppliers, but it is common to find painters preparing and applying their own grounds as a part of their painting procedure.

PL. 61. RICHARD ANUSZKIEWICZ. *All Things Do Live in the Three*. 1963. Canvas, 21⅞ x 35⅞″. Collection Mrs. Robert M. Benjamin, New York.

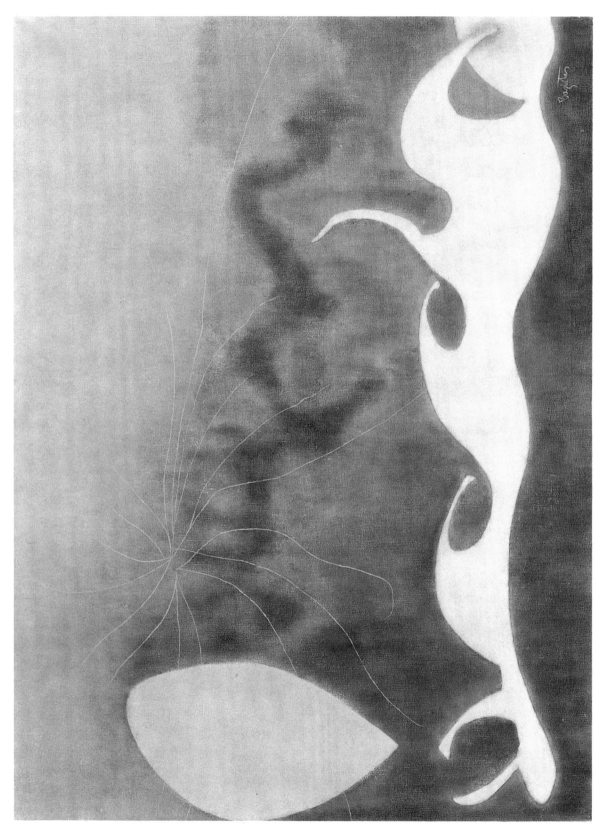

PL. 62. WILLIAM BAZIOTES. *The Beach.* 1955. Canvas, 36 x 48". Whitney Museum of American Art, New York.

PL. 63. JOSEF ALBERS.
Above: *Study for an Early
Diary*. 1955. Canvas. 15″
square. The Sheldon Memorial
Art Gallery, University of
Nebraska, Lincoln.

Below: *Homage to the Square:
"Ascending."* 1955. Oil on
composition board, 43½″
square. Whitney Museum
of American Art, New York.

PL. 64. ANDREW WYETH. *Christina's World.* 1948. Tempera on gesso panel, 32¼ x 47¾". The Museum of Modern Art, New York.

COLOR THEORY

APPENDIX IV

Any discussion of color inevitably depends upon the ability of the communicators to identify and describe the particular qualities which give each color its distinctive appearance. In painting these qualities are a function of the source of illumination used to light the surface of the work and the coloring matter in or on that surface. Color theory, as applied to light from a direct source, is somewhat different from that applied to color as perceived from reflected surfaces. Because most of the present-day use of color in the visual arts is reflected color, this appendix will be concentrated on a description of this theory. The reader should note that some artists work with colored light on translucent screens or in the medium of motion pictures, and in these instances a color theory concerned with direct light sources must be applied to understand the way in which color effects are produced and controlled.

Many systems have been developed for the description of color. Most of them employ a theoretical model of a three-dimensional solid as a graphic device for the representation of the three qualities in color which, it is generally agreed, affect the appearance of any individual color. These qualities are identified as *hue ; lightness,* or *value* ; and *brilliance,* or *saturation.*

HUE

The hue of a color is a function of the wavelength of the light which is reflected from a surface to the retina of the eye. The spectrum of wavelengths and their corresponding hue varies from waves about 1/33000 inch long, which are seen as red, to those about 1/67000 inch long, which are seen as violet. At certain points along the spectrum most people with normal vision will identify narrow bands at which the change of wavelength will appear to produce a change in the quality of the color. These bands have been identified by the commonly used words "red," "orange," "yellow," "green," "blue," and "violet." Actually many people can identify intermediate bands which seem to differ enough from the bands juxtaposed to them to require separate identities, so that "yellow-orange" and "red-orange," "yellow-green" and "blue-green," "blue-violet" and "red-violet" are also used to make distinctions of color quality. For the trained color observer, even more precise identifications of isolated wavelength bands are possible, and each identifiable band on the spectrum is called a "hue."

VALUE

On a scale beginning with black and progressively lightening to white, a hue such as yellow is seen to have a degree of lightness close to the white pole. Other hues in the blue or violet family match points on the scale nearer black. This measure of lightness in a color is called its "value." As noted, not all hues have the same value; each of them may be altered in value to be lighter or darker. With paint, if the artist wishes to raise the value of a color, he may do so directly by the addition of white. When transparent paints are being used, the artist may add vehicle and thin the paint, dispersing the particles of pigment so that more of the white ground shows through the paint film, thereby giving the optical effect of a lighter value. Similarly, hues may be darkened to a lower value through the admixture of black, or, in the case of transparent paint, by applying the thinned paint over a dark ground.

SATURATION

It is possible to produce an area of color which is yellow in hue, very light in value, and extremely bright. This same light-hued yellow may be made to appear dull and grayed. This difference in brilliance is said to be a difference in the degree of "saturation" in a color.

In paint, each hue has a different ultimate degree of saturation, for the pigments available to produce the color and the binding medium have limits as to the brilliance of color they can produce. All hues, however, can be reduced in brilliance until they reach the lowest levels of saturation. At that point they become neutralized and appear as grays which cannot be identified with any hue family.

When two hues of paint are combined and their combination produces a neutral gray, the hues are said to be "complementary." Some disagreement exists about the precise identification of complementary hues, but in broad terms red is complemented by a hue in the green or blue-green area, yellow by violet or blue-violet, and blue by orange. By varying the proportions of a complementary mixture of hues, different degrees of saturation may be produced.

THE COLOR SOLID

A theoretical model of the three color qualities, hue, value, and saturation, may be constructed so that the hues are represented as circling a vertical axis (Diag. 77). This axis represents a value scale with black at the bottom and white

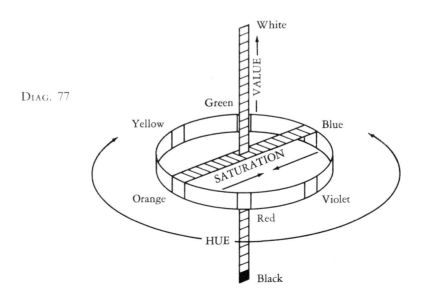

Diag. 77

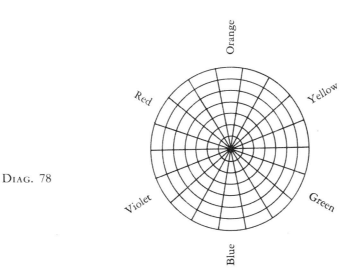

Diag. 78

at the top. Changes in saturation are expressed across the circle, so that the blue-orange complementary group is shown with the most brilliant color at the outer edge of the hue circle and neutrality is indicated at the center point, a step on the vertical axis. The orange and blue segments get progressively grayer as they move in toward the center.

A horizontal slice through the color solid shows all the hues at a constant value level with variations in saturation indicated from outer edge to the center (Diag. 78).

A vertical slice through the color solid shows two complementary hues juxtaposed along the value axis. These hues vary in value along the vertical axis, and a variation in saturation is indicated along a horizontal axis (Diag. 79).

The model described above is a simplified concept. It does not represent the differences in value and saturation between pure hues. A more precise model could be constructed, but it would not differ in essentials from that drawn here.

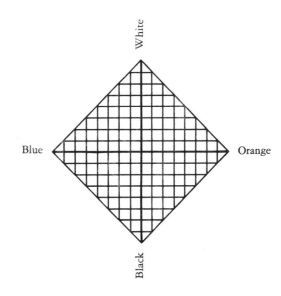

Diag. 79

SCULPTURE: Materials

APPENDIX V

Clay and wax are the most common modeling materials. Both allow the artist to make quick and spontaneous sketches. They may also be used for prolonged, careful studies, for they have the properties of remaining pliable for long periods of time. Because of the pliability of these materials and their ease in handling, the artist can use a variety of tools, including his fingers, to shape the forms of his sculpture (Fig. 60). Usually the modeling material is built up over a skeletal structure of wire or wood called an "armature," but aside from this preliminary necessity, there are few restrictions to modeling even for the uninitiated amateur.

Statues of clay or wax are not generally considered permanent forms of sculpture. Special clays may sometimes be baked at a high temperature to result in a hardened form of the material called "terra cotta," but it is usually necessary for the artist to transfer the form of his modeled work into a more permanent material. This is done through the process of casting. A negative mold is made of the original clay model, which in turn is used to produce the finished permanent work in metal or some hard, stonelike substance. Often a clay model is cast in plaster, but this material is not really permanent, for it is subject to chipping, breakage, and moisture damage under normal conditions, so that the plaster cast is usually considered only a step in the metal-casting process.

Casting is rather intricate and need not be discussed here. Those who are interested will find ample descriptions of both *sandcasting* and the *lost-wax process* of metal casting in books devoted exclusively to the processes of sculpture. It is, however, important to note that a sculptor who works in any of the modeling techniques, with the idea that his work will eventually be cast in another material, must visualize the finished appearance of his work, not as it appears in its modeled form, but as it will appear in its final cast form. He must be able to envision the surface as a metal surface, with a texture and reflective quality considerably different from that of clay. Metal may be polished or treated with chemical solutions to produce variations of color and texture in the finished object, and the sculptor must be aware of these potentials. Some examples of cast sculpture duplicate every fingerprint of the sculptor in the modeling material; others are highly polished mirrorlike works, with surfaces filed and meticulously finished, after they were cast, to produce machinelike, precise sculpture which seems to deny the touch of the human hand. (See Figs. 57, 59, 137, 150, 167.)

DIRECT PLASTER SCULPTURE

It is possible for a sculptor to work directly in plaster, rather than in clay or wax. To do this, he constructs an armature, which he then covers with plaster mixed to a thick, creamy consistency. By continued application of plaster, one layer over another, it is possible to build up a piece of sculpture and maintain a very precise control over the forms. The material is soft enough to allow the artist to remove excess parts easily, and he may always add additional plaster wherever he wishes it. Direct plaster sculpture, like cast plaster, is not considered permanent and requires casting in metal or imitation stone if the artist wishes to preserve it.

DIRECT METAL SCULPTURE

In direct metal sculpture the sculptor builds up his forms piece by piece. He may make changes as he goes along, adding or subtracting parts or whole sections, until he is satisfied with the appearance of the entire piece. He may combine different materials, fitting or riveting them together. He may even design his pieces so that they can articulate, be set in motion mechanically or through the action of the wind. (See Figs. 157, 159, 160.)

After the constructive process is completed, it is possible for the artist to paint the separate parts or apply metal coatings to all or part of the construction. By using the heat of his torch, he may melt bronze, silver, or other metals, so that they will adhere to the surfaces he has constructed, adding variations in color and texture to his forms. (See Figs. 152, 153, Pl. 18.)

In hammered sculpture the artist uses sheets of a ductile metal, usually copper or lead. He fastens these sheets so that both sides are exposed for working. Then, with hammers of different shapes, he beats the metal from one or the other side, pushing out some portions and recessing others, until the entire composition is completed (Fig. 151). Sculpture of this type is characterized by an allover hammered surface. Often the examples of this work are not sculpture in the round. That is, they are designed to be seen from a front position, rather than from any direction in a 360-degree circle about the work.

PLASTICS IN SCULPTURE

With the introduction of the wide range of plastics available today, the chemist has provided the sculptor with still another medium. Many sculptors are using plastics both as a preliminary and a final material in the production of their work.

Transparent plastics permit the artist to organize forms so that they may be seen through other forms. Surfaces which would once have been hidden from the viewer until he walked around to the other side of the piece may be made visible from all sides; their forms can become a part of the composition from any viewpoint.

Edges and planes of plastic sheets may be warped and formed into sensuous shapes by the application of heat, and, as in welded-metal sculpture, small elements may be joined into intricate combinations of forms. Some plastics are light, strong, and inexpensive. Their use permits the sculptor to fabricate large pieces of some complexity, which may be handled with ease.

A relatively new process for the casting of metals requires that the artist produce a Styrofoam version of his sculpture. Styrofoam is a light-weight, cellular material which may be purchased in sheets of varying thickness or in large blocks. It may be carved, heated, and bent or warped; it may be cemented or pinned into large constructions. The surface of the sculpture may be left in the natural, rather porous state of the material or coated with wax. When the model is complete, it is encased in a heat-resistant material like sand; channels are cut for the liquid metal to enter the mold, and other channels are provided for the escape of gases. The hot metal is poured directly into the mold with the Styrofoam still inside. The heat vaporizes the plastic, leaving a cavity that is filled almost instantly by the metal. With the the removal of the mold, the sculpture is complete, save for the final patina and chasing.

Fiberglass fabrics and fibers combined with polyester or epoxy resins can be formed into sculptural masses by building the material up over armatures or by forcing the fabric-resin combination into negative molds. Fiberglass may be carved or burnished; it may have textural materials imbedded in it, and color may be added as an integral component (Fig. 62). When hardened, Fiberglass-resin sculpture is extremely strong, weatherproof, and light-weight. (See Pl. 21.)

A combination of polyester and epoxy resins with other materials lends itself to the construction of relief compositions. Many painters have begun to experiment with these materials, intrigued by the possibilities of adding three-dimensional sections to the flat surface of their work. As a result, the dividing line between painting and relief has become fuzzy (Fig. 174).

SUBTRACTIVE SCULPTURE

In subtractive, or carved, sculpture the artist eliminates the excess portions of a block of material until he is satisfied with the shape and the textures of the remaining forms. Woods of all sorts, marble, granite, even field stone and precious jewels have been used by contemporary sculptors and those in the past.

Many different types of chisels, hammers, and rasps, or files, are used by carvers to reduce the original raw material to the finished piece of sculpture. Some materials resist the edge of the cutting tool and require a considerable expenditure of strength and energy to reduce them to final form. Others are more susceptible to cutting, but may draw the chisels along defined paths controlled by their structure. Each type of stone and wood has its own characteristics, and the carver must learn to recognize and exploit them.

Some sculptors who carve consider the block as having an inner form which is covered by a film of excess material. They feel that carving is a way of "releasing the form from the block." That is, they attempt to recognize in each raw block of material the forms which should be exposed in the completed work. These forms may suggest human or animal subjects, or they may be seen as abstract arrangements of concavities and convexities, edges and planes, which appeal to the esthetic sensibilities of the artist (Fig. 165).

The artist who works this way is keenly aware of the peculiarities of each new block he begins. The shape, the color, the hardness, and the texture of the original material make their imprint on the final appearance of the sculpture. A skilled craftsman must have a knowledge of the potentials of the material he selects. He must be aware of the way in which its surface can be treated. Most important, he must be sure of what he wishes to do with the block.

Errors are difficult to correct in carved sculpture. Sometimes pieces of wood may be glued back in place when they have been removed too hastily, but it is impossible to attach a piece of stone once the chisel has slipped. Each stroke of the mallet must be carefully calculated and often preceded by models and drawings which clarify the artist's intentions to himself.

Some sculptors work directly on the block; others make full-scale models and have them transferred to the final material by a mechanical means called "pointing." Pointing enables the artist or an assistant to reproduce the form of a piece of sculpture by measuring it accurately and transferring those measurements to the raw block. The process is not complex, but it is time-consuming. Here again, it is possible for those who wish a detailed account of the technique to refer to a standard volume on the craft of sculpture. Although the process is widely used, some sculptors find the results lacking in sensitivity to the qualities of the material.

WOOD SCULPTURE

Wood, as a material, is still fairly close to the living forms of nature. The grain of a wooden block carries traces of the life of the tree from which it was cut. The growth of the tree, its structure and shape, are a part of the material. Their obvious presence almost forces him to include their movements and patterns into the total conception of his work.

Every type of wood cuts differently. It varies in softness from the receptive surface of yellow pine to the stonelike resistance of lignum vitae and coca-bola, which are so hard that they chip like granite. Some woods may be carved to hard edges; others require that the forms be smooth and large. Their color and the stains they will accept vary considerably and are often a consideration in the selection by an artist. (See Figs. 131, 133, 140, 161.)

WOOD CONSTRUCTIONS

There are limits to the size of a single piece of wood available to the sculptor. If he wishes to produce a large piece of sculpture in wood, it is often necessary to join sections of wood. By gluing small pieces together a large laminated block may be formed. Such a block may then be carved in the same way as any wood block. The joints between the laminated sections will show, and the sculptor may include them in his composition or ignore them. Some sculptors use flat planks of wood shaped by power tools and laminated into geometric solids, which are then joined into spatial constructions (Fig. 156).

Another form of joined wood sculpture is produced when the artist constructs open structures of separate pieces jointed and glued together. Each piece may be shaped to contrast or harmonize with the other parts of the composition. This form of sculpture requires that the artist employ many of the cabinetmaker's skills to achieve the structural and esthetic details necessary to the finished work (Fig. 155, Pl. 19).

STONE SCULPTURE

Much of what has been said of wood sculpture applies equally to sculpture in stone. The major differences are in the less obvious grain of stone as compared to wood and the usually greater resistance to carving. Because the carver must work so much harder at cutting into his material, it is not unusual to find that he does less carving. As a consequence, stone sculpture tends to be more blocky and stiffer than sculpture in wood. This is not always the case, but it can be noted as a characteristic of much stone sculpture (Figs. 142, 144, 146, 162, 163). The surface which can be developed on a piece of stone can also have an influence on the forms given to the material. Marble, which may be beautifully polished, lends itself to smooth, sensuous forms (Figs. 52, 129, 130, 136, 147). Limestone, on the other hand, has a rough, nonreflective surface and is particularly suited to large, massive forms with hard edges and strongly defined planes (Fig. 51).

In wood carving and stone carving the artist can decide on the degree of influence which the material will have on the appearance of the finished piece. In some periods in history artists appeared to care little about the natural qualities of the materials they used. They selected those materials which would permit the greatest ease of execution and were the most permanent. In our own time many artists emphasize the significance of the material in the concept of their work. A term often heard is "truth to materials." It is difficult in the light of past history to state unequivocally that a significant piece of sculpture must be "true to its materials." Such a contention would eliminate the sculpture of fifth-century Greece and the statues in the Gothic cathedrals of the twelfth and thirteenth centuries, for the original texture and color of the material were often changed by paint and gilt. Nevertheless, it must be recognized that it is possible to admire and enjoy the appearance of a well-rubbed piece of walnut or the glistening reflections of a handsomely figured piece of marble. If an artist does exploit the inherent qualities of his material in his work and can integrate them with the other aspects of his conception, there is no reason to neglect this facet of sculpture in the appreciation of this form of art.

SELECTED BIBLIOGRAPHY

ARCHITECTURE

Fletcher, Banister, *A History of Architecture on the Comparative Method,* Charles Scribner's Sons, N.Y., 1961.

Giedeon, Siegfried, *Space, Time and Architecture,* Harvard University Press, Cambridge, Mass., 1963.

Gropius, Walter, *Scope of Total Architecture,* P. F. Collier, Inc., New York, 1962.

Hamlin, Talbot F., *Architecture through the Ages,* G. P. Putnam's Sons, New York, 1940–53.

— — — *Forms and Functions of Twentieth Century Architecture,* Columbia University Press, N.Y., 1952.

Neutra, Richard, *Survival through Design,* Oxford University Press, New York, 1954.

Pevsner, Nikolaus, *An Outline of European Architecture,* Penguin Books, Inc., Baltimore, 1957.

Rasmussen, Steen Eiler, *Experiencing Architecture,* The M.I.T. Press, Cambridge, Mass., 1962.

Richards, J. M., *An Introduction to Modern Architecture,* Penguin Books, Inc., Baltimore, 1940.

Sullivan, Louis, *Kindergarten Chats and Other Writings,* George Wittenborn, Inc., New York, 1947.

Ware, Dora, and Betty Beatty, *A Short Dictionary of Architecture,* Philosophical Library, Inc., N.Y., 1945.

Wright, Frank Lloyd, *The Future of Architecture,* Horizon Press, Inc., New York, 1953.

COLOR

Albers, Josef, *Interaction of Color,* Yale University Press, New Haven, 1963.

Birren, Faber, *The Story of Color,* The Crimson Press, Westport, Conn., 1941.

Itten, Johannes, *The Art of Color,* Reinhold Publishing Corporation, New York, 1961.

Munsell, Albert Henry, *A Color Notation,* Munsell Color Co., Baltimore, 1946.

Ostwald, Wilhelm, *Color Science,* Winsor and Newton, London, 1931–33.

Seitz, William C., *The Responsive Eye,* The Museum of Modern Art, New York, 1965.

Wright, W. D., *The Measurement of Color,* Hilger and Watts, London, 1958.

COMMUNICATION

Hall, E. T., *The Silent Language,* Doubleday & Company, Inc., Garden City, N.Y., 1959.

McLuhan, Marshall, and Edmund Carpenter, *Explorations in Communication,* Beacon Press, Boston, 1960.

Ogden, C. K., and I. A. Richards, *The Meaning of Meaning,* Harcourt, Brace, & World Inc., New York, 1930.

Ulman, Stephen, *Words and Their Use,* Philosophical Library, Inc., New York, 1951.

Urban, Wilbur Marshall, *Language and Reality,* The Macmillan Company, New York, 1939.

Whorf, Benjamin Lee, *Language, Thought and Reality,* Technology Press and John Wiley & Sons, N.Y., 1956.

DRAWING

Blake, Vernon, *The Art and Craft of Drawing,* Oxford University Press, London, 1927.

Moskowitz, Ira, *Great Drawings of All Time,* Shorewood Publishers, Inc., New York, 1962.

Rosenberg, Jakob, *Great Draftsmen from Pisanello to Picasso,* Harvard University Press, Cambridge, 1959.

Tolnay, Charles de, *History and Technique of Old Master Drawings,* H. Bittner & Co., New York, 1943.

Watrous, James, *The Craft of Old Master Drawings,* University of Wisconsin Press, Madison, Wisc., 1957.

HISTORY OF ART SURVEYS

Fleming, William, *Arts and Ideas,* rev., Holt, Rinehart and Winston, Inc., New York, 1963.

Gombrich, E. H., *The Story of Art,* Phaidon Publishers, New York, 1954.

Hauser, Arnold, *The Social History of Art,* 4 vols., Vintage Books, New York, 1957.

Janson, H. W., *History of Art,* Prentice-Hall, Inc., Englewood Cliffs, N.J., 1962.

Lee, Sherman, *A History of Far Eastern Art,* Prentice-Hall, Inc., Englewood Cliffs, N.J., 1964.

Myers, Bernard, *Art and Civilization,* McGraw-Hill, New York, 1957.

Newton, Eric, *European Painting and Sculpture,* Penguin Books, Inc., Baltimore, 1964.

Robb, David M., and J. J. Garrison, *Art in the Western World,* Harper & Row Publishers, N.Y., 1963.

Sewall, John Ives, *A History of Western Art,* rev., Holt, Rinehart and Winston, Inc., New York, 1961.

Upjohn, Everard, Paul S. Wingert, and Jane Gaston Mahler, *History of World Art,* Oxford University Press, New York, 1958.

PAINTING

Canaday, John, *Mainstreams of Modern Art,* Holt, Rinehart and Winston, Inc., New York, 1959.

Chaet, Bernard, *Artists at Work,* Webb Books, Cambridge, Mass., 1960.

Doerner, Max, *The Materials of the Artist and Their Use in Painting, with Notes on the Techniques of the Old Masters,* Harcourt, Brace, & World, N.Y., 1949.

Jensen, Lawrence N., *Synthetic Painting Media,* Prentice-Hall, Inc., Englewood Cliffs, N.J., 1964.

Levey, Michael, *A Concise History of Painting,* Frederick A. Praeger, Inc., New York, 1962.

Mayer, Ralph, *The Painter's Craft,* D. Van Nostrand Co., Inc., Princeton, N.J., 1948.

Robb, David M., *The Harper History of Painting,* Harper & Brothers, New York, 1951.

PERCEPTION AND VISION

Ames, A., C. A. Proctor, and Blanche Amos, "Vision and the Technique of Art," *Proceedings of the American*

Academy of Arts and Sciences, Vol. 58, No. 1, February, 1923.

Brandt, Herman F., *The Psychology of Seeing*, Philosophical Library, Inc., New York, 1945.

Buswell, Guy Thomas, *How People Look at Pictures: A Study of the Psychology of Perception*, University of Chicago Press, Chicago, 1935.

Gibson, James J., *Perception of the Visual World*, Houghton Mifflin Company, Boston, 1950.

Gregory, R. L., *Eye and Brain, The Psychology of Seeing*, McGraw-Hill, New York, 1966.

Vernon, M. D., *A Further Study of Visual Perception*, Cambridge University Press, London, 1952.

Young, J. Z., *Doubt and Certainty in Science*, Oxford University Press, London, 1950.

PHILOSOPHY OF ART AND CRITICISM

Bird, Milton, *A Study in Aesthetics*, Harvard University Press, Cambridge, Mass., 1932.

Bosanquet, Bernard, *A History of Aesthetics*, Meridian Books, New York, 1957.

Carritt, E. F., *Philosophies of Beauty*, Oxford University Press, New York, 1931.

Cassirer, Ernest, *An Essay on Man*, Doubleday & Company, Garden City, N.Y., 1956.

Chandler, Albert, *Beauty and Human Nature*, Appleton-Century-Crofts, New York, 1934.

Dewey, John, *Art as Experience*, G. P. Putnam's Sons, New York, 1934.

Fiedler, Conrad, *On Judging Works of Art*, University of California Press, Berkeley, Calif., 1949.

Jarritt, James L., *The Quest for Beauty*, Prentice-Hall, Inc., Englewood Cliffs, N.J., 1957.

Langer, Susanne K., *Problems of Art*, Charles Scribner's Sons, New York, 1957.

Munro, Thomas, *The Arts and Their Inter Relations*, The Liberal Arts Press, New York, 1949.

Osborne, Harold, *Aesthetic and Criticism*, Philosophical Library, Inc., New York, 1955.

Pepper, Stephen C., *The Basis of Criticism in the Arts*, Harvard University Press, Cambridge, 1941.

Rader, Melvin, *A Modern Book of Esthetics*, Holt, Rinehart and Winston, Inc., New York, 1951.

Read, Herbert, *The Meaning of Art*, Penguin Books, Inc., Baltimore, 1964.

PSYCHOLOGY OF ART

Arnheim, Rudolph, *Art and Visual Perception*, University of California Press, Berkeley, Calif., 1954.

Eng, Helga, *The Psychology of Children's Drawings*, Routledge and Kegan Paul, Ltd., London, 1954.

Gombrich, E. H., *Art and Illusion*, Pantheon Books, Inc., New York, 1960.

Lowenfeld, Viktor, *The Nature of Creative Activity*, Harcourt, Brace & World, Inc., New York, 1939.

Ogden, Robert, *The Psychology of Art*, The Macmillan Company, New York, 1939.

Schaefer-Simmern, Henry, *The Unfolding of Artistic Activity*, University of California Press, Berkeley, 1948.

SCULPTURE

Giedeon-Welcker, Carola, *Contemporary Sculpture*, George Wittenborn, Inc., New York, 1955.

Ramsden, E. H., *Twentieth Century Sculpture*, Pleiades Books, London, 1949.

Read, Herbert, *The Art of Sculpture*, Pantheon Books, Inc., New York, 1956.

— — — *A Concise History of Modern Sculpture*, Frederick A. Praeger, Inc., New York, 1965.

Rich, Jack C., *The Materials and Methods of Sculpture*, Oxford University Press, New York, 1947.

Ritchie, Andrew C., *Sculpture of the Twentieth Century*, The Museum of Modern Art, New York, 1953.

Seymour, Charles, *Tradition and Experiment in Modern Sculpture*, American University Press, Washington, D.C., 1949.

Struppeck, Jules, *The Creation of Sculpture*, Holt, Rinehart and Winston, Inc., New York, 1952.

Valentiner, W. R., *Origins of Modern Sculpture*, George Wittenborn, Inc., New York, 1946.

PRINTS AND PRINTMAKING

Heller, Jules, *Printmaking Today*, Holt, Rinehart and Winston, Inc., New York, 1958.

Hind, Arthur Mayger, *A History of Engraving and Etching from the 15th Century to the Year 1914*, Dover Publications, New York, 1963.

— — — *An Introduction to the History of Woodcut*, Constable & Co., Ltd., London, 1935.

Ivins, William Mills, *Prints and Visual Communication*, Harvard University Press, Cambridge, 1953.

Peterdi, Gabor, *Printmaking*, The Macmillan Company, New York, 1961.

Sachs, Paul Joseph, *Modern Prints and Drawings*, Alfred A. Knopf, Inc., New York, 1954.

Sternberg, Harry, *Silk Screen Printing*, McGraw-Hill, New York, 1942.

Watson, Ernest W., *The Relief Print*, Watson-Guptill Publications, New York, 1945.

Weddige, Emil, *Lithography*, International Textbook Company, Scranton, Pa., 1966.

STATEMENTS BY ARTISTS

Butler, Reg, *Creative Development*, Horizon Press, Inc., New York, 1963.

Cellini, Benvenuto, *Autobiography of Benvenuto Cellini*, Doubleday & Company, Garden City, N.Y., 1960.

Dali, Salvador, *The Secret Life of Salvador Dali*, The Dial Press, New York, 1960.

Goldwater, Robert John, and Marco Treves, *Artists on Art*, Pantheon Books, Inc., New York, 1947.

Herbert, Robert, *Modern Artists on Art*, Prentice-Hall, Inc., Englewood Cliffs, N.J., 1964.

Holt, Elizabeth G., *A Documentary History of Art*, Doubleday & Company, Garden City, N.Y., 1958.

Kandinsky, Wassily, *On the Spiritual in Art*, The Solomon R. Guggenheim Foundation, New York, 1946.

Klee, Paul, *Paul Klee on Modern Art*, Faber & Faber, Ltd., London, 1949.

MacCurdy, Edward, *The Notebooks of Leonardo da Vinci*, G. Braziller, New York, 1955.

Mondrian, Piet, *Plastic Art and Pure Plastic Art*, George Wittenberg, Inc., New York, 1947.

Protter, Eric, *Painters on Painting*, Grosset & Dunlap, New York, 1963.

Shahn, Ben, *The Shape of Content*, Vintage Books, N.Y., 1960.

Williams, Hiram, *Notes for a Young Painter*, Prentice-Hall, Inc., Englewood Cliffs, N.J., 1964.

Americans 1963, The Museum of Modern Art, N.Y., 1963.

Fifteen Americans, The Museum of Modern Art, N.Y., 1952.

The New Decade, 22 European Painters and Sculptors, The Museum of Modern Art, New York, 1955.

INDEX

References are to page numbers, except for colorplates, which are identified by plate numbers. Roman numbers refer to the text; **bold face** page numbers locate black-and-white illustrations. The names of artists are given in CAPITALS. Titles of art are printed in *italics*; roman type is used for descriptive citations and titles of examples in architecture. Illustrations are listed by artist, by title, and under the general reference for the art form (Architecture, Painting, Photography, Sculpture, etc.). Items indexed under general categories are listed by national or regional area and then chronologically (Architecture, American 20th century).

Sensory information: 40, 43, 51
Serigraphy: 318, 319
SEURAT, GEORGES, *Entrance to the Harbor, Port-en-Essin:* **42**
Severn Bridge: see DARBY
Sewing: 29
Shading: 41, 178
SHAHN, BEN: 158, 309; *Miner's Wives,* Pl. 38; *The Passion of Sacco and Vanzetti,* **309**
SHARAKU, TOSHUSAI: 178; *Iwai Hanshiro IV as Chihaya,* Pl. 43
SHUNSHO, KATSUKAWA: 154; *Woman in Red,* **155**
Silverpoint: 313
SISLEY, ALFRED: 178; *Flood at Port-Marly,* Pl. 46
SKIDMORE, OWINGS, and MERRILL, Lever House: **296**
Skill: 25
SMEATON, JOHN, *Eddystone Light:* **297**
Solomon R. Guggenheim Museum: see WRIGHT
SOUTINE, CHAIM: *Portrait of Kisling,* Pl. 34
Space: 41; illusion of, 107, 131; in architecture, 89, 93; in sculpture, 78–81, 216; two-dimensional, 100, 107
Spectrum: 327
Squinch: 284
Standing Female Nude: see NADELMAN
Standing Woman: see LACHAISE
STANKIEWICZ, RICHARD: 200; *Marionette,* **201**
Starry Night: see VAN GOGH
Statue of Liberty: see BARTHOLDI
STEIG, WILLIAM, *That's a Brave Little Man:* **151**
Still Life with Fishes: see PICASSO
Still Life with Instruments: see LIPCHITZ
Story of Jacob and Esau: see GHIBERTI
Studies for the Libyan Sibyl: see MICHELANGELO
Study for a painting in progress: see NICOLAÏDES

SUGARMAN, GEORGE: 83, 217; *C Change,* Pl. 19
Sullivan, Louis: 257
Sunflowers: see MONET; VAN GOGH
Supports for paintings: 321
Surrealism: 239–43
Surrender at Breda: see VELÁZQUEZ
Swirls and Eddies of a Tennis Stroke: see EDGERTON
Symbols: 5, 36, 37, 64, 70, 109, 149; in architecture, 261; visual, 40, 243

Taharqa: see Sculpture, Egyptian
Taliesin West: see WRIGHT
Tampoco (Nor These): see GOYA
Tea Time: see METZINGER
Tempera: 321
Temptation of Christ: see Sculpture, French 12th century
Tension, force of: 272
Terra cotta: 198, 330
Texture: 36; in architecture, 99; in sculpture, 81; in two-dimensional art, 107
Theseum: see Architecture, Greek
Thirty-one Rods, Each with a Ball: see BURY
Tiger Hunt: see RUBENS
TINGUELY, JEAN, *Homage to New York: A Self-constructing and Self-destroying Work of Art:* **204**
Tolstoi, Lev: 22
Torso: see GONZALES
Torso of a Young Man: see BRANCUSI
Towne House: see Architecture, American 18th century
Trans World Flight Center: see SAARINEN
Transfiguration of Christ: see DUCCIO; Easter Column; Gospel Book of Otto III
Treasury of Atreus: see Architecture, Pre-Greek
Tree II: see MONDRIAN
Truss: 290
Two Sculptures: see DAUMIER
Typography: 63

Union Tank Car Company Dome: see FULLER
Unity: 109, 110–12; and variety in two-dimensional art, 143; through contrast, 114; through movement and continuity, 120
Universal Penman Initials: **62**
Untitled Drawing (1955): see CICERO
Upturned Head (Head of a Recumbent Figure): see MATISSE
Urban, Wilbur: 33

Value, in color: 119, 328
Values: 18 (see Esthetic judgments)
VAN DER ROHE, LUDWIG MIES, Seagram Building: **94**, 95

VAN GOGH, VINCENT: 32, 33, 102, 223; *Crows over a Wheatfield,* Pl. 53; *Sunflowers,* **102**; *The Starry Night,* Pl. 12
Variation Number 7: Full Moon: see LIPPOLD
Variety: 111
Vaults: 279–83
Vehicle, in paint: 320, 321
VELÁZQUEZ: 164; *The Surrender at Breda,* Pl. 39
VERMEER: 40; *Girl Asleep,* Pl. 15
View of Venice, Piazza and Piazzetta San Marco: see CANALETTO
VIGNOLA, GIACOMO, Church of the Gesù: 270, **271**
Violin and Pipe with the World "Polka": see BRAQUE
Violin and Pitcher: see BRAQUE
Virgin and Child: see Sculpture, French 13th century
Virgin and Child Enthroned: see MASACCIO
Vision of St. John the Divine: see EL GRECO
Visual weight: 116–17, 120
Vitruvius: 256
Voussoir: 30

Walking Man: see GIACOMETTI
Wall and lintel: 216
Walls: 296
Watercolor: 321
Wax, in sculpture: 81, 330
Weaving: 29
Westminster Abbey, section and plan: **150**
Wheatfields: see RUYSDAEL
WHEELER, DENNIS, *Banner of Leadership,* 64; *Fresh as Spring,* **64**
Woman in Red: see SHUNSHO
Woman I: see DEKOONING
Woodcut: 141–43, 315, 319
Woodworth, Robert: 111
"Wounded to the Rear," One More Shot: see ROGERS
WRIGHT, FRANK LLOYD: 99, 255–57, 263; Kaufman House, "Falling Water," **100**; Taliesin West, Pl. 22, **98**; The Solomon R. Guggenheim Museum, **254**, 254–57
Writing, decorative: 53
WYETH, ANDREW: *Christina's World,* Pl. 64

Young, J. Z.: 14, 50

ZORACH, WILLIAM: 210; *Head of Christ,* **211**
Zuccone: see DONATELLO

SOURCES OF PHOTOGRAPHS

Alinari, Florence: Figs. 170, 171, 207, 208, 214
Alinari–Art Reference Bureau, Ancram, N.Y.: Figs. 87, 94, 112, 137–140, 166, 191, 192, 207, 208
American Museum of Natural History, The, New York: Figs. 70, 144
Arteaga Photos, St. Louis, Mo.: Fig. 201
Avery Architecture Library, Columbia University, New York: Fig. 225
Baker, Oliver, New York: Figs. 153, 161, 176
Beville, Henry B., Washington, D.C.: Pl. 24
Bibliothèque Nationale, Archives, Paris: Fig. 229
Blomstrann, E. Irving, New Britain, Conn.: Figs. 9, 11, 85
Bodley Head, The, London: Fig. 105
Brandt, Bill, New York: Fig. 105
Brenwasser, New York: Fig. 173
Brogi–Art Reference Bureau, Ancram, N.Y.: Fig. 165
Burckhardt, Rudolph, New York: Figs. 156, 175
Byron, Museum of the City of New York: Fig. 5
Chicago Architectural Photographing Company: Fig. 231
Clements, Geoffrey, New York: Figs. 31, 155
Crameri, L., Graubünden, Switzerland: Fig. 4
Croton Watch Co., Inc.: Fig. 241
Cusati, E. de, New Haven: Figs. 163, 164
Eastman Kodak Company, Rochester, N.Y.: Fig. 36
Elisofon, Eliot, New York: Fig. 211
Ferrari, John A., Philadelphia: Pl. 19
Fischbach Gallery, New York: Pl. 19
Fototeca Unione, Rome: Figs. 220, 222
Frantz, Alison, Athens: Figs. 10, 213, 217, 219
French Cultural Services, New York: Fig. 179
French Government Tourist Office, New York: Fig. 2
Fuller, R. Buckminster: Figs. 237–239
Gahr, David, New York: Fig. 159
Georges, Alexandre, Pomona, N.Y.: Fig. 65
Giraudon, Paris: Figs. 75, 224
Giraudon–Art Reference Bureau, Ancram, N.Y.: Fig. 46
Green Studio, Ltd., The, Dublin: Fig. 48
Grippi and Waddell Gallery, New York: Fig. 62
Guerrero, P. E., New York: Figs. 76, 77; Pl. 22
Hahn, Ernst, Zurich: Fig. 143
Harmon, Mamie, New York: Figs. 13–16, 90, 244
Hedrich-Blessing, Chicago: Figs. 79, 209
Hirmer Fotoarchiv, Munich: Figs. 178, 212, 226
House and Home, New York: Figs. 206, 227
Hubbard, Courtlandt V. D., Philadelphia: Fig. 206
Italian Information Service, New York: Figs. 207, 208
Juley, Peter A., & Son, New York: Fig. 108
Kantonales Tiefbauamt, Graubünden, Switzerland: Fig. 4
Knobler, Nathan, Mansfield Center, Conn.: Figs. 6, 114–121, 202–205
Life Magazine, © Time, Inc., New York: Fig. 1
Marburg–Art Reference Bureau, Ancram, N.Y.: Fig. 181

Marlborough–Gerson Gallery, New York: Fig. 173
Massachusetts Institute of Technology, Cambridge, Mass.: Fig. 104
Matter, Herbert, New York: Fig. 158
McDonald's System, Inc., Chicago: Fig. 73
Modernage, New York: Fig. 199
Moore, Henry, Much Hadham, Herts.: Fig. 58
Morse, Ralph, New York: Fig. 1
Musées Nationaux, Service Photographique, Château de Versailles, Seine-et-Oise: Pl. 46
Museum of Modern Art, The, New York: Figs. 78, 91, 157, 173; Pls. 27, 61
National Parks Service, U.S. Department of the Interior: Figs. 184, 199, 200
Old Sturbridge Village, Sturbridge, Mass.: Figs. 63, 64
Pennsylvania State University, Department of Physics: Fig. 37
Piaget, St. Louis, Mo.: Fig. 19
Pollitzer, Eric, New York: Pl. 30
Port of New York Authority: Fig. 210
Portland Cement Association, Chicago: Fig. 234
Radio Times Hulton Picture Library, London: Fig. 233
Rowe, Abbie, National Parks Service: Fig. 200
Saint Patrick's Information Service, New York: Fig. 74
Scala, Florence: Figs. 52, 54–56; Pls. 3, 23
Science Museum, London: Fig. 228
Seagram, Joseph E., and Sons, New York: Fig. 71
Sherwin Greenberg, McGranahan & May, Inc., Buffalo: Fig. 33
Smith, William Stevenson, Harvard University, Cambridge, Mass.: Fig. 179
Society for the Preservation of New England Antiquities, The, Boston: Fig. 215
Stable Gallery, The, New York: Fig. 154
Staempfli Gallery, New York: Fig. 167
Stephen Radich Gallery, New York: Fig. 12
Stoedtner, Dr. Franz, Düsseldorf: Figs. 165, 221
Stoller, Ezra, Associates, Rye, N.Y.: Figs. 66–69, 72
Trans World Airlines: Figs. 69, 72
Uht, Charles, New York: Figs. 27, 133, 134, 141, 142
U. S. Department of Agriculture: Fig. 38
Wachtel, Dr. Allen W., University of Connecticut, Storrs, Conn.: Fig. 34
Wehmeyer, Herman, Hildesheim: Fig. 167
Wide World Photos, New York: Figs. 98, 235, 236
Wyatt, A. J., Philadelphia: Pls. 11, 34, 35, 38
Works by Degas, Gauguin, Klee, Lipchitz, Matisse, Monet, Picasso, Rodin, Soutine: © SPADEM, by French Reproduction Rights, Inc.
Works by Arp, Brancusi, Braque, Derain, Dubuffet, Giacometti, Kandinsky: © ADAGP, by French Reproduction Rights, Inc.